POPULAR MUSIC

The Popular Music Series

Popular Music, 1980–1989 is a revised cumulation of and supersedes Volumes 9 through 14 of the *Popular Music* series, all of which are still available:

Volume 9, 1980–84
Volume 10, 1985
Volume 11, 1986
Volume 12, 1987
Volume 13, 1988
Volume 14, 1989

Popular Music, 1920–1979 is also a revised cumulation of and supersedes Volumes 1 through 8 of the *Popular Music* series, of which Volumes 6 through 8 are still available:

Volume 1, 2nd ed., 1950–59
Volume 2, 1940–49
Volume 3, 1960–64
Volume 4, 1930–39
Volume 5, 1920–29
Volume 6, 1965–69
Volume 7, 1970–74
Volume 8, 1975–79

Popular Music, 1900–1919 is a companion volume to the revised cumulation.

This series continues with:

Volume 15, 1990
Volume 16, 1991
Volume 17, 1992
Volume 18, 1993
Volume 23, 1998
Volume 19, 1994
Volume 20, 1995
Volume 21, 1996
Volume 22, 1997
Volume 24, 1999

Other Books by Gary Graff

MusicHound Country: The Essential Album Guide

MusicHound Folk: The Essential Album Guide

MusicHound Jazz: The Essential Album Guide

MusicHound Lounge: The Essential Album Guide

MusicHound R&B: The Essential Album Guide

MusicHound Rock: The Essential Album Guide

ISSN 0886-442X

VOLUME 25

2000

POPULAR MUSIC

An Annotated Guide to American Popular Songs,
ncluding Introductory Essay, Lyricists and Composers Index,
Important Performances Index,
Awards Index, and List of Publishers

GARY GRAFF
Editor

GALE GROUP

THOMSON LEARNING

Detroit • New York • San Diego • San Francisco
Boston • New Haven, Conn. • Waterville, Maine
London • Munich

Gary Graff, *Editor*

Gale Group Staff

Jolen Marya Gedridge and Michael T. Reade, *Co-Editors*
Andrew C. Claps and Lynn U. Koch, *Associate Editors*
Rachel J. Kain and Michael D. Lesniak, *Assistant Editors*
John F. McCoy, *Contributing Editor*
Rita Runchock, *Managing Editor*

Dorothy Maki, *Manufacturing Manager*
Stacy Melson, *Buyer*

Michael Logusz, *Graphic Artist*

Venus Little, *Manager, Database Applications, ESS*
Charles Beaumont, *Senior Programmer/Analyst*

This book is printed on acid-free paper that meets the minimum requirements of American National Standard for Information Sciences—Permanence Paper for Printed Library Materials, ANSI Z39.48-1984.

Library of Congress Catalog Card Number 85-653754
ISBN 0-7876-3312-7
ISSN 0886-442X

Printed in the United States of America

10 9 8 7 6 5 4 3 2 1

Contents

About the Book and How to Use It vii
Popular Music in 2000 xi
Song Listings, A-Z 1
Lyricists & Composers Index 117
Important Performances Index 147
Awards Index 171
List of Publishers 173

About the Book and How to Use It

This volume is the twenty-fifth of a series whose aim is to set down in permanent and practical form a selective, annotated list of the significant popular songs of our times. Other indexes of popular music have either dealt with special areas, such as jazz or theater and film music, or been concerned chiefly with songs that achieved a degree of popularity as measured by the music-business trade indicators, which vary widely in reliability.

Annual Publication Schedule

The first nine volumes in the *Popular Music* series covered sixty-five years of song history in increments of five or ten years. With Volume 10, a new, annual publication schedule was initiated, making background information available as soon as possible after a song achieves prominence. Yearly publication also allows deeper coverage—approximately five hundred songs—with additional details about writers' inspiration, uses of songs, album appearances, and more.

Indexes Provide Additional Access

Three indexes make the valuable information in the song listings even more accessible to users. The Lyricists & Composers Index shows all the songs represented in *Popular Music, 2000,* that are credited to a given individual. The Important Performances Index tells at a glance which albums, musicals, films, television shows, or other media are represented in the volume. The "Performer" category—first added to the index as "Vocalist" in the 1986 volume—allows the user to see which songs an artist has been associated with this year. The index is arranged by broad media category, then alphabetically by show or album title, with the songs listed under each title. Finally, the Awards Index provides a list of songs nominated for awards by the American Academy of Motion Picture Arts and Sciences (Academy Award) and the American Academy of

Recording Arts and Sciences (Grammy Award). Winning songs are indicated by asterisks.

List of Publishers

The List of Publishers is an alphabetically arranged directory that provides addresses—when available—for the publishers of songs represented in *Popular Music, 2000*. Also noted is the organization that handles performance rights for the particular publisher: in the United States, the American Society of Composers, Authors, and Publishers (ASCAP) or Broadcast Music, Inc. (BMI); in Canada, the Society of Composers, Authors, and Music Publishers of Canada (SOCAN); and in Europe, the Society of European Songwriters and Composers (SESAC).

Tracking Down Information on Songs

Unfortunately, the basic records kept by the active participants in the music business are often casual, inaccurate, and transitory. There is no single source of comprehensive information about popular songs, and those sources that do exist do not publish complete material about even the musical works with which they are directly concerned. Four of the primary proprietors of basic information about popular music are the major performing-rights societies: ASCAP, BMI, SOCAN, and SESAC. Although these organizations have considerable information about the songs of their own writer and publisher members, and also issue indexes of their own songs, their files and published indexes are designed primarily for clearance identification by commercial users of music. Their publications of annual or periodic lists of their "hits" necessarily include only a small fraction of their songs, and the facts given about these are also limited. ASCAP, BMI, SOCAN, and SESAC are, however, invaluable and indispensable sources of data about popular music. It is just that their data and special knowledge are not readily accessible to the researcher.

Another basic source of information about musical compositions and their creators and publishers is the Copyright Office of the Library of Congress. A computerized file lists each published, unpublished, republished, and renewed copyright of songs registered with the Office. It takes between six months and a year from the time of application before songs are officially registered (in some cases, songs have already been released before copyright registration begins). This file is helpful in determining the precise date of the declaration of original ownership of musical works, but since some authors, composers, and publishers have been known to employ rather makeshift methods of protecting their works legally, there are songs listed in *Popular Music* that might not be found in the Library of Congress files.

Selection Criteria

In preparing the original volumes for this time period, the staff was faced with a number of separate problems. The first and most important of these was that of selection. The stated aim of the project—to offer the user as comprehensive and accurate a listing of significant popular songs as possible—has been the guiding criterion. The purpose has never been to offer a judgment on the quality of any songs or to indulge a prejudice for or against any type of popular music. Rather, it is the purpose of *Popular Music* to document those musical works that (1) achieved a substantial degree of popular acceptance, (2) were exposed to the public in especially notable circumstances, or (3) were accepted and given important performances by influential musical and dramatic artists.

Another problem was whether or not to classify the songs as to type. Most works of music are subject to any number of interpretations, and although it is possible to describe a particular performance, it is more difficult to give a musical composition a label applicable not only to its origin but also to its subsequent musical history. In fact, the most significant versions of some songs are often quite at variance with the songs' origins. Citations for such songs in *Popular Music* indicate the important facts about not only the songs' origins but also their subsequent lives, rather than assigning an arbitrary and possibly misleading label.

Research Sources

The principal sources of information for the titles, authors, composers, publishers, and dates of copyright of the songs in this volume were the Copyright Office of the Library of Congress, ASCAP, BMI, SOCAN, SESAC, and individual writers and publishers. Data about best-selling recordings were obtained principally from three sources: *Billboard* magazine, Rock on the Net (http://www.rockonthenet.com), and the Recording Industry Association of America (RIAA). For historical notes; information about foreign, folk, public domain, and classical origins; and identification of theatrical, film, and television introducers of songs, the staff relied upon album notes, web sites such as All Music Guide (http://www.allmusic.com) and CDNOW (http://www.cdnow.com), newspaper and magazine articles, and other materials.

About the Book and How to Use It

Contents of a Typical Entry

The primary listing for a song includes

- title and alternate title(s)
- country of origin (for non-U.S. songs)
- author(s) and composer(s)
- current publishers, copyright date
- annotation on the song's origins or performance history

Title. The full title and alternate title or titles are given exactly as they appear on the Library of Congress copyright record. Since even a casual perusal of the book reveals considerable variation in spelling and punctuation, it should be noted that these are the colloquialisms of the music trade. The title of a given song as it appears in this series is, in almost all instances, the one under which the song is legally registered.

Foreign Origin. If a song is of foreign origin, the primary listing indicates the country of origin after the title. Additional information may be noted, such as the original title, copyright date, writer, publisher in country of origin, or other facts about the adaptation.

Authorship. In all cases, the primary listing reports the author(s) and composer(s). The reader may find variations in the spelling of a songwriter's name. This results from the fact that some writers used different forms of their names at different times or in connection with different songs. In addition to this kind of variation in the spelling of writers' names, the reader will also notice that in some cases, where the writer is also the performer, the name as writer may differ from the form of the name used as performer.

Publisher. The current publisher or publishers are listed. Since *Popular Music* is designed as a practical reference work rather than an academic study, and since copyrights more than occasionally change hands, the current publisher is given instead of the original copyright holder. If a publisher has, for some reason, copyrighted a song more than once, the years of the significant copyright subsequent to the year of the original copyright are also listed after the publisher's name.

Annotation. The primary listing mentions significant details about the song's history, including performer; album, film, or other production in which the song was introduced or featured; any other performers appearing on the song; best selling or number-one chart status; record company; awards; and other relevant data. The name of a performer may be listed differently in connection with different songs, especially over a period of years. The name listed is the form of the name given in connection with a particular performance or record. Dates are provided for important recordings and performances.

Popular Music in 2000

It was the first year of the new millennium—a time of expected change and new sounds, sights, and ventures. Maybe the world wouldn't be altered overnight, but at the dawn of the twenty-first century, we surely expected to feel a step closer to the space cars of *The Jetsons* and to be going, *Star Trek* style, where no man (or woman) had gone before.

Music during 2000 did not break quite so much ground, however. In fact, the first year of the twenty-first century seemed more like a continuation of the final year of the twentieth, with the biggest marks being made by albums that were actually released in 1999. Consider:

Santana's *Supernatural,* the June 1999 all-star project that vaulted legendary guitarist Carlos Santana and his band back into the spotlight, reigned even greater the following year—producing eight Grammy Awards and spawning the top-selling single of the year, "Maria Maria," which, along with the smash "Smooth," made Santana only the fifth act ever to have two singles in the year-end charts. *Supernatural* was also the Number 2 album of the year.

Florida hard-rock quartet Creed's sophomore album, *Human Clay,* started strong when it was released in the fall of 1999, but thanks to the endurance of the first single, "Higher," and the blockbuster roll of "With Arms Wide Open," which front man Scott Stapp wrote for his infant son, Creed and *Human Clay* affixed themselves to the pop consciousness throughout 2000, logging in at Number 6 on the both the Billboard album and artist year-end charts.

The R&B vocal group Destiny's Child watched its prophetically titled 1999 release *The Writing's on the Wall* explode in 2000—ironically, about the same time the group lost two of its founding members and ultimately finished the year as a trio. Hits such as "Say My Name" and "Jumpin, Jumpin" pushed the album into the multi-platinum stratosphere. The group's fortunes certainly weren't hurt by "Independent Women Part I," commissioned as the theme song for the film adaptation of the TV series *Charlie's Angels.* By the time the dust settled, the group was Billboard's Number 1 act for the year.

Pop sensation Britney Spears' 1999 debut album, *...Baby One More Time,* hung tough in the new year, spinning off a few more hits, including "From the Bottom of My Broken Heart," before making way for her sophomore effort, *Oops!...I Did It Again.*

Christina Aguilera, Spears' former Mickey Mouse Club mate, pushed her self-titled late '99 debut into one of 2000's best sellers with her own string of hits—"What a Girl Wants," "I Turn to You," and "Come On Over Baby (All I Want Is You)"—and a burgeoning reputation as the best pure singer of the new pop revolution. By the end of the year, she had also released a Christmas collection and a Spanish-language album.

Meanwhile, Backstreet Boys continued to ride the success of 1999's *Millennium* into 2000, and was arguably hotter at the start of the year than when it released its next effort, *Black & Blue,* in November.

This should not imply that 2000 was bereft of its own success stories, however. After all, another comely pop quintet, 'N Sync, set a new record for first-week sales when its *No Strings Attached* sold more than 2.4 million copies and went on to become the year's Number 1 seller. Spears' *Oops!...I Did it Again* blew in with first-week sales of 1.3 million, but the anti-pop of controversial rapper Eminem made the biggest run at the boys, with 1.76 million copies of *The Marshall Mathers LP* moving in its first week of availability.

While rap continued to dance with the teenyboppers at the top of the charts—thanks to Eminem and his mentor, Dr. Dre, along with Sisqó, DMX, and Jay-Z—a more traditional form of rock crept back into vogue. With Santana and Creed making it safe to play guitars for young listeners again, groups such as Foo Fighters, Vertical Horizon, 3 Doors Down, Five for Fighting, and Nine Days filled the earnest-yet-melodic realm once populated by Hootie & the Blowfish, Gin Blossoms, and Toad the Wet Sprocket, while Blink-182 made sure that punk rock wasn't left out of the mix.

But, despite all that, music's biggest story of the year was not necessarily the music itself.

Napster Steals the Music Scene

While the Baha Men asked the musical question "Who Let the Dogs Out?" much of the barking in 2000 was directed at the Internet file-sharing service Napster. Using improved MP3 technology, which allowed computer users to download high-quality digital audio files, Napster became the most popular of several music-swapping services, with an estimated fifty million users. Not surprisingly, this did not sit well with the music industry, which feared a great potential for lost sales, particularly when users exchanged brand-new releases—sometimes even before their release date.

Some populist-minded artists supported the concept, including Limp Bizkit and Cypress Hill, which, during the summer of 2000, played a Napster-sponsored tour of small theaters. But the opposition quickly mobilized. The Washington, D.C.-based Recording Industry Association of America (RIAA), which represents record companies, sued Napster for copyright infringement and sought an injunction against the company, claiming the service "is causing irreparable harm to...the entire music industry" and is at least partly responsible for decreased CD sales.

A number of artists lined up behind the RIAA, including heavy-metal heroes Metallica and hip-hop impresario Dr. Dre, who filed their own suits against Napster and declared "a desire to put Napster out of business," as Metallica drummer Lars Ulrich wrote during an Internet chat. Other artists treaded more cautiously, perhaps not wanting to experience the same backlash Metallica received after it revealed the names of more than three hundred thousand Napster users, forcing the company to bar them from the site.

"Everybody kinda looks like a [jerk] to me," said Green Day's Billie Joe Armstrong. "Lars looks like a [jerk]. Napster looks like [a jerk]. We want to make music, they want to sell music, so let's just...figure it out...I think there's a lot of people that are broke that need to get paid. I think they have a right to argue [against Napster], but not the bigger sort of rock stars that have been getting paid for years."

Nikki Sixx of Mötley Crüe, which has been generous with providing free music to fans via its Web site, declared Metallica and Dre's action "an embarrassment to rock 'n' roll" and called them "puppets strung along by record companies, attorneys and managers who don't have the ability to go in and stop something as powerful as the Internet."

But the majority of artists tacitly supported efforts to eliminate, or at least neutralize, on-line file sharing. Jimmy Buffett noted, "It's probably the most serious thing that can undermine an artist's catalog...if all of a sudden there's not value there 'cause everyone can get what you have for free." And Eminem remarked: "When I worked 9 to 5, I expected to get a paycheck every week. It's the same with music; if I'm putting my heart and all my time into my music, I expect to get rewarded for that. And if you can afford to have a computer, you can afford to pay $16 for my CD."

Chino Moreno, of the popular, but hardly multi-platinum, hard-rock group the Deftones, pointed out that rich mega-acts such as Metallica aren't the only artists hurt by Napster and similar services. "Every record sale that we make, it counts with us," says Moreno. "We could lose a lot of record sales from this. I don't think people think they're directly affecting us by just trading music with other people; I would hope that anybody who was gonna download our record would still buy it, but you don't know."

The war raged into 2001, when the industry was successful in winning injunctions against Napster and—to the surprise of no one—began making deals with the company to use the technology for its own means. "I think the labels will be sure there's some way of having control," said Mötley Crüe's Sixx, "because control is their middle name, isn't it?"

Corporate Flux and Government Action

Napster and the Internet weren't the only major issues facing the music industry in 2000. Consolidation continued unabated as AOL merged with Time Warner, home of the Warner Music Group (Warner Bros., Atlantic, Elektra, and others), though that deal effectively scotched Time Warner's plans to acquire the EMI Group. Seagram, which, in 1999, formed the world's largest music company, the Universal Music Group, was itself acquired by the French company Vivendi SA for $34 billion.

Clear Channel Communications, which, in 1999, became America's largest radio-station owner, paid $1.4 billion for SFX Entertainment, the country's largest concert promoter and facility operator for an unparalleled entertainment conglomerate. The acquisition immediately led to concerns of potential anti-competitive practices. Contributing to the alarm was SFX founder Robert Sillerman's bid to form a new management company, FXM, which would acquire The Firm, whose artists include 'N Sync, Backstreet Boys, and Limp Bizkit. That sale never went through, however.

In other major acquisitions, MTV owner Viacom scooped up Black Entertainment Television (BET) and The Box, folding the latter into its M2 video channel.

There were several notable changes in record company front offices—particularly in the wake of the Universal Music Group and AOL Time Warner conglomerations—but none had the profile of Arista Records' shocking ouster of founder Clive Davis as its president. Despite Davis's long success with artists such as Whitney Houston, and more recent triumphs, such as spearheading Santana's *Supernatural* project, Arista's parent company, the Bertelsmann Group (BMG), enforced a mandatory "retirement" on Davis, mostly as a means of keeping hotshot R&B/pop producer L. A. Reid in the fold. While Reid took the helm at Arista after BMG bought a controlling interest in his La Face Records, Davis negotiated enough capital to start another label, J Records, which took a few Arista signings (Luther Vandross, Olivia), developed new talent such as Alicia Keys and O-Town, and became the home base for Wyclef Jean's Clef Records imprint.

The federal government, meanwhile, continued to look into lyrical content and CD pricing; and the Federal Trade Commission ruled that labels had to abandon a Minimum Advertised Price (MAP) policy that was instituted in 1999 to keep large retail chains, such as Best Buy and Circuit City, from selling CDs at below-wholesale prices to lure customers into their stores.

Teen Pop: Overstaying Its Welcome?

Led by 'N Sync, Spears, and Aguilera, teen pop maintained its hold on the music world throughout much of 2000. Supported by marketing devices that their forebears never imagined—from fast-food-chain tie-ins to ubiquitous Internet programs and general-interest TV outlets such as Nickelodeon and the Disney Channel—these artists continued to soar in a multi-million-selling strata that eclipsed every other genre.

But there were signs of wear in this world, however. While a few new pop tarts emerged—including Jessica Simpson, Pink, LFO, Mandy Moore, and BBMak—the landscape was littered with myriad others who represented typical record company attempts to cash in on a trend. No Authority asked, "Can I get your number, baby?" but most audiences said no, as they did to a slew of others, such as 5ive, Innosense, Bosson, soulDecision, and a legion of faceless, soundalike acts.

And, in a new peak of commercially generated cynicism, two TV shows—*Making the Band* and *Popstars*—surfaced to manufacture new groups in front of the entire viewing audience.

There was also some disappointment that Backstreet Boys' *Black & Blue* didn't do better when it was released in time for the holiday gift-giving season. First-week sales of 1.6 million are nothing to scoff at, of course, but the expectations were far greater. Ninety-eight Degrees' *Revelation* was that the world wasn't exactly waiting for its new album, while the quick death of the Spice Girls' third album, *Forever,* proved the British phenom's stay to be anything but.

"Yeah, pop is definitely not going to be as big in the next few years as it has been," predicted 'N Sync's Lance Bass. "I mean, it's been enormous. It's terrible for a new pop group or pop act right now; all the new pop artists are kinda getting lost in the dust. Nobody really cares anymore…So a lot of the baby acts will be disappearing."

Ladies and Gentlemen…The Beatles

Back on the radar in a big way in 2000 was the original boy band—the Beatles. The group's hits collection *1,* which collected the Fab Four's twenty-seven Number 1 hits, took the planet by storm, topping charts in nearly three dozen countries and selling more than twenty million copies worldwide. Tales circulated about parents and children bonding over the communal joys of "I Want to Hold Your Hand" and "Hey Jude," while pundits marveled over the statement of consistent quality that *1* represented.

"The Beatles were together for what, eight or nine years? And they got 27 Number 1 songs, and every song gets better…You suddenly go 'Where...did these guys get their inspiration from?'" said hard rocker Ozzy Osbourne. "It's timeless music. I think in another 150, 200 years to come, they'll look back at the Beatles and still go 'Man, these guys really had something special.'"

The success of *1* took some of its makers by surprise, however. "You can't imagine that," said Beatles drummer Ringo Starr. "We're not sitting around in 1964 saying, 'Wow, in 2001 people are still gonna be buying these songs.' It just rolls on. It's incredible. You know it's gonna be received really well, but you don't know it's gonna be received like *that.*"

But Paul McCartney said he always had an inkling that the group was making music that would endure. "I remember in the '60s, [having] a discussion with a cousin of mine who's a bit older, and he was asking me 'Do you think the Beatles stuff will ever last and become standards?' And I —it was a very bold move of me then, 'cause it was just a fresh off the skillet kind of thing—I said 'I think it will.' He said 'What, you mean like Sinatra standards and all that?' I said 'Yeah.' That was a little cheeky of me to say it then, but it's amazingly gratifying to see I was right."

Advertising: A New Way to Market Music?

Pop music has long had an ambivalent relationship with the advertising community. On one hand, performers welcomed the increased exposure and substantial fees; on the other, they feared and loathed charges of "selling out." In 2000, however, some of those barriers came crashing down as artists found that advertising could be more than just pitching products, but actually a vehicle to market music shunned by radio or video outlets.

The most prominent case study was Sting's "Desert Rose." Though the former Police-man took home two trophies at the 2000 Grammy Awards, sales for his *Brand New Day* were sluggish, and the response to "Desert Rose"—a Middle Eastern–tinged single featuring Algerian singer Cheb Mami—was lukewarm. Then Sting let Jaguar use the song and portions of its video for a TV commercial.

"That was a calculated risk," Sting acknowledged. "It happened in a very organic way; they saw our video in which I was in the back of a brand new Jaguar, and they said 'That's what we'd like as our commercial. Can we use it?' And we said 'Yes'; I mean, you couldn't have paid for more promotion than that. It costs millions to have that kind of promotion. So we said 'OK, we're going to try to put this song out to as many people as possible, people who wouldn't necessarily hear it.' That kind of opened the floodgates, really; once people recognized the song, radio was much more amenable, and we ended up playing the Super Bowl! So a song which might have had a limited audience ended up with a huge audience, which pleased me because it's an unusual song."

Moby, meanwhile, was able to place every song on his eclectic, critically acclaimed *Play* in ads and films, which helped boost the album to platinum sales. The Gap proved to be a continuing source of exposure for artists, making use in 2000 of tracks by Badly Drawn Boy, Red House Painters, and Low, as well as by country insurgent Dwight Yoakam, who delivered his rendition of Queen's "Crazy Little Thing Called Love" to the clothing chain before he even put it on an album. And older songs—from the Who's "Baba O'Riley" to David Bowie's "Heroes"—found renewal in ads for car companies, technology services, and other products.

Hip-Hop and R&B Stay Strong

Hip-hop continued to maintain the foothold on mass tastes it gained during the mid-'90s. In 2000, it continued to seep into the mainstream cultural soundtrack, showing up everywhere from commercials and movie music to roller-rink PA systems and even rock music, as urban and suburban youths mined a shared—though usually independent—affection for the music's irresistible beats and naughty-by-nature lyricism. Seven of the top ten male artists of the year—Eminem, Dr. Dre, DMX, Sisqó,

Nelly, Jay-Z, and Juvenile—were rappers, while an eighth, genre-splicer Kid Rock, employed rap as a significant element in many of his songs.

Explained producer-performer Dr. Dre: "It's real simple; the music is hot, and it's interesting. And the stuff that we're doing right now is very different than anything anybody else is doing. And I think when it's good, then no matter who you are, where you're from, what color you are, you're gonna get into it, straight up. That's all there is to it; everybody enjoys this music."

Dre, who was part of the groundbreaking gangsta rap troupe N.W.A., added some spice to the pop pot with *2001,* his first album in seven years and an all-star joint that featured the likes of Eminem and Snoop Dogg. Dre used the occasion to launch the highly successful Up in Smoke tour, a multi-act bill that became one of the most successful hip-hop road shows ever staged—though the N.W.A. reunion that closed each night's performance did not transpire on record by the end of the year.

Eminem was part of the Up in Smoke package—and arguably its hottest performer, thanks to the success of his second full-length effort, *The Marshall Mathers LP*. With no subject too reverent for attack, the Detroit rapper courted the ire of the conservative right, the Moral Majority, and the Gay & Lesbian Alliance Against Defamation (GLAAD) as he fiercely fired on targets such as late celebrities Gianni Versace and Sonny Bono; paralyzed actor Christopher Reeve; popsters 'N Sync, Aguilera, and Spears (who said she was "flattered" to be in his song and considered Eminem "brilliant"); and even his own mother, who filed a $10 million defamation suit against him. Even Dr. Dre was offed on two of the album's songs—and he's a friend.

Defending his work as "morbid humor," Eminem explained: "A lot of people ask me, 'You joke so much, you say so much..., when do we know you're joking and when do we know you're not? When do we know to take you seriously?' You don't. It's your guess—am I serious or am I not? It's kinda like that mystique I want to leave about me. It's the only real mystique I've got. As far as my personal life, it's all out there."

Indeed it was. During 2000, Eminem's on-and-off relationship with wife Kim—the mother of their daughter, Hailie, and the subject of particularly disturbing songs on each of his albums—took some dark turns, including a suicide attempt by Kim when the Up in Smoke tour played Detroit. And Eminem was arrested on gun-possession and assault charges in two different locations on the same day in June, first when he encountered an employee of rival rap troupe Insane Clown Posse, and later when he found Kim kissing another man at a bar near their home. He was placed on probation for both incidents.

Eminem wasn't the only rapper to experience a few hard knocks in 2000. Bad Boy founder Sean "Puffy" Combs was arrested at the end of the year after a shooting incident in a New York City nightclub, while Lil' Kim's much-hyped *Notorious K.I.M.* album failed to live up to expectations. Making up for that, however, was the refreshing appearance of St. Louis rapper Nelly and his St. Lunatics collective, and continuing hits from Missy "Misdemeanor" Elliott, DMX and his Ruff Ryders (Eve, the Lox, Drag-On), Jay-Z and the Roc-A-Fella crew (UGK, Beanie Sigel), the So So Def gang (Jagged Edge, Da Brat, Lil' Bow Wow), and Juvenile's Cash Money posse (Big Tymers, Lil' Wayne). The Wu-Tang Clan came back into collective form with *The W,* and let's not forget Sisqó and his ubiquitous ode to material-saving fashions, "Thong Song."

More traditional forms of R&B held their own on the urban scene, however—often crossing over to the mainstream pop charts, as well. Macy Gray continued her reign as new soul treasure, while Erykah Badu resurfaced after a long break with the exemplary *Mama's Gun.* Joe ("I Wanna Know") and Donnell Jones ("Where I Wanna Be") set hearts throbbing, as did D'Angelo with "Untitled (How Does It Feel)" and the other steamy material from his *Voodoo* album. Soundtrack hits helped Aaliyah ("Try Again" and "I Don't Wanna," from *Romeo Must Die*) and Janet Jackson ("Doesn't Really Matter," from *Nutty Professor II: The Klumps*) bridge the gaps between their next albums, while Toni Braxton made a defiant comeback with "He Wasn't Man Enough."

Pop in Cowboy Clothing?

Thanks to a surge of success by Tim McGraw, Lonestar, Toby Keith, a resurgent Alan Jackson, and a stalwart George Strait, men regained a bit of the foothold they'd lost in country music in recent years, but it was still the women ruling the roost. The Dixie Chicks and Faith Hill were the genre's most dominant artists, while newcomers SHeDAISY marked their turf with a string of hits. The specter of Shania Twain stayed strong, too, as her album *Come on Over* topped seventeen million in sales to become the best-selling solo album by a female artist in the history of recorded music and achieve a tie for fifth place on the all-time list with the soundtrack to the film *The Bodyguard.*

But the debate continued to rage about whether it was truly country music dominating the country charts, as detractors disparaged hits by Hill and Twain as mere pop songs released by Nashville divisions of major labels. "I turn on the radio and don't hear what I think sounds like country coming from my country music radio stations," grumbled Travis Tritt, one of many genre veterans pushed out of the spotlight by the new breed of mega-sellers. "It's like this big cookie cutter sound."

Hill, however, was quick to defend herself and her work—primarily the album *Breathe,* which debuted at Number 1 on the Billboard charts and sold more than five million copies. The title track was the trade magazines' Song of the Year for all formats.

"I don't forget where I come from; I'm just growing," said Hill, who was named Female Vocalist of the Year by both the Country Music Association and the Academy of Country Music. "I'm not trying to be Shania. I'm not trying to be Whitney Houston or anybody like that. I'm just being who I am, and I have an incredible respect for the establishment of country music and what it's all about, and just country music, period. It molded and shaped who I am today. But so did a lot of other sounds.

"I just wanted to continue to grow as a musician. I'm still inspired by music and growing and developing myself. I just wanted to continue on that path. I just want to be an artist. I just want to be respected as an artist that's trying to do great music. I don't want to be pegged as anything. Just an artist. I don't see a crime in that."

But even the Dixie Chicks, whose massive pop success owed a lot to heavy airplay, expressed concern over country radio's seeming narrow-mindedness. The group's Emily Robinson lamented that "there is another world of this great music that people who only listen to the radio don't realize is out there, unless you're listening to a specifically Texas radio station or you're listening to public radio, and I think the masses need to hear this music. It's frustrating sometimes that the country format doesn't include more of that."

Indeed, the music being made under the mainstream country radar in 2000 was not only some of the best of its kind, but also the best of *any* kind of music being made in the United States. So, while the soundalikes of Keith Urban, Toby Keith, Brad Paisley, Chad Brock, Kenny Chesney, and Tracy Lawrence were duking it out to be the next ten-gallon superstar, those who dug a little deeper were rewarded with rich fare such as Steve Earle's stellar *Transcendental Blues,* Emmylou Harris's *Red Dirt Girl,* Terri Clark's *Fearless,* Allison Moorer's *The Hardest Part,* and grizzled veteran Merle Haggard's *If I Could Only Fly.*

There was some good news for the country fringe, however, when Lee Ann Womack's critically celebrated *I Hope You Dance* was nominated for a Grammy Award for Best Country Album, giving country-radio programmers and Nashville label executives a rare moment of pause as they pondered whether the masses were hearing—and craving—something they weren't delivering.

Latin Music Still Hot

In 1999, Latin music was "Livin' la Vida Loca," as Ricky Martin's massive success brought a taste of that huge worldwide market to America's mainstream pop scene. The good news in 2000 was that Latin music sales continued to grow, and the music was even considered to have enough commercial spunk for CBS to spin off a separate Latin Grammy Awards program for prime time.

The question, however, was whether anyone was noticing.

Yes, Martin was a big deal. Santana and, to a lesser extent, Christina Aguilera also contributed to Latin music's increased profile. But the year did not yield the plethora of new hitmakers that was anticipated in the wake of Martin's ascent, though a couple of artists did manage to make a dent.

Marc Anthony, who already enjoyed a reputation as one of the world's great modern salsa singers and had won solid reviews for his work in Paul Simon's Broadway dud *The Capeman,* made a strong transition into the pop charts. His self-titled English debut album was a double-platinum hit that spun off singles such as "I Need to Know" and "You Sang to Me." And Enrique Iglesias, son of '80s Latin crossover pioneer Julio Iglesias, brought his international success onto American shores with his million-selling *Enrique* album and a chain of hits that included "Bailamos," "Rhythm Divine," "Be with You," and "Could I Have This Kiss Forever," a duet with Whitney Houston.

But, like the predicted electronic-music boom that came before it, things seem to flatten out quickly, leaving us wondering about the true commercial potential of singers such as Elvis Crespo, Jaci Velasquez, and Shakira, and the group Mana. Even the previously unstoppable Martin showed signs of slowing down, as his *Sound Loaded* album was a surprisingly soft follow-up to the colossal success of 1999's *Ricky Martin.* Some of Latin music's purveyors, though, including the younger Iglesias, were glad to see gradual growth rather than wholesale mania.

"I don't want them to make Latino music a trend," he explained. "I guess I'm so scared of trends, and I want it to last. I want it to be there for a long time, not just for people to think it's one music and that's it. There's so many different styles within Latino music. I want people to discover it little by little. But it's not like people are hearing salsa music on every corner. I don't think it's ever going to be like that."

Rock 'n' Roll: The Beast Lives

Amidst all the genre stratification, what was going on in rock 'n' roll, the area most affected by taste shifts during the last half of the '90s? There were actually signs of hope from several different directions, as guitar-wielding groups began to find favor from the same young audience that embraced 'N Sync, Britney Spears, and others of that ilk.

Taking advantage of this newfound audience was a legion of new, young, and seemingly interchangeable bands that offered as much melody and as many hooks as any teen pop act, whether it was 3 Doors Down with "Kryptonite" and "Loser," Vertical Horizon with "Everything You Want," Nickelback with "Leader of Men," or Nine Days with "If I Am" and "Absolutely (Story of a Girl)." Creed, of course, was the hands-down champion in making rock part of the popular mainstream again—thanks to a string of hits that included "Higher," "With Arms Wide Open," "What If," and "Are You Ready?"—and its crunchy, semi-metal sound opened a few doors for headier groups such as Godsmack, Staind, Fuel, and U.P.O.

Rock's more extreme edge was also healthy. Limp Bizkit's *Chocolate Starfish and the Hot Dog Flavored Water* debuted at Number 1, selling slightly fewer than 1.1 million copies in its first week of release, on its way to sales of more than four million copies. Korn's angst-fired *Issues* scorched listeners with tracks such as "Falling Away from Me" and "Make Me Bad," and the ageless AC/DC proved its enduring mettle with *Stiff Upper Lip*. The Red Hot Chili Peppers kept its 1999 release, *Californication,* alive with the title track and "Otherside," while the likes of Foo Fighters ("Learn to Fly") and Filter ("Take a Picture") checked in from the so-called alternative end of the spectrum.

Kid Rock backed off of his roiling rock 'n' rap blend for the tender "Only God Knows Why," though his "American Bad Ass" put him back on familiar stomping ground. But nobody changed pace more than Britain's Radiohead, who, with *Kid A,* delivered a highly anticipated work that eschewed standard melodic and songwriting conventions, replacing them with ambient sonic pastiches and skewed, formless arrangements.

"Our goal was really not to do what we've done before—it's really as simple as that—and not to go over old ground," said guitarist Ed O'Brien. "A lot of the time it didn't feel right to pick up the guitar and do kind of what we've done before. It just felt like we didn't have a choice; this is the record we had to make. There wasn't mass amounts of thinking behind it; it was just 'We're not gonna go over old ground.'"

The rock scene also welcomed some newcomers and left some veteran favorites in flux during 2000. Papa Roach and Linkin Park were fresh rap-rock arrivals, while A Perfect Circle, co-founded by Tool front man Maynard James Keenan, took off on the strength of songs such as "Judith." Meanwhile, the annual heavy-metal tour Ozzfest spun off two solid contenders, Disturbed and Incubus. But Metallica—a group potent enough to be referred to as "the mighty..."—was left reeling when bassist Jason Newsted left after the release of the ambitious orchestral live album *S&M,* while Rage Against the Machine front man Zack de la Rocha's departure prior to the release of the pioneering rap-rock outfit's covers album, *Renegades,* made its future uncertain, even though his bandmates promised to soldier on.

—Gary Graff
Editor

A

Aaron's Party (Come Get It)
Words and music by Brian Kierulf and Joshua Schwartz.
Kierulf, 2000/Mugsy Boy Publishing, 2000/Zomba Enterprises, 2000/ Mcud Music, 2000.
Best-selling record by Aaron Carter from the album *Aaron's Party (Come Get It)* (Jive, 2000).

Absolutely (Story of a Girl)
Words and music by John Hampson.
WB Music Publishing, 2000/Hazel Songs, 2000.
Best-selling record by Nine Days from the album *The Madding Crowd* (Sony/Epic, 2000).

Adam's Song
Words and music by Thomas Delonge and Mark Hoppus.
EMI-April Music, 1999/Fun with Goats Music, 1999.
Best-selling record by Blink-182 from the album *Enema of the State* (Uni/MCA, 1999).

Again
Words and music by Leonard Kravitz.
Miss Bessie Music, 2000.
Best-selling record by Lenny Kravitz from the album *Greatest Hits* (EMD/Virgin, 2000).Nominated for a Grammy Award, Best Rock Song, 2000.

All or Nothing
Words and music by Ontario Haynes, John Rhone, Aleese Simmons, Latrelle Simmons, Sherree Ford-Payne, Shante Frierson, and Enchante Minor.
J Rhone Music, La Cresenta, 2000/Andre'sia Music, 2000/E Two Music, 2000.
Introduced by Athena Cage on the soundtrack album *Save the Last Dance* (Uni/Hollywood, 2000).

All This Time
Words and music by Lalah Hathaway and Marcus Miller.
Famous Music Corp., 2000.
Introduced by Lalah Hathaway and Marcus Miller on the soundtrack album *The Ladies Man* (Uni/DreamWorks, 2000).

A.M. Radio
Words and music by Arthur Alexakis, Joseph Broussard, Greg Eklund, Craig Montoya, Carol Washington, and Ralph Williams.
Common Green Music, 2000/Evergleam Music, 2000/Montalupis Music, 2000/Caraljo Music Inc., 2000/Malaco Music Co., 2000.
Introduced by Everclear on the album *Songs from an American Movie, Vol. One: Learning How to Smile* (EMD/Capitol, 2000).

American Bad Ass
Words and music by James Hetfield, Kid Rock (pseudonym for Robert Ritchie), and Lars Ulrich.
Atlantic Recording Corp., England, 2000/Thirty Two Mile Music, 2000/Warner-Tamerlane Music, 2000/Creeping Death Music, 2000.
Best-selling record by Kid Rock from the album *The History of Rock* (Lava/Atlantic, 2000).

American Pie
Words and music by Don McLean.
Benny Bird Co., Inc., Camden, 1971/Songs of Universal, 1971.
Best-selling record as Revived by Madonna in the film and on the soundtrack album *The Next Best Thing* (WEA/Warner Bros., 2000).

Angel's Eye
Words and music by Martin Frederiksen, Anthony Perry, and Steven Tyler (pseudonym for Steven Tallarico).
EMI-April Music, 2000/EMI-Blackwood Music Inc., 2000/Pearl White Music, 2000/Demon of Screamin Music, 2000/JuJu Rhythms, 2000.
Introduced by Aerosmith on the soundtrack album *Charlie's Angels* (Sony/Columbia, 2000).

Another Dumb Blonde
Words and music by Antonina Armato and Timothy James.
EMI-April Music, 2000/Tom Sturges Music, 2000/Bedknobs and Broomsticks Music, 2000/Warner-Tamerlane Music, 2000/EMI Music Publishing, 2000/Armo Music Corp., 2000.
Best-selling record by Hoku from the soundtrack album *Snow Day* (Uni/Geffen, 2000). Later featured on the album *Hoku* (Uni/Geffen, 2000).

Another Nine Minutes
Words and music by Timothy Buppert, William Crain, and Tom Douglas.
Sony ATV Songs LLC, Nashville, 1999/Chrysalis Music Group, 1999/

Tiny Buckets O'Music, 1999/Nick 'n Ash Music, 1999/Tree Publishing Co., Inc., 1999.
Best-selling record by Yankee Grey from the album *Untamed* (Monument/Sony, 1999).

Another Way
Words and music by Paul Matthias.
BMG Songs Inc., 2000.
Introduced by Paul van Dyk on the album *Out There and Back* (Mute, 2000).

Around the World (La La La La La) (German)
English words and music by Alex Christensen, Peter Koenemann, Aleksei Potekhin, and Sergei Zhukov.
EMI-Blackwood Music Inc., 2000/Diana Music Corp., 2000/Edition Alex C Music, 2000/Rock Willows Music, 2000.
Best-selling single by ATC (BMG, 2000).

As If
Words and music by Shelly Peiken and Guy Roche.
Manuiti LA Music, Encino, 2000/Hidden Pun Music, 2000/Sushi Too Music, 2000.
Introduced by Blaque featuring Joey Fatone Jr. on the soundtrack album *Bring It On* (Sony/Epic, 2000).

As We Lay
Words and music by Billy Beck and Larry Troutman.
Sony ATV Songs LLC, Nashville, 1984/Saja Music Co., 1984/Songs of Lastrada, 1984.
Revived by Kelly Price on the album *Mirror Mirror* (Uni/Def Jam, 2000).

B

Baby Don't Cry (Keep Ya Head Up II)
Words and music by Rufus Cooper, DJ Soulshock, Malcolm Greenidge, Kenneth Karlin, Carsten Schack, and Tupac Shakur.
WB Music Publishing, 1996/Universal-MCA Music Publishing, 1996/EMI-Blackwood Music Inc., 1996/Songs of Universal, 1996/EMI Blackwood Music Canada Ltd., 1996/Joshua's Dream Music, 1996/Full of Soul Music, 1996/Soulvang Music, 1996/Suge Publishing, 1996/Jungle Fever Music, 1996.
Best-selling record by 2Pac featuring Outlawz from the album *Still I Rise* (Uni/Interscope, 1999).

Baby U Are
Words and music by Craig Cooper and Gerald Levert.
Coopick Music, Los Angeles, 2000/Divided Music, 2000.
Best-selling record by Gerald Levert from the album *G* (WEA/Elektra, 2000).

Babylon
Words and music by David Gray.
Chrysalis Music Group, 1999.
Best-selling record by David Gray from the album *White Ladder* (BMG/RCA, 1999).

Back Here
Words and music by Mark Barry, Christian Burns, Stephen McNally, and Philip Thornalley.
BMG Songs Inc., 2000/EMI-April Music, 2000/Strong Songs, 2000/BMG Music Publishing Ltd., 2000.
Best-selling record by BBMak from the album *Sooner or Later* (Uni/Hollywood, 2000).

Bad Boyz
Words and music by David Jones, Barrington Levy, Iggy Pop (pseudonym for James Osterberg), Lamont Porter, and Shyne (pseudonym for Jamaal Barrow).

Ez Elpee Music, Bronx, 2000/Tintoretto Music, New York, 2000/Jones Music America, 2000/Universal-Polygram Intl Tunes, 2000/Bug Music, 2000/James Osterberg Music, 2000/Screen Gems-EMI Music Inc., 2000/Solomon's Works Music, 2000/EMI Music Publishing Ltd., 2000.
Best-selling record by Shyne featuring Barrington Levy from the album *Shyne* (BMG/Arista/Bad Boy, 2000).

Bad Man
Words and music by Robert Kelly.
R. Kelly Music, 2000/Zomba Enterprises, 2000.
Best-selling record by R. Kelly from the soundtrack album *Shaft (2000)* (BMG/Arista/La Face, 2000).

Bad Religion
Words and music by Salvatore Erna and Tommy Stewart.
Universal-MCA Music Publishing, 1998/Meeengya Music, 1998/MCA Music Publishing, 1998/Harvey Scott Music, 1998.
Re-introduced by Godsmack on the album *Godsmack* (Uni/Universal, 1999).

The Bad Touch
Words and music by James Franks.
Hey Rudy Music Publishing, 2000/Universal Songs of Polygram Intl., 2000.
Best-selling record by Bloodhound Gang from the album *Hooray for Boobies* (Uni/Geffen, 2000).

Bag Lady
Words and music by Erykah Badu (pseudonym for Erica Wright), Brian Bailey, Ricardo Brown, Nathaniel Hale, Isaac Hayes, Craig Longmiles, Harold Martin, and Andre Young.
Irving Music Inc., 2000/Irving Music Inc.-East Memphis, 2000/Nate Dogg Music, 2000/Warner-Tamerlane Music, 2000/WB Music Publishing, 2000/Antraphil Music, 2000/Divine Pimp Music, 2000/Aftermath Music, 2000.
Number one song by Erykah Badu from the album *Mama's Gun* (Uni/Motown, 2000).Nominated for a Grammy Award, Best R&B Song, 2000.

Bang the Drum Slowly
Words and music by Guy Clark and Emmylou Harris.
EMI-April Music, 2000/Almo Music Corp., 2000/EMI April Canada, 2000/Poodlebone Music, 2000.
Introduced by Emmylou Harris on the album *Red Dirt Girl* (WEA/Atlantic/Nonsuch, 2000).

Be with You
Words and music by Paul Barry, Enrique Iglesias, and Mark Taylor.
Right Bank Music, Encino, 1999/EMI-April Music, 1999/Enrique Iglesia Music, 1999.
Number one song by Enrique Iglesias from the album *Enrique* (Uni/ Interscope, 1999).

Be Yourself
Words and music by Skye Edwards, Paul Godfrey, and Ross Godfrey.
Chrysalis Songs, 2000.
Introduced by Morcheeba on the album *Fragments of Freedom* (WEA/ London/Sire, 2000).

Beat from Underground
Words and music by Roderick Taylor.
Rats God Music, 2000.
Introduced by the fictional band Beyond Gravity in the television movie and on the soundtrack album *At Any Cost* (WEA/Warner Bros., 2000).

Beautiful Day
Words and music by Bono (pseudonym for Paul Hewson), Adam Clayton, The Edge (pseudonym for David Evans), and Larry Mullen.
Universal-Polygram Intl Tunes, 2000/Polygram International Music B.V., 2000.
Best-selling record by U2 from the album *All That You Can't Leave Behind* (Uni/Interscope, 2000).Won Grammy Awards.

Beautiful Women
Words by Kandi Burruss, words and music by Michael McCary, Nathan Morris, Wanya Morris, and Shawn Stockman, music by Kevin Briggs.
Shek' Em Down Music, 2000/Vanderpool Publishing, 2000/Ensign Music, 2000/Black Panther Publishing, 2000/Shawn Patrick Publishing, 2000/Aynaw Music, 2000/Kandacy Music, 2000/Air Control Music, 2000/EMI-April Music, 2000/Hitco Music, 2000/EMI April Canada, 2000/Hitco South, 2000/Music of Windswept, 2000.
Introduced by Boyz II Men on the album *Nathan Michael Shawn Wayna* (Uni/Universal, 2000).

Because You Love Me
Words and music by Kostas Lazarides and John Sherrill.
Sony ATV Songs LLC, Nashville, 1998/Nothing But the Wolf Music, Nashville, 1998/Universal-Polygram Intl Tunes, 1998/Tree Publishing Co., Inc., 1998/Universal Songs of Polygram Intl., 1998/Seven Angels Music, 1998/Little Big Town Music, 1998/Songs of Polygram, 1998.
Best-selling record by Jo Dee Messina from the album *I'm Alright* (WEA/Atlantic/Curb, 1998).

Been There
Words and music by Clint Black and Steven Wariner.
Blackened Music, 1999/Steve Wariner Music, 1999.
Best-selling record by Clint Black featuring Steve Wariner from the album *D'lectrified* (BMG/RCA, 1999). Also featured on the Steve Wariner album *Faith in You* (EMD/Capitol, 2000).

Bent
Words and music by Robert Thomas.
Bidnis Inc Music, 2000/EMI-Blackwood Music Inc., 2000.
Number one song by Matchbox Twenty from the album *Mad Season* (WEA/Atlantic/Lava, 2000).Nominated for a Grammy Award, Best Rock Song, 2000.

The Best Day
Words and music by Carson Chamberlain and Dean Dillon.
Acuff Rose Music, 2000/Everything I Love Music, 2000/Universal Songs of Polygram Intl., 2000.
Number one song by George Strait from the album *Latest Greatest Straitest Hits* (Uni/MCA Nashville, 2000).

Best Friend
Words and music by Christopher Cross, Todd Gaither, Puff Daddy (pseudonym for Sean Combs), and Mario Winans.
Butter Jinx Music, Los Angeles, 1999/BMG Songs Inc., 1999/EMI-April Music, 1999/Justin Combs Publishing, 1999/Yellow Man Music, 1999/September Six Music, 1999.
Best-selling record by Puff Daddy featuring Mario Winans, Hezekiah Walker, and the Love Fellowship Crusade Choir from the album *Forever* (BMG/Arista/Bad Boy, 1999).

Best of Intentions
Words and music by Travis Tritt.
Post Oak Publishing, New York, 2000.
Number one song by Travis Tritt from the album *Down the Road I Go* (Sony/Columbia, 2000).

The Best Man I Can Be
Words and music by James Harris, Terry Lewis, and James Wright.
EMI-April Music, 1999/Flyte Tyme Tunes, 1999/Ji Branda Music Works, 1999/Minneapolis Guys Music, 1999.
Best-selling record by Ginuwine featuring R. L., Tyrese, and Case from the film and soundtrack album *The Best Man* (Sony/Columbia, 1999).

The Best of Me
Words and music by Teron Beal, Jimmy Cozier, Kasseem Dean, Mya Harrison, J. Phillips, and Mashonda Tifrere.
Karima Music, New York, 2000/Swizz Beats Publishing, Atlanta, 2000/

Warner-Tamerlane Music, 2000/Teron Beal Songs, 2000/Warner-Chappell Music, 2000/Jae'wans Music, 2000/Siyeeda's Publishing, 2000/BMG Songs Inc., 2000/Art of War Publishing, 2000.
Best-selling record by Mya featuring Jadakiss from the album *Fear of Flying* (Uni/Interscope, 2000).

Better Off Alone
Words and music by Kalmani (pseudonym for Eelke Kalberg) and Pronti (pseudonym for Sebastian Molijn).
Pentagon Lipservices Two PSW Music, 2000/Universal Songs of Polygram Intl., 2000/Violent Publishing, 2000/SODRAC, 2000.
Best-selling record by Alice Deejay from the album *Who Needs Guitars Anyway?* (Uni/Universal, 2000).

Between Me and You
Words and music by Ja Rule (pseudonym for Jeffrey Atkins), Irving Lorenzo, and Robert Mays.
Lil Rob Entertainment, Springfields, 2000/DJ Irv, 2000/Ensign Music, 2000/White Rhino Music, 2000.
Best-selling record by Ja Rule featuring Christina Milian from the album *Rule 3:36* (Uni/Def Jam, 2000).

Big Pimpin'
Words by Jay-Z (pseudonym for Shawn Carter) and Kyambo Joshua, music by Timothy Mosley.
Virginia Beach Music, 1999/WB Music Publishing, 1999/EMI-Blackwood Music Inc., 1999/Lil Lu Lu Publishing, 1999.
Best-selling record by Jay-Z featuring UGK from the album *Vol. 3: The Life & Times of Shawn Carter* (Uni/Def Jam, 1999).

Black Light Blue
Words and music by Bill Bottrell, Roger Fritz, Jay Joyce, Shelby Lynne, and Dorothy Overstreet.
Magnasong, 2000/Ignorant, 2000/Irving Music Inc., 2000/Songs of Dreamworks, 2000.
Introduced by Shelby Lynne on the album *I Am Shelby Lynne* (Uni/Island, 2000).

Bloodflowers
Words and music by Jason Cooper and Robert Smith, music by Simon Gallup, Roger O'Donnell, and Perry Bamonte.
Fiction Songs Ltd., 2000.
Introduced by the Cure on the album *Bloodflowers* (WEA/Elektra, 2000).

Bloodstains
Words and music by Michael Palm.
Covina High Music, Palm Desert, 1981/Peermusic Ltd., Los Angeles,

1981.
Revived by the Offspring on the soundtrack album *Ready to Rumble* (WEA/Atlantic, 2000).

Blue Moon
Words and music by Gary Leach and Mark Tinney.
Acrynon Publishing, 1998/WCR Publishing, 1998.
Best-selling record by Steve Holy from the album *Blue Moon* (Curb, 2000).

Blue Skies for Everyone
Words and music by Robert Schneider.
Bug Music, 2000/Shokorama Music, 2000.
Introduced by Bob Schneider on the soundtrack album *Gun Shy* (Uni/Hollywood, 2000).

Bodhisattva
Words and music by Donald Fagen.
Universal-MCA Music Publishing, 1982.
Revived by the Brian Setzer Orchestra on the soundtrack album *Me, Myself & Irene* (WEA/Elektra, 2000).

Bohemian like You
Words and music by Courtney Taylor.
Dandy Warhol Music, Los Angeles, 2000.
Introduced by Dandy Warhols on the album *Thirteen Tales from Urban Bohemia* (EMD/Capitol, 2000).

Born to Fly
Words and music by Sara Evans, Marcus Hummon, and Darrell Scott.
Careers-BMG Music, Beverly Hills, 2000/Floyd's Dream Music, Nashville, 2000/Sony ATV Songs LLC, Nashville, 2000/Chuch Wagon Gourmet Music, 2000/Famous Music Corp., 2000/Tree Publishing Co., Inc., 2000.
Number one song by Sara Evans from the album *Born to Fly* (BMG/RCA, 2000).

Boss of Me
Words and music by John Flansburgh and John Linnel.
Fox Film Music Corp., 2000/New Enterprises Music, 2000.
Introduced by They Might Be Giants in the television show and on the soundtrack album *Malcolm in the Middle* (BMG/Restless, 2000).

Bounce with Me
Words and music by Bryan-Michael Cox, Da Brat (pseudonym for Shawntae Harris), and Jermaine Dupri.
Babyboys Little Pub Co, 2000/So So Def Music, 2000/Throwin' Tantrums Music, 2000/EMI-April Music, 2000/Air Control Music, 2000/TCF Music Publishing, 2000/Fox Tunes, 2000/New Monarchy

Music, 2000/New Regency Music, 2000/Noontime South, 2000.
Number one song Introduced by Lil' Bow Wow on the soundtrack album *Big Momma's House* (Sony/Columbia, 2000). Later featured on the Lil' Bow Wow album *Beware of Dog* (Sony/Columbia, 2000).

Breadline
Words and music by Marty Friedman, Dave Mustaine, and Bud Prager.
Adam Martin Music, 1999/EMI-Blackwood Music Inc., 1999/Mustaine Music, 1999/Windfall Music Enterprises, 1999.
Introduced by Megadeth on the album *Risk* (EMD/Capitol, 1999). Featured in a publicservice announcement for the National Coalition for the Homeless.

Break Stuff
Words and music by Wesley Borland, Fred Durst, Dimant Leor, Brendan O'Brien, John Otto, and Samuel Rivers.
Charlie Noble Music, Atlanta, 1999/Big Bizkit Music, 1999/Zomba Enterprises, 1999.
Best-selling record by Limp Bizkit from the album *Significant Other* (Uni/Interscope, 1999).

Break You Down
Words and music by Ullrich Hepperlin, Jason Miller, Michael Miller, and James O'Connor.
Trinity of Relative Evil Music, Los Angeles, 2000/Warner-Tamerlane Music, 2000.
Introduced by Godhead featuring Marilyn Manson on the soundtrack album *Dracula 2000* (Sony/Columbia, 2000).

Breakout
Words and music by David Grohl, Oliver Hawkins, and Nate Mendel.
Flying Earform Music, Culver City, 1999/Living Under a Rock Music, 1999/EMI-Virgin Songs, 1999/MJ Twelve Music, 1999.
Best-selling record by the Foo Fighters from the album *There Is Nothing Left to Lose* (BMG/RCA, 1999).

Breathe
Words and music by Stephanie Bentley and Holly Lamar.
Cal IV Entertainment Inc., Nashville/Hope Chest Music, 1999/Universal Songs of Polygram Intl., 1999.
Number one song by Faith Hill from the album *Breathe* (WEA/Warner Bros., 1999).Nominated for Grammy Awards, Best Country Song, 2000 and Song of the Year, 2000.

Breathe and Stop
Words and music by Robert Bell, Ronald Bell, George Brown, Roy Handy, Cleveland Horne, Robert Mickens, Q-Tip (pseudonym for Kamaal Fareed), Clarence Redd, Gene Redd, Claydes Smith, Dennis

Thomas, Richard Westfield, and James Yancey.
EPHCY Music, 1999/Stephanye Music, 1999/U Betta Like My Muzic, 1999/Zomba Enterprises, 1999/Universal-Polygram Intl Tunes, 1999/ Warner-Tamerlane Music, 1999.
Introduced by by Q-Tip on the album *Amplified* (BMG/Arista, 1999). Later featured on the soundtrack album *Save the Last Dance* (Uni/ Hollywood, 2000).

Breathless
Words and music by Andrea Corr, Caroline Corr, James Corr, Sharon Corr, and Robert Lange.
Universal-Polygram Intl Tunes, 2000/Zomba Enterprises, 2000/Universal Songs of Polygram Intl., 2000/Universal-MCA Music Publishing, 2000.
Best-selling record by Corrs from the album *In Blue* (WEA/Atlantic/ Lava, 2000).

Bring Your Lovin' Back Here
Words and music by Benjamin Attewell, Ian Ball, Paul Blackburn, William Gray, and Oliver Peacock.
Warner/Chappell Music Canada Ltd., 2000.
Introduced by Gomez on the album *Abandoned Shopping Trolley Hotline* (EMD/Virgin, 2000).

Broadway
Words and music by John Rzeznik.
Corner of Clark and Kent, 1998/EMI-Virgin Songs, 1998.
Best-selling record by the Goo Goo Dolls from the album *Dizzy Up the Girl* (WEA/Warner Bros., 1998).

Buffalo Springfield Again
Words and music by Neil Young.
Silver Fiddle Music, 1998.
Introduced by Neil Young on the album *Silver & Gold* (WEA/Warner Bros., 2000).

Burning Inside
Words and music by Paul Barker, Christopher Connelly, Allen Jourgensen, and William Rieflin.
Spurburn Music, Austin, 1990/Warner-Tamerlane Music, 1990.
Revived by Static X featuring Burton C. Bell on the soundtrack album *The Crow: Salvation* (Koch, 2000).

Butterfly
Words and music by Flea (pseudonym for Michael Balzary), Seth Binzer, John Frusciante, Anthony Kiedis, Bret Mazur, and Chad Smith.
Crazytown Music, Encino, 1999/Moebetoblame Music, 1999/Screen

Gems-EMI Music Inc., 1999.
Introduced by Crazy Town featuring the Red Hot Chili Peppers on the album *The Gift of Game* (Sony/Columbia, 1999).

Buy Me a Rose
Words and music by Jim Funk and Erik Hickenlooper.
Blue Plate Music Publishing, 1999/Rex Benson Music, 1999/Stone Forest Music, 1999/Tripptunes, 1999.
Number one song by Kenny Rogers featuring Alison Krauss and Billy Dean from the album *She Rides Wild Horses* (Dreamcatcher, 1999). Featured on an episode of the television series *Touched by an Angel.*

By Your Side
Words and music by Paul Denman, Andrew Hale, Stuart Matthewman, and Sade (pseudonym for Helen Adu).
Sony ATV Songs LLC, Nashville, 2000/Angel Music Ltd., 2000.
Introduced by Sade on the album *Lovers Rock* (Sony/Epic, 2000).

Bye Bye Bye
Words and music by Andreas Carlsson, Kristian Lundin, and Jacob Schulze.
Zomba Enterprises, 2000/Grantsville Publishing, 2000.
Best-selling record by 'N Sync from the album *No Strings Attached* (BMG/Jive/Silvertone, 2000).Nominated for a Grammy Award, Record of the Year, 2000.

C

Californication

Words and music by Flea (pseudonym for Michael Balzary), John Frusciante, Anthony Kiedis, and Chad Smith.

Moebetoblame Music, 1999.

Best-selling record by the Red Hot Chili Peppers from the album *Californication* (WEA/Warner Bros., 1999).Nominated for a Grammy Award, Best Rock Song, 2000.

Callin' Me

Words and music by Zane Copeland, Irving Folmar, Kenneth Jones, and Dominick Warren.

Painkiller Publishing, 2000/Tycon Music, 2000.

Best-selling record by Lil' Zane featuring 112 from the album *Young World: The Future* (EMD/Priority, 2000).

Can I Get Your Number (A Girl like You)

Words and music by Joseph Belmaati, Mich Hansen, and Stephen Migliore.

Emerald Forest, Ventura, 2000/Warner-Tamerlane Music, 2000/Finger Lickin Good Music, 2000.

Introduced by No Authority on the album *No Authority* (WEA/Warner Bros., 2000).

Can't Fight the Moonlight

Words and music by Diane Warren.

Realsongs, 2000.

Best-selling record by LeAnn Rimes from the film and soundtrack album *Coyote Ugly* (WEA/Atlantic/Curb, 2000).

Can't Go for That

Words and music by Sara Allen, Calvin Broadus, Melissa Elliott, Brycyn Evans, Warren Griffin, N. Hale, Daryl Hall, Roosevelt Harrel, and John Oates.

Irving Music Inc., 2000/Songs of Windswept Pacific, 2000/Unichappell Music Inc., 2000/My Own Chit Publishing, 2000/Hot Cha Music,

2000/Nature's Finest Music, 2000/Geomantic Music, 2000/Nuevo Dia Publishing, 2000.
Best-selling record by Tamia from the album *A Nu Day* (WEA/Elektra, 2000). Based on the 1981 Hall and Oates hit "I Can't Go for That (No Can Do)."

Can't Stay
Words and music by David Hollister and Eugene Peoples.
Cherry River Music, New York, 1999/Gee Jaz Music, 1999/Ma Ma Bev's Music, 1999/Oh My God Music, 1999/Universal-Polygram Intl Tunes, 1999/Polygram International Music, 1999/Songs of Dreamworks, 1999.
Best-selling record by Dave Hollister from the album *Ghetto Hymns* (Uni/DreamWorks, 1999).

The Captain
Words and music by Kasey Chambers.
Gibbon Music Publishing, 1999.
Introduced by Kasey Chambers on the album *The Captain* (WEA/ Warner Bros., 2000). Also appeared in an episode of the HBO original series *The Sopranos*.

Careful (Click, Click)
Words and music by Robert Diggs, Lamont Hawkins, Darryl Hill, Jason Hunter, and Elgin Turner.
Careers-BMG Music, Beverly Hills, 2000/Diggs Family Music, New York, 2000/Wu-Tang Publishing, 2000.
Introduced by the Wu-Tang Clan on the album *The W* (Sony/Columbia, 2000).

Carlene
Words and music by Charles Black, Rory Bourke, and Phillip Vassar.
Rory Bourke Music, Nashville, 2000/EMI-April Music, 2000/Phil Vassar Music, 2000/EMI-Blackwood Music Inc., 2000/Flybridge Tunes, 2000.
Best-selling record by Phil Vassar from the album *Phil Vassar* (Arista, 2000).

Case of the Ex (Watcha Gonna Do)
Words and music by Traci Hale, Thabiso Nkhereanye, and Christopher Stewart.
Famous Music Corp., 2000/Hale Yeah Music, 2000/Mo Better Grooves Music, 2000/Tunes on the Verge of Insanity, 2000/Peertunes LTD, 2000/Tabulous Music, 2000/Hitco South, 2000.
Best-selling record by Mya from the album *Fear of Flying* (Uni/ Interscope, 2000).

The Chain of Love
Words and music by Jonathan Barnett and Rory Feek.
Melanie Howard Music, Nashville, 1999/Pugwash Music, 1999/Waterdance Music, 1999.
Best-selling record by Clay Walker from the album *Live, Laugh, Love* (Giant, 1999).

Change (In the House of Flies)
Words and music by Stephen Carpenter, Chi Cheng, Abran Cunningham, and Camilo Moreno.
My Rib Is Broke, 2000/WB Music Publishing, 2000.
Introduced by the Deftones on the album *White Pony* (WEA/Warner Bros., 2000). Later featured on the soundtrack album *Little Nicky* (WEA/Warner Bros., 2000).

Change Your Mind
Words and music by Jeff Beres, Ken Block, Andrew Copeland, Ryan Newell, and Mark Trojanowski.
Crooked Chimney Music, Gainesville, 2000/Songs of Universal, 2000.
Introduced by Sister Hazel on the album *Fortress* (Uni/Universal, 2000).

Cherchez Laghost
Words and music by Stony Browder, Ghostface Killah (pseudonym for Dennis Coles), August Darnell, and Lawrence Parker.
Browder and Darnell Publishing, Beverly Hills, 2000/Zomba Enterprises, 2000/Rainyville Music, 2000.
Introduced by Ghostface Killah on the album *Supreme Clientele* (Sony, 2000).

C'mon People (We're Making It Now)
Words and music by Richard Ashcroft.
EMI-Virgin Songs, 2000/EMI Virgin Music Ltd., 2000.
Introduced by Richard Ashcroft on the album *Alone with Everybody* (EMD/Virgin, 2000).

Cold Day in July
Words and music by Richard Leigh.
EMI U Catalogue, 1981/United Artists Music Co., Inc., 1981/Lion Hearted Music, 1981.
Best-selling record by the Dixie Chicks from the album *Fly* (Sony/Monument, 1999).

Come On, Come On
Words and music by Gregory Camp, Paul Delisle, Steven Harwell, and Kevin Iannello.
Warner-Tamerlane Music, 1999/Squish Moth Music, 1999/Smash Mouth Music, 1999.
Introduced by Smash Mouth on the album *Astro Lounge* (Uni/

Interscope, 1999). Later featured on the soundtrack album *Snow Day* (Uni/Geffen, 2000).

Come On Over Baby (All I Want Is You)
Words and music by Johan Aberg, Christina Aguilera, Chaka Blackmon, Raymond Cham, Eric Dawkins, Ronald Fair, Shelly Peiken, Pauli Reinikainen, and Guy Roche.
Manuiti LA Music, Encino, 1999/Christina Aguilera Music, Santa Monica, 1999/BMG Songs Inc., 1999/Chrysalis Music Group, 1999/ Dreamworks Songs, 1999/Celebrity Status Entertainment, 1999/E D Duz It Music, 1999/Peermusic III LTD, 1999/Shellayla Songs, 1999/ Eclectic Music Co., 1999/Vibe Like That Music, 1999/Hidden Pun Music, 1999/Sushi Too Music, 1999.
Number one song by Christina Aguilera from the album *Christina Aguilera* (BMG/RCA, 1999). Spanish-language version, "Ven Conmigo (Solamente Tu)," featured on *Mi Reflejo* (BMG/U.S. Latin, 2000).

Connect
Words and music by DJ Hurricane (pseudonym for Wendell Fite), Cameron Gipp, Pharoahe Monch (pseudonym for T. Mcnair), and Xzibit (pseudonym for Alvin Joiner).
EMI-April Music, 2000/Get the Bo, 2000/Merokee Music, 2000.
Best-selling record by DJ Hurricane featuring Xzibit, Big Gipp, and Pharoahe Monch from the album *Don't Sleep* (TVT, 2000).

Could I Have This Kiss Forever
Words and music by Diane Warren.
Realsongs, 1999.
Introduced by Enrique Iglesias and Whitney Houston on the album *Enrique* (Uni/Interscope, 1999). Later featured on the Whitney Houston album *The Greatest Hits* (BMG/Arista, 2000).

Couldn't Last a Moment
Words and music by Jeffrey Steele and Danny Wells.
Yellow Desert Music, Nashville, 2000/Irving Music Inc., 2000/My Life's Work Music, 2000/Songs of Windswept Pacific, 2000.
Best-selling record by Collin Raye from the album *Tracks* (Sony/Epic, 2000).

A Country Boy Can Survive
Words and music by Hank Williams, Jr.
Bocephus Music, Nashville, 1981.
Revived by Chad Brock featuring Hank Williams Jr. and George Jones on the album *Yes!* (WEA/Warner Bros., 2000). Also featured on the Hank Williams Jr. compilation *The Bocephus Box: 1979-1999* (WEA/ Atlantic/Curb, 2000).

Country Comes to Town
Words and music by Toby Keith.
Tokeco Tunes, Nashville, 1999.
Best-selling record by Toby Keith from the album *How Do You Like Me Now?!* (Uni/DreamWorks, 1999).

Country Grammar (Hot Shit)
Words by Nelly (pseudonym for Cornell Haynes), music by Jason Epperson.
BMG Songs Inc., 2000/Jay E's Basement, 2000/Universal-MCA Music Publishing, 2000/Jackie Frost Music, 2000.
Best-selling record by Nelly from the album *Country Grammar* (Uni/Universal, 2000).

Cousin Dupree
Words and music by Walter Becker and Donald Fagen.
Freejunket Music, 1999/Len Freedman Music, 1999/Zeon Music, 1999.
Introduced by Steely Dan on the album *Two Against Nature* (WEA/Warner Bros, 2000).

Cowboy Take Me Away
Words and music by Marcus Hummon and Martie Seidel.
Careers-BMG Music, Beverly Hills, 1999/Floyd's Dream Music, Nashville, 1999/Woolly Puddin' Music, 1999.
Number one song by the Dixie Chicks from the album *Fly* (Sony/Monument, 1999).

Crash and Burn
Words and music by Darren Hayes and Daniel Jones.
WB Music Publishing, 1999.
Best-selling record by Savage Garden from the album *Affirmation* (Sony/Columbia, 1999).

Crazy for This Girl
Words and music by Jeff Cohen and Jaron Lowenstein.
As You Wish Music, New York, 2000/EMI-Blackwood Music Inc., 2000/Tzitzis What We Do Music, 2000.
Best-selling record by Evan and Jaron from the album *Evan and Jaron* (Sony/Columbia, 2000).

Cruisin'
Words and music by William Robinson and Marvin Tarplin.
Bertam Music Co., 1979/Jobete Music Co., 1979/Bertam Music Publishing, 1979.
Revived by Huey Lewis and Gwyneth Paltrow in the film and on the soundtrack album *Duets* (Uni/Hollywood, 2000).

Cry Like a Baby
Words and music by Kasey Chambers.

Gibbon Music Publishing, 1999.
Introduced by Kasey Chambers on the album *The Captain* (WEA/Warner Bros., 2000).

Crybaby
Words and music by Mariah Carey, Timothy Gatling, Gene Griffin, Aaron Hall, Howie Hersh, Trey Lorenz, Edward Riley, Lloyd Smith, and Snoop Dogg (pseudonym for Calvin Broadus).
Rye Songs, Philadelphia, 1999/Sony ATV Songs LLC, Nashville, 1999/Smitty's Son, 1999/Donril Music, 1999/EMI-Virgin Music, 1999/Zomba Enterprises, 1999/Cal-Gene Music, 1999/EMI-Virgin Songs, 1999/My Own Chit Publishing, 1999/Cal Rock Music, 1999/WB Music Publishing, 1999.
Best-selling record by Mariah Carey featuring Snoop Dogg from the album *Rainbow* (Sony/Columbia, 1999).

D

Daddy Won't Sell the Farm
Words and music by Robin Branda and Steve Fox.
Kreditkard Music, Nashville, 1999/Penny Annie Music, 1999.
Best-selling record by Montgomery Gentry from the album *Tattoos & Scars* (Sony/Columbia, 1999).

Dance with Me
Words and music by Richard Adler and Jerry Ross.
J & J Ross Co., 2000/Lakshmi Puja Music, 2000.
Best-selling record by Debelah Morgan from the album *Dance with Me* (WEA/Atlantic, 2000).

Dance Tonight
Words and music by Ali Jones-Muhammad, Dawn Robinson, and Raphael Saadiq.
Stratinum Songs, 2000/Watermelon Girl Music, 2000/Zomba Enterprises, 2000/Ensign Music, 2000/Cool Abdul Music, 2000/Ugmoe Music, 2000.
Best-selling record by Lucy Pearl from the album *Lucy Pearl* (Uni/Beyond, 2000).

Dancin'
Words and music by Delvis Damon, Edward Ferrell, Clifton Lighty, Darren Lighty, Balewa Muhammad, and Edward Riley.
Eddie F. Music, Closter, 2000/Donril Music, 2000/WB Music Publishing, 2000/Zomba Enterprises, 2000/Jahque Joints, 2000/Universal-Polygram Intl Tunes, 2000/Rusty Knuckles Music, 2000/Dowhatigotta Music, 2000.
Introduced by Guy on the album *III* (Uni/MCA, 2000).

Dancing in the Moonlight
Words and music by Sherman Kelly.
St. Nathanson Music, Brooklyn, 1970/EMI United Catalogue, 1970.
Revived by Toploader on the album *Onka's Big Monka* (Sony International, 2000).

Dancing Queen
Words and music by Stig Anderson, Benny Andersson, and Bjoern Ulvaeus.
EMI-Grove Park Music, 1976/Universal Songs of Polygram Intl., 1976.
Best-selling record as Revived by the A*Teens on the album *The Abba Generation* (Uni/MCA, 1999). Later featured on the soundtrack album *Miss Congeniality* (TVT, 2000).

Daydream Believer
Words and music by John Stewart.
Screen Gems-EMI Music Inc., 1967.
Revived by Mary Beth Maziarz on the soundtrack album *Songs from Dawson's Creek, Volume 2* (Sony/Columbia, 2000).

Deadly Assassins
Words and music by Louis Freeze, Alan Maman, and Eric Schrody.
A. Maman Music, 2000.
Introduced by Everlast featuring B-Real on the album *Eat at Whitey's* (Tommy Boy, 2000).

Dear Lie
Words and music by Babyface (pseudonym for Kenneth Edmonds) and T-Boz (pseudonym for Tionne Watkins).
Ecaf Music, Philadelphia, 1999/Sony ATV Songs LLC, Nashville, 1999/EMI-April Music, 1999/EMI April Canada, 1999/Grunge Girl Music, 1999.
Best-selling record by TLC from the album *Fanmail* (BMG/Arista/La Face, 1999).

Deck the Halls
Words and music by Kristyn Osborn and Philip Symonds.
Without Anna Music, Nashville, 1999.
Revived by SHeDAISY on the album *Brand New Year* (Uni/Hollywood, 2000).

Deep Inside
Words and music by Mary Blige, Kevin Deane, Tara Geter, Elton John, and Bernard Taupin.
Dick James Music Ltd., London, England, 1999/EMI-April Music, 1999/Universal Songs of Polygram Intl., 1999/Mary J. Blige Music, 1999/Universal-MCA Music Publishing, 1999/Gyz Muzik, 1999.
Best-selling record by Mary J. Blige from the album *Mary* (Uni/MCA, 1999).

Deep Inside of You
Words and music by Kevin Cadogan and Stephan Jenkins.
Careers-BMG Music, Beverly Hills, 1999/EMI-Blackwood Music Inc., 1999/3EB Publishing, 1999/Cappagh Hill Music, 1999.

Introduced by Third Eye Blind on the album *Blue* (WEA/Elektra, 1999). Later featured on the soundtrack album *Me, Myself & Irene* (WEA/Elektra, 2000).

Demons

Words and music by Fatboy Slim (pseudonym for Norman Cook), Macy Gray, R. Jackson, Natalie Hinds, Natalie McIntyre, and Bill Withers.

Universal-MCA Music Publishing, 2000/Zomba Enterprises, 2000/Universal-Polygram Intl Tunes, 2000/Interior Music, 2000/Happy Mel Boopy's Cocktail Lounge, 2000.

Introduced by Fatboy Slim featuring Macy Gray on the album *Halfway Between the Gutter and the Stars* (EMD/Astralwerks, 2000).

Desert Rose

Words and music by Sting (pseudonym for Gordon Sumner).

EMI-Blackwood Music Inc., 1999/Magnetic Music Publishing Co., 1999.

Best-selling record by Sting featuring Cheb Mami from the album *Brand New Day* (Uni/A&M, 1999).

Devil's Pie

Words and music by D'Angelo (pseudonym for Michael Archer) and DJ Premier (pseudonym for Chris Martin).

EMI-April Music, 1998/Universal-Polygram Intl Tunes, 1998/Ah Choo Music, 1998/Gifted Pearl, 1998.

Introduced by D'Angelo on the soundtrack album *Belly* (Uni/Def Jam, 1998). Later featured on the D'Angelo album *Voodoo* (EMD/Virgin, 2000).

Dirt Ball

Words and music by Joseph Bruce.

Psychopathic Music Publishing, 2000.

Introduced by Insane Clown Posse featuring Twiztid on the soundtrack album *Heavy Metal 2000* (BMG/Restless, 2000).

Do It Again (Put Ya Hands Up)

Words by Dwight Grant, Jay-Z (pseudonym for Shawn Carter), and Kyambo Joshua, music by Dana Stinson.

Hitco South, 1999/Shakur al Din Music, 1999/EMI-Blackwood Music Inc., 1999/Lil Lu Lu Publishing, 1999.

Best-selling record by Jay-Z featuring Beanie Sigel and Amil from the album *Vol. 3: The Life & Times of Shawn Carter* (Uni/Def Jam, 1999).

Do You

Words and music by Robert Bell, Ronald Bell, Donald Boyce, George Brown, DMX (pseudonym for Earl Simmons), Irving Lorenzo, Robert Mickens, Larry Ogletree, Claydes Smith, Dennis Thomas, and

Richard Westfield.
Boomer X Publishing, New York, 2000/DJ Irv, 2000/Warner-Tamerlane Music, 2000/Ensign Music, 2000/Dead Game Publishing, 2000/Famous Music Corp., 2000/Second Decade Music, 2000/Gang Music Ltd., 2000.
Best-selling record by Funkmaster Flex featuring DMX from the album *Mix Tape, Volume 4: 60 Minutes of Funk* (Loud, 2000).

Doesn't Really Matter
Words and music by James Harris, Janet Jackson, and Terry Lewis.
Black Ice Publishing, Calabasa, 2000/EMI-April Music, 2000/Flyte Tyme Tunes, 2000.
Number one song by Janet Jackson from the soundtrack album *Nutty Professor II: The Klumps* (Uni/Def Jam, 2000).

Don't Call Me Baby
Words and music by Giuseppe Chierchia, April Coates, Jerry Cohen, Gene McFadden, Duane Morrison, Andrew Van Dorsselaer, and John Whitehead.
Universal-MCA Music Publishing, 2000/Warner-Tamerlane Music, 2000/Mijac Music, 2000/Crisler Edizioni Musicali SR, 2000.
Best-selling single by Madison Avenue. Later featured on the album *The Polyester Embassy* (Sony/Columbia, 2000).

Don't Give Up
Words and music by Bryan Adams, Chicane (pseudonym for Nicholas Bracegirdle), and Raymond Hedges.
Realsongs, 2000/Warner-Tamerlane Music, 2000/Warner/Chappell Music Canada Ltd., 2000/19 Music, 2000/Bryan Adams Publishing, 2000/Badams Music Ltd., 2000/Nick Bracegirdle Publishing, 2000.
Best-selling single by Chicane featuring Bryan Adams. Later featured on the album *Behind the Sun* (Sony/Columbia, 2000).

Don't Mess with My Man
Words and music by Ali Jones-Muhammed, Conesha Owens, Dawn Robinson, and Raphael Saadiq.
Tenom Music, Anitoch, 2000/Cool Abdul Music, 2000/Ugmoe Music, 2000/Ensign Music, 2000/Stratinum Songs, 2000/Watermelon Girl Music, 2000/Zomba Enterprises, 2000.
Introduced by Lucy Pearl on the album *Lucy Pearl* (Uni/Beyond, 2000).

Don't Say You Love Me
Words and music by James Bralower, Marit Larsen, Marion Ravn, and Peter Zizzo.
Fancy Footwork Music, Roslyn, 1999/Lissome Songs, Minneapolis, 1999/Pez, Old Brookeville, 1999/Warner-Chappell Music, 1999/Vaporeon Music, 1999/Mewtwo Music, 1999/Warner-Tamerlane Music, 1999/Connotation Music, 1999.

Best-selling record by M2M from the soundtrack album *Pokemon: The First Movie* (WEA/Atlantic, 1999). Later featured on the album *Shades of Purple* (WEA/Atlantic, 2000).

Don't Think I'm Not
Words and music by Kevin Briggs, Kandi Buruss, Bernard Edwards, and Katrina Willis.
3rd I Musicworks, Los Angeles, 2000/Air Control Music, 2000/EMI-April Music, 2000/Kandacy Music, 2000/Shek' Em Down Music, 2000/Silliwak, 2000.
Best-selling record by Kandi from the album *Hey Kandi* (Sony/Columbia, 2000).

Down with the Sickness
Words and music by Dan Donegan, David Draiman, Steve Kmak, and Michael Wengren.
WB Music Publishing, 2000.
Introduced by Disturbed on the album *The Sickness* (WEA/Warner Bros., 2000).

Dramacide
Words and music by R. Aguilar, K. Bailey, Big Punisher (pseudonym for Christopher Rios), Kool G Rap (pseudonym for Nathaniel Wilson), D. Matthews, A. Williams, and J. Wright.
Let Me Show You Music, New York, 2000/For My Son Publishing, 2000.
Introduced by the X-ecutioners featuring Big Punisher and Kool G. Rap on the soundtrack album *Black and White* (Sony/Columbia, 2000).

Drive
Words and music by Brandon Boyd, Michael Einziger, Alex Katunich, Chris Kilmore, and Jose Pasillas.
EMI-April Music, 1999/Hunglikeyora, 1999.
Introduced by Incubus on the album *Make Yourself* (Sony/Epic, 1999).

E

Early Mornin' Stoned Pimp
Words and music by Martin Gross and Kid Rock (pseudonym for Robert Ritchie).
Thirty Two Mile Music, 1996/Warner-Tamerlane Music, 1996.
Re-introduced by Kid Rock on the album *The History of Rock* (WEA/Atlantic, 2000). Also featured on the soundtrack album *Road Trip* (Uni/DreamWorks, 2000).

Elite
Words and music by Stephen Carpenter, Chi Cheng, Abran Cunningham, and Camilo Moreno.
My Rib Is Broke, 2000/WB Music Publishing, 2000.
Introduced by the Deftones on the album *White Pony* (WEA/Warner Bros., 2000).

Every Story Is a Love Story
Words by Timothy Rice, music by Elton John.
Wonderland Music, 1997/Happenstance Music, 1997/Sixty Four Square Music, 1997/Evadon Ltd., 1997.
Featured on the original Broadway cast recording of *Elton John and Tim Rice's Aida* (Uni/Disney/Duplicate Numbers, 2000).

Everything Is Different Now
Words and music by Scott Crago, Timothy Drury, and Don Henley.
Warner-Tamerlane Music, 2000/Wisteria Music, 2000/Third Lug Music, 2000.
Introduced by Don Henley on the album *Inside Job* (WEA/Warner Bros., 2000).

Everything in Its Right Place
Words and music by Radiohead.
Warner-Chappell Music, 2000.
Introduced by Radiohead on the album *Kid A* (EMD/Capitol, 2000).

Everything You Want

Words and music by Matthew Scannell.

Mascan Music, 1999/WB Music Publishing, 1999.

Number one song by Vertical Horizon from the album *Everything You Want* (BMG/RCA, 1999).

Ex-Girlfriend

Words and music by Thomas Dumont, Tony Kanal, and Gwen Stefani.

Universal-MCA Music Publishing, 2000/World of the Dolphin Music, 2000.

Best-selling record by No Doubt from the album *Return of Saturn* (Uni/Interscope, 2000).

Exterminator

Words and music by Martin Duffy, Bobby Gillespie, Jim Hunt, Andrew Innes, Duncan Mackay, Darrin Mooney, Gary Mounfield, and Robert Young.

EMI-Blackwood Music Inc., 2000/Complete Music (England), 2000/EMI Music Publishing Ltd., 2000.

Introduced by Primal Scream on the album *XTRMNTR* (EMD/Astralwerks, 2000).

F

Fa Fa (Never Be the Same Again)
Words and music by Adam Gardner, Ryan Miller, and Brian Rosenworcel.
Universal-Polygram Intl Tunes, 1999/Low Crawl Music, 1999.
Introduced by Guster on the album *Lost and Gone Forever* (WEA/London/Sire, 1999).

Faded
Words and music by Trevor Guthrie.
EMI-April Music, 1999.
Best-selling record by soulDecision featuring Thrust from the album *No One Does It Better* (Uni/MCA, 2000).

Feelin' So Good
Words and music by Big Punisher (pseudonym for Christopher Rios), Puff Daddy (pseudonym for Sean Combs), Fat Joe (pseudonym for Joseph Cartagena), George Logios, Jennifer Lopez, Cory Rooney, and Steven Standard.
Let Me Show You Music, New York, 1999/Cori Tiffani Music, Great Neck, 1999/Sony ATV Songs LLC, Nashville, 1999/Jelly's Jams L.L.C. Music, New York, 1999/Nuyorican Publishing, Los Angeles, 1999/STD Music Publishing, Brooklyn, 1999/EMI-April Music, 1999/Sony Songs Inc., 1999/EMI April Canada, 1999/Joseph Cartegena Music, 1999/Justin Combs Publishing, 1999.
Best-selling record by Jennifer Lopez featuring Big Punisher and Fat Joe from the album *On the 6* (Sony/Work, 1999).

Feels like Love
Words and music by Vince Gill.
Vinny Mae Music, 2000.
Best-selling record by Vince Gill from the album *Let's Make Sure We Kiss Goodbye* (Uni/MCA Nashville, 2000).Nominated for a Grammy Award, Best Country Song, 2000.

Fever Dog

Words and music by Cameron Crowe, Russell Hammond, and Nancy Wilson.

Beatle Boots Music, Bellevue, 1999/Edge of Reality Music, Santa Monica/SKG Music Publishing LLC, 1999.

Introduced by the fictional band Stillwater in the film and on the soundtrack album *Almost Famous* (Uni/DreamWorks, 2000).

Flowers on the Wall

Words and music by Lewis DeWitt.

Unichappell Music Inc., 1966/Wallflower Music, 1966.

Best-selling record as Revived by Eric Heatherly on the album *Swimming in Champagne* (Uni/Mercury Nashville, 2000).

A Fool in Love

Words and music by Randy Newman.

Universal-MCA Music Publishing, 2000/SKG Music Publishing LLC, 2000/Randy Newman Music, 2000.

Introduced by Randy Newman in the film and on the soundtrack album *Meet the Parents* (Uni/DreamWorks, 2000).Nominated for an Academy Award, Best Original Song of the Year, 2001.

For Heaven's Sake 2000

Words and music by Dennis Coles, Mitchell Diggs, Robert Diggs, Oli Grant, Darryl Hill, Jason Hunter, Tommy Iommi, Robert Marlette, Ozzy Osbourne (pseudonym for John Osbourne), and Elgin Turner.

Careers-BMG Music, Beverly Hills, 2000/Diggs Family Music, New York, 2000/Blizzard Music, Palm Coast, 2000/Vallallen, New York, 2000/Wu-Tang Publishing, 2000/Black Lava, 2000.

Introduced by the Wu-Tang Clan featuring Ozzy Osbourne and Tony Iommi on the various-artists album *Loud Rocks* (Sony/Columbia, 2000). Based on the song "For Heaven's Sake" from the Wu-Tang album *Wu-Tang Forever* (Loud/RCA, 1997).

Forgot about Dre

Words by Melvin Bradford and Eminem (pseudonym for Marshall Mathers), words and music by Dr. Dre (pseudonym for Andre Young).

Eight Mile Style Music, 1999/Ain't Nothing but Funkin', 1999/WB Music Publishing, 1999/Hard Working Black Folks, 1999.

Best-selling record by Dr. Dre featuring Eminem from the album *2001* (Uni/Interscope, 1999).

4 Sho Sho

Words and music by RZA (pseudonym for Robert Diggs).

Careers-BMG Music, Beverly Hills, 2000/Diggs Family Music, New York, 2000/Ramecca Publishing, 2000.

Introduced by North Star featuring RZA on the soundtrack album *Ghost Dog: The Way of the Samurai* (Sony/Epic, 2000).

Freakin' It

Words and music by Samuel Barnes, Lennie Bennett, Bernard Edwards, Marilyn McLeod, Jean Olivier, Nile Rodgers, Pamela Sawyer, and Willard Smith.

Sony ATV Songs LLC, Nashville, 1999/Sony ATV Tunes LLC, Nashville, 1999/O' Brook Music, Los Angeles, 1999/Treyball Music, Los Angeles, 1999/Slam U Well Music, New York, 1999/Bernard's Other Music, 1999/Ekop Publishing LLC, 1999/Sony Songs Inc., 1999/Warner-Tamerlane Music, 1999/Enot Publishing LLC, 1999/ Jobete Music Co., 1999.

Best-selling record by Will Smith from the album *Willennium* (Sony/ Columbia, 1999).

Free

Words and music by James Harris, Mya Harrison, Terry Lewis, Alexander Richbourg, and Tony Tolbert.

Urban Warfare, New York, 2000/Ella and Gene's Son's Music, Edina, 2000/Street Warfare Publishing, New York, 2000/EMI-April Music, 2000/Flyte Tyme Tunes, 2000/EMI-Blackwood Music Inc., 2000/EMI April Canada, 2000/EMI Blackwood Music Canada Ltd., 2000/Who Knows Music, 2000.

Introduced by Mya on the album *Fear of Flying* (Uni/Interscope, 2000).

From the Bottom of My Broken Heart

Words and music by Eric White.

Zomba Enterprises, 1999/4MW, 1999.

Best-selling record by Britney Spears from the album *...Baby One More Time* (BMG/Jive/Silvertone, 1999).

Funeral Flights

Words and music by Michael Doling, John Fahnestock, and B. Dez Fafara.

Big Scary Tree Publishing, 2000.

Introduced by Strait Up featuring B. Dez Fafara on the album *Strait Up* (EMD/Virgin, 2000).

G

G'd Up
Words and music by Tracey Davis, Kevin Gilliam, Danny Means, Snoop Dogg (pseudonym for Calvin Broadus), and Keiwan Spillman.
Tray Tray's Music, Fontana, 2000/Black Fountain Music, 2000/My Own Chit Publishing, 2000.
Best-selling record by Tha Eastsidaz featuring Snoop Dogg from the album *Snoop Dogg Presents Tha Eastsidaz* (TVT/Doggy Style, 2000).

Get Your Roll On
Words and music by Byron Thomas and Bryan Williams.
Money Mack Music, 2000.
Best-selling record by the Big Tymers from the album *I Got That Work* (Uni/Universal, 2000).

Gettin' in the Way
Words and music by Vidal Davis and Jill Scott.
Blue's Baby Music, 2000/EMI-April Music, 2000/Jat Cat Music Publishing, 2000/Touched by Jazz Music, 2000.
Best-selling record by Jill Scott from the album *Who Is Jill Scott? Words and Sounds, Vol. 1* (Sony/Epic, 2000).

Girls Dem Sugar
Words and music by Beenie Man (pseudonym for Moses Davis), Chad Hugo, and Pharrell Williams.
EMI-Blackwood Music Inc., 2000/Waters of Nazareth Publishing, 2000/EMI April Canada, 2000/Chase Chad Music, 2000/EMI Music Publishing Ltd., 2000.
Best-selling record by Beenie Man featuring Mya from the album *Art and Life* (EMD/Virgin, 2000).

Give Me Just One Night (Una Noche)
Words and music by Anders Bagge, Arnthor Birgisson, and Huentenau Ogalde.
Chrysalis Music Group, 2000/EMI-April Music, 2000/Universal-Polygram Intl Tunes, 2000.

Best-selling record by 98 Degrees from the album *Revelation* (Uni/Universal, 2000).

Give Me You
Words and music by Diane Warren.
Realsongs, 1999.
Best-selling record by Mary J. Blige from the album *Mary* (Uni/MCA, 1999).

Gladys and Lucy
Words and music by Victoria Williams.
Careers-BMG Music, Beverly Hills, 2000/Mumblety Peg, 2000.
Introduced by Victoria Williams on the album *Water to Drink* (WEA/Atlantic, 2000).

Glitter in Their Eyes
Words and music by Oliver Ray and Patti Smith.
Hierophany Music, New York, 2000/Druse Music Inc., 2000.
Introduced by Patti Smith on the album *Gung Ho* (BMG/Arista, 2000).

Go!
Words and music by Melanie Chisolm and William Wainwright.
Rondor Music, 1999/EMI-Full Keel Music, 1999/EMI Music Publishing Ltd., 1999.
Introduced by Melanie C on the album *Northern Star* (EMD/Virgin, 1999). Later featured on the soundtrack album *Whatever It Takes* (Uni/Hollywood, 2000).

Go Let It Out
Words and music by Noel Gallagher.
Sony ATV Songs LLC, Nashville, 2000.
Introduced by Oasis on the album *Standing on the Shoulder of Giants* (Sony/Epic, 2000). Live version featured on the album *Familiar to Millions* (Sony/Epic, 2000).

Go Monkey Go
Words and music by Gerald Casale and Robert Mothersbaugh.
Recombinant Music, 2000.
Introduced by Devo on the soundtrack album *Heroes & Villains: Music Inspired by the Powerpuff Girls* (WEA/Rhino, 2000).

Go On
Words and music by Anthony Martin and Mark Nesler.
Baby Mae Music, Austin, 2000/Glitterfish, Nashville, 2000/Buna Boy Music, 2000/Hamstein Cumberland Music, 2000.
Best-selling record by George Strait from the album *George Strait* (Uni/MCA Nashville, 2000).

Godless
Words and music by Shawn Albro and Christopher Weber.
Back from the Edge, West Hollywood, 2000/Shame on You, Hollywood, 2000/Foot in the Door, West Hempstead, 2000/Famous Music Corp., 2000.
Introduced by U.P.O. on the album *No Pleasantries* (Sony/Epic, 2000).

Good Life
Words and music by Boots.
EMI Blackwood Music Canada Ltd., 2000.
Introduced by the Getaway People on the album *Turnpike Diaries* (Sony/Columbia, 2000).

Goodbye Earl
Words and music by Dennis Linde.
EMI-Blackwood Music Inc., 1999/Rising Gorge Music, 1999.
Best-selling record by the Dixie Chicks from the album *Fly* (Sony/Monument, 1999).

Goodbye Lament
Words and music by David Grohl, Anthony Iommi, and Robert Marlette.
Vallallen, New York, 2000/Twenty Seven Songs, New York, 2000/Music of Windswept, 2000/EMI-Virgin Songs, 2000/MJ Twelve Music, 2000/Universal-MCA Music Publishing, 2000/Songs of Windswept Pacific, 2000/Black Lava, 2000.
Introduced by Tony Iommi featuring Dave Grohl on the album *Iommi* (EMD/Priority/Divine, 2000). Also featured on the soundtrack album *Blair Witch 2: Book of Shadows* (EMD/Priority, 2000).

Got to Get It
Words and music by Marquis Collins, Sisqo (pseudonym for Mark Andrews), James Travis, and Alvin West.
Hot as Fire, Baltimore, 1999/Urban Warfare, New York, 1999/K Money Music, Baltimore, 1999/Sony ATV Songs LLC, Nashville, 1999/Al West Publishing, 1999/WB Music Publishing, 1999.
Best-selling record by Sisqo featuring Make It Hot from the album *Unleash the Dragon* (Uni/Def Jam, 1999).

Got It All
Words and music by Sheldon Harris, Jadakiss (pseudonym for Jason Phillips), Eve Jeffers, Sean Lassiter, and Barry Reese.
Ruff Ryders Entertainment, New York, 2000/Larsiny, Philadelphia, 2000/Teflon Hitz, Scarsdale, 2000/Till Death Do Us Part, Philadelphia, 2000/Blondie Rockwell Music, 2000/EMI-April Music, 2000/Jae'wans Music, 2000/Justin Combs Publishing, 2000.
Best-selling record by Eve and Jadakiss from the various-artists album *Ryde or Die, Vol. 2* (Uni/Interscope, 2000).

Gotta Tell You
Words and music by Anders Bagge, Arnthor Birgisson, and Samantha Mumba.
Chrysalis Music Group, 2000/Air Chrysalis Scandinavia, 2000/Warner-Tamerlane Music, 2000/Murlyn Songs, 2000/Universal-Polygram Intl Tunes, 2000/Warner/Chappell Music Canada Ltd., 2000.
Best-selling record by Samantha Mumba from the album *Gotta Tell You* (Uni/Interscope, 2000).

Grace Kelly Blues
Words and music by Mark Everett.
Almo Music Corp., 1999/Sexy Grandpa Music, 1999.
Introduced by the Eels on the album *Daisies of the Galaxy* (Uni/DreamWorks, 2000).

Graduation (Friends Forever)
Words and music by Josh Deutsch and Colleen Fitzpatrick.
Blanc E Music, New York, 1999/Warner-Tamerlane Music, 1999/Big Black Jacket Music, 1999.
Best-selling record by Vitamin C from the album *Vitamin C* (WEA/Elektra, 1999).

Gravel Pit
Words and music by Dennis Coles, Robert Diggs, Lamont Hawkins, Paulisa Moorman, and Clifford Smith.
Careers-BMG Music, Beverly Hills, 2000/Universal-Polygram Intl Tunes, 2000/Wu-Tang Publishing, 2000.
Introduced by the Wu-Tang Clan on the album *The W* (Sony/Columbia, 2000).

The Great Beyond
Words and music by Peter Buck, Michael Mills, and Michael Stipe.
Temporary Music, 2000.
Introduced by R.E.M. in the film and on the soundtrack album *Man on the Moon* (WEA/Warner Bros., 1999).Nominated for a Grammy Award, Best Song Written for a Movie, 2000.

Green Grass Vapors
Words and music by Stefanie Bolton and Aaron Lyles.
Silly Bo Music, Memphis, 1999/Universal-Polygram Intl Tunes, 1999/Dat Nigga Funky, 1999.
Introduced by Angie Stone on the album *Black Diamond* (BMG/Arista, 1999).

Grinch 2000
Words and music by Busta Rhymes (pseudonym for Trevor Smith), Theo Geisel, and Albert Hague.
EMI Robbins Catalog Inc., 2000.

Introduced by Busta Rhymes and Jim Carrey on the soundtrack album *How the Grinch Stole Christmas* (Uni/Interscope, 2000).

The Ground Beneath Her Feet

Words and music by Bono (pseudonym for Paul Hewson), Adam Clayton, The Edge (pseudonym for David Evans), Larry Mullen, and Salman Rushdie.

Polygram International Music B.V., 2000/Blue Mountain Music Ltd., 2000/Universal Music Publishing Int. Ltd., 2000.

Introduced by U2 featuring Daniel Lanois in the film and on the soundtrack album *Million Dollar Hotel* (Uni/Interscope, 2000).

Gung Ho

Words by Patti Smith, music by Jay Dee Daugherty, Lenny Kaye, Oliver Ray, and Tony Shanahan.

Hierophany Music, New York, 2000/Druse Music Inc., 2000/Slea Head Music, 2000.

Introduced by Patti Smith on the album *Gung Ho* (BMG/Arista, 2000).

H

The Hardest Part of Breaking Up (Is Getting Back Your Stuff)
Words and music by Brian Kierulf and Joshua Schwartz.
Kierulf, 2000/Mugsy Boy Publishing, 2000/Zomba Enterprises, 2000.
Introduced by 2ge+her on the album *2ge+her: Again* (TVT Records, 2000).

Have a Cigar
Words and music by Roger Waters.
Warner-Tamerlane Music, 1975/Roger Waters Music Overseas Ltd., 1975.
Revived by Foo Fighters and Brian May on the soundtrack album *Music from and Inspired by M:I-2* (Uni/Hollywood, 2000).

He Did That
Words and music by Lil' Mac, Master P (pseudonym for Percy Miller), Donald Robertson, and Silkk the Shocker (pseudonym for Zyshonne Miller).
Big P Music, 2000.
Introduced by Silkk the Shocker featuring Master P and Mac on the single *He Did That* (EMD/Priority, 2000).

He Wasn't Man Enough
Words and music by Lashawn Daniels, Fred Jerkins, Rodney Jerkins, and Harvey Mason.
BMG Songs Inc., 2000/EMI-April Music, 2000/EMI-Blackwood Music Inc., 2000/Ensign Music, 2000/Fred Jerkins Publishing, 2000/Rodney Jerkins Music, 2000.
Number one song by Toni Braxton from the album *The Heat* (BMG/Arista/La Face, 2000).Nominated for a Grammy Award, Best R&B Song, 2000.

Heavy Metal Machine
Words and music by Billy Corgan.
Faust's Haus Music, 2000.

Introduced by Smashing Pumpkins on the album *MACHINA/The Machines of God* (EMD/Virgin, 2000).

Hemorrhage (In My Hands)
Words and music by Carl Bell and David Jolicoeur.
Pener Pig Publishing, 2000/Universal Songs of Polygram Intl., 2000.
Best-selling record by Fuel from the album *Something like Human* (Sony/550 Music, 2000).

Hey Papi
Words and music by Jay-Z (pseudonym for Shawn Carter), Memphis Bleek (pseudonym for Malik Cox), and Timothy Mosley.
Virginia Beach Music, 2000/WB Music Publishing, 2000/EMI-Blackwood Music Inc., 2000/Lil Lu Lu Publishing, 2000/EMI Blackwood Music Canada Ltd., 2000.
Best-selling record by Jay-Z featuring Memphis Bleek and Amil from the soundtrack album *Nutty Professor II: The Klumps* (Uni/Def Jam, 2000).

Highlife
Words and music by Louis Freeze, Lawrence Muggerud, and Senen Reyes.
Soul Assassin Music, Los Angeles, 2000/Hits from Da Bong Music, Seattle, 2000/Phreakas Ada Phunk, Cypress, 2000/BMG Songs Inc., 2000.
Introduced by Cypress Hill on the album *Skull & Bones* (Sony/Columbia, 2000).

Home
Words and music by John April, Aaron Lewis, Michael Mushok, and Jonathan Wysocki.
Greenfund, 1999/I'm Nobody Music, 1999/My Blue Car Music, 1999/Pimp Yug, 1999/WB Music Publishing, 1999.
Introduced by Staind on the album *Dysfunction* (WEA/Elektra, 1999).

How Do You Like Me Now?!
Words and music by Chuck Cannon and Toby Keith.
Tokeco Tunes, Nashville, 1999/Wacissa River Music, Nashville, 1999.
Number one song by Toby Keith from the album *How Do You Like Me Now?!* (Uni/DreamWorks, 1999).

How Many Licks?
Words and music by Lil' Kim (pseudonym for Kimberly Jones), Sisqo (pseudonym for Mark Andrews), and Mario Winans.
Undeas Music, Brooklyn, 2000/Butter Jinx Music, Los Angeles, 2000/Notorious Kim Music, 2000/Warner-Tamerlane Music, 2000/EMI Blackwood Music Canada Ltd., 2000/WB Music Publishing, 2000/Janice Combs Music, 2000/Yellow Man Music, 2000/Marsky Music,

2000.
Best-selling record by Lil' Kim featuring Sisqo from the album *Notorious K.I.M.* (WEA/Atlantic, 2000).

Hurricane
Words and music by Bob Dylan (pseudonym for Robert Zimmerman) and Jacques Levy.
Jackelope Publishing, Hamilton, 1975/Ram's Horn Music Co., Inc., 1975.
Featured in the film and on the soundtrack album *The Hurricane* (Uni/MCA, 2000).

I

(I Can't Get No) Satisfaction
Words and music by Michael Jagger and Keith Richards.
ABKCO Music Inc., 1965.
Revived by Britney Spears on the album *Oops!...I Did It Again* (BMG/Jive/Silvertone, 2000).

I Disappear
Words and music by James Hetfield and Lars Ulrich.
Creeping Death Music, 2000.
Introduced by Metallica in the film *Mission: Impossible 2* and on the accompanying soundtrack album, *Music from and Inspired by M:I-2* (Uni/Hollywood, 2000).

I Don't Wanna
Words and music by Phalon Alexander, Johnta Austin, Kevin Hicks, and Darnley Scantlebury.
Chrysalis Music Group, 1999/Naked Under My Clothes Music, 1999/Bubba Gee Music, 1999/Kevin Hicks Music, 1999/Warner-Tamerlane Music, 1999/Scantz Music, 1999/Noontime Tunes, 1999/KDH Publishing, 1999/Noontime South, 1999.
Best-selling record by Aaliyah from the soundtrack album *Romeo Must Die* (EMD/Virgin, 2000).

I Don't Wanna Kiss You Goodnight
Words and music by Dane DeViller, Benjamin Groff, Sean Hosein, Stephen Kipner, and Darryl Zero.
Careers-BMG Music, Beverly Hills, 1999/On Board Music, Santa Monica, 1999/BMG Songs Inc., 1999/EMI-April Music, 1999/Bubalas Publishing, 1999/Brill Building Songs, 1999/Stephen A. Kipner Music, 1999/Banana Tunes Music, 1999.
Best-selling record by LFO from the album *LFO* (BMG/Arista, 1999).

I Hope You Dance
Words and music by Mark Sanders and Tia Sillers.
Choice Is Tragic Music, 2000/Universal-MCA Music Publishing, 2000/

Soda Creek Songs, 2000/Ensign Music, 2000.
Number one song by Lee Ann Womack featuring Sons of the Desert from the album *I Hope You Dance* (Uni/MCA Nashville, 2000).Won a Grammy Award for Best Country Song 2000. Nominated for a Grammy Award, Song of the Year, 2000.

I Knew I Loved You
Words and music by Darren Hayes and Daniel Jones.
WB Music Publishing, 1999.
Number one song by Savage Garden from the album *Affirmation* (Sony/ Columbia, 1999).

I Like It
Words and music by Dallas Austin and Gary White.
Cyptron Music, 2000/EMI-Blackwood Music Inc., 2000/Soundtron Tunes, 2000.
Best-selling record by Sammie from the album *From the Bottom to the Top* (EMD/Capitol, 2000).

I Lost It
Words and music by James Olander and Joe Thrasher.
Major Bob Music, 2000/Taxicaster Music, 2000/Warner-Tamerlane Music, 2000.
Best-selling record by Kenny Chesney from the album *Greatest Hits* (BMG/BNA Entertainment, 2000).

I Need a Hot Girl
Words and music by Lil' Wayne (pseudonym for D'Wayne Carter), Chris Dorsey, Terius Gray, B. W. Thomas, Virgil, and Bryan Williams.
Money Mack Music, 1999.
Best-selling record by the Hot Boy$ featuring the Big Tymers from the album *Guerilla Warfare* (Uni/Universal, 1999).

I Need You
Words and music by Ty Lacy and Dennis Matkosky.
Ariose Music, Brentwood, 2000/Baldy Baldy Music, Nashville, 2000/ EMI-April Music, 2000.
Best-selling record by LeAnn Rimes from the television miniseries *Jesus*.

I Still Got to Have It
Words and music by Monica Arnold, Bryan-Michael Cox, Jermaine Dupri, Peter Gabriel, and Nas (pseudonym for Nasir Jones).
EMI-April Music, 2000/TCF Music Publishing, 2000/So So Def Music, 2000/Babyboys Little Pub Co, 2000/EMI April Canada, 2000/New Regency Music, 2000/Fox Tunes, 2000/New Monarchy Music, 2000/ Ill Will, 2000/Mondeenise Productions, 2000.

Introduced by Jermaine Dupri and Nas featuring Monica on the soundtrack album *Big Momma's House* (Sony/Columbia, 2000).

I Think God Can Explain
Words and music by Waymon Boone.
Hit & Run Music, 1999.
Introduced by Splender on the album *Halfway down the Sky* (Sony/Columbia, 1999). Later featured on the soundtrack album *Songs from Dawson's Creek, Volume 2* (Sony/Columbia, 2000).

I Think I'm in Love with You
Words and music by John Mellencamp, Cory Rooney, and Daniel Shea.
Cori Tiffani Music, Great Neck, 1999/Sony ATV Songs LLC, Nashville, 1999/Second Generation Rooney Tunes, Great Neck, 1999/Songs of Universal, 1999/EMI-Full Keel Music, 1999/Dan Shea Music, 1999.
Introduced by Jessica Simpson on the album *Sweet Kisses* (Sony/Columbia, 1999). Later featured on the soundtrack album *Songs from Dawson's Creek, Volume 2* (Sony/Columbia, 2000).

I Try
Words and music by Macy Gray, Jinsoo Lim, Natalie McIntyre, Jeremy Ruzumna, and David Wilder.
Children of the Forest Music, Los Angeles, 1999/Mel Boopie Music, Los Angeles, 1999/Ooky Spinalton Music, 1999/EMI-April Music, 1999/Roastitoasti Music, 1999/Zomba Enterprises, 1999/Jinsoo Lim Music, 1999.
Best-selling record by Macy Gray from the album *On How Life Is* (Sony/Epic, 1999).Nominated for Grammy Awards, Record of the Year, 2000 and Song of the Year, 2000.

I Turn to You
Words and music by Diane Warren.
Realsongs, 1999/WB Music Publishing, 1999.
Best-selling record by Christina Aguilera from the album *Christina Aguilera* (BMG/RCA, 1999). Spanish-language version, "Por Siempre Tu," featured on the album *Mi Reflejo* (BMG/U.S. Latin, 2000).

I Wanna Be with You
Words and music by Tiffany Arbuckle, Shelly Peiken, and Keith Thomas.
Sony ATV Tunes LLC, Nashville, 2000/Yellow Elephant Music, 2000/Hidden Pun Music, 2000/Sushi Too Music, 2000/EMI-Blackwood Music Inc., 2000/Shoecrazy Publishing, 2000/Hidden Kuu Music, 2000.
Best-selling record by Mandy Moore from the album *I Wanna Be with You* (Sony/550 Music, 2000).

I Wanna Know
Words and music by Jolyon Skinner and Joe Thomas.
563 Music Publishing, 1999/Conversation Tree Entertainment, 1999/Zomba Enterprises, 1999/Foray Music, 1999/Fade 2 Black Music, 1999/Jo Skin Music, 1999.
Best-selling record by Joe from the soundtrack album *The Wood* (BMG/Jive/Silvertone, 1999). Later featured on the Joe album *My Name Is Joe* (BMG/Jive/Silvertone, 2000).

I Want to Be a Millionaire
Words and music by Jemma Cooper, Jack Elliot, Keith Strachan, and Matthew Strachan.
Jack D. Elliot Music, New York, 2000/Jemma K. Cooper Music, New York, 2000/Universal-Polygram Intl Tunes, 2000/WB Music Publishing, 2000/Fozman Music LLC, 2000.
Introduced by Jack and Jemma on the soundtrack album *Who Wants to Be a Millionaire: The Album* (Uni/Disney, 2000).

I Will Love Again
Words and music by Paul Barry and Mark Taylor.
Right Bank Music, Encino, 1999.
Best-selling record by Lara Fabian from the album *Lara Fabian* (Sony/Columbia, 2000).

I Will...But
Words and music by Jason Deere and Kristyn Osborn.
Without Anna Music, Nashville, 1999/Lehsem Songs, 1999/Magnolia Hill Music, 1999.
Best-selling record by SHeDAISY from the album *The Whole Shebang* (Uni/Lyric Street, 1999).

I Wish
Words and music by Robert Kelly.
R. Kelly Music, 2000/Zomba Enterprises, 2000.
Number one song by R. Kelly from the album *TP-2.com* (BMG/Jive/Silvertone, 2000).

I Wish
Words and music by Mike City.
Mike City Music, 2000.
Number one song by Carl Thomas from the album *Emotional* (BMG/Arista/Bad Boy, 2000).

I Won't Back Down
Words and music by Jeffrey Lynne and Thomas Petty.
EMI-April Music, 1989/Gone Gator Music, 1989.
Revived by Johnny Cash featuring Tom Petty on the album *American III: Solitary Man* (Sony/Columbia, 2000).

If I Am
Words and music by John Hampson.
Hazel Songs, 2000/WB Music Publishing, 2000.
Introduced by Nine Days on the album *The Madding Crowd* (Sony/Epic, 2000). Later featured on the soundtrack album *Songs from Dawson's Creek, Volume 2* (Sony/Columbia, 2000).

If I Don't Tell You Now
Words and music by Diane Warren.
Realsongs, 2000.
Introduced by Ronan Keating on the album *Ronan* (Polygram International, 2000).

If You Don't Wanna Love Me
Words and music by LaTocha Scott and Christopher Stewart.
Famous Music Corp., 2000/Juicy Time, 2000/Mo Better Grooves Music, 2000/Tunes on the Verge of Insanity, 2000.
Best-selling record by Tamar from the album *Tamar* (Uni/DreamWorks, 2000).

If You're Gone
Words and music by Robert Thomas.
Bidnis Inc Music, 2000/EMI-Blackwood Music Inc., 2000.
Best-selling record by Matchbox Twenty from the album *Mad Season* (WEA/Atlantic/Lava, 2000).

I'll Be
Words and music by Diane Warren.
Realsongs, 1999.
Best-selling record by Reba McEntire from the album *So Good Together* (Uni/MCA Nashville, 1999).

I'll Go
Words and music by Steven Hurley and Rahsaan Patterson.
Silktone Songs, Olympia Fields, 2000/Chrysalis Music Group, 2000/ Ecstasoul Music, 2000.
Introduced by Donnell Jones on the soundtrack album *Love & Basketball* (New Line, 2000).

I'm like a Bird
Words and music by Nelly Furtado.
Nelstar Publishing, 2000.
Introduced by Nelly Furtado on the album *Whoa, Nelly!* (Uni/ DreamWorks, 2000).

I'm Gonna Make You Love Me
Words and music by Gary Louris and Taylor Rhodes.
Taylor Rhodes Music, 2000/Absinthe Music, 2000/Warner-Tamerlane Music, 2000.

Introduced by the Jayhawks on the album *Smile* (Sony/Columbia, 2000). Later featured on the soundtrack album *Songs from Dawson's Creek, Volume 2* (Sony/Columbia, 2000).

I'm Leavin' Now
Words and music by John Cash.
Johnny Carter Cash Music, 1985.
Introduced by Johnny Cash featuring Merle Haggard on the album *American III: Solitary Man* (Sony/Columbia, 2000).

I'm Outta Love
Words and music by Louis Biancaniello, Anastacia Newkirk, and Samuel Watters.
Sony ATV Tunes LLC, Nashville, 2000/Universal-MCA Music Publishing, 2000/EMI April Canada, 2000/SMY Music, 2000/ Breakthrough Creations, 2000/Po Ho Productions, 2000.
Introduced by Anastacia on the single *I'm Outta Love* (Sony/Columbia, 2000).

I'm Still Your Daddy
Words and music by Merle Haggard.
Merle Haggard Music, 2000.
Introduced by Merle Haggard on the album *If I Could Only Fly* (Anti/ Epitaph, 2000). Later featured in the film and on the soundtrack album *The Gift* (Will Records, 2001).

Immortally Insane
Words and music by Darrel Abbott, Vincent Abbott, Philip Anselmo, and Rex Brown.
Warner-Tamerlane Music, 2000/Cota Music, 2000/VDPR Music, 2000.
Introduced by Pantera on the soundtrack album *Heavy Metal 2000* (BMG/Restless, 2000).

Incomplete
Words and music by Anthony Crawford, Kristin Hudson, and Montell Jordan.
Hudson Jordan Music, Tarzana, 1999/Almo Music Corp., 1999/Famous Music Corp., 1999/Montel Jordan Music, 1999/Shep and Shep Publishing, 1999.
Number one song by Sisqo from the album *Unleash the Dragon* (Uni/ Def Jam, 1999).

Independent Women Part I
Words and music by Samuel Barnes, Beyonce Knowles, Jean Olivier, and Mark Rooney.
Sony ATV Tunes LLC, Nashville, 2000/Colpix Music, Philadelphia, 2000/Cori Tiffani Music, Great Neck, 2000/Sony ATV Songs LLC, Nashville, 2000/Beyonce Publishing, 2000/Ekop Publishing LLC,

2000/New Columbia Pictures Music, 2000/Enot Publishing LLC, 2000.
Number one song by Destiny's Child from the soundtrack album *Charlie's Angels* (Sony/Columbia, 2000).Nominated for a Grammy Award, Best Song Written for a Movie, 2000.

Into the Void
Words and music by Michael Reznor.
Leaving Hope Music, Cleveland, 1999/TVT Music, NYC, 1999.
Introduced by Nine Inch Nails on the album *The Fragile* (Uni/Interscope, 1999).

Intro (Shaolin Finger Jab)/Chamber Music
Words and music by Dennis Coles, Robert Diggs, Gary Grice, Lamont Hawkins, Darryl Hill, Jason Hunter, Clifford Smith, Elgin Turner, and Raekwon (pseudonym for Corey Woods).
Careers-BMG Music, Beverly Hills, 2000/BMG Songs Inc., 2000/Wu-Tang Publishing, 2000.
Introduced by the Wu-Tang Clan on the album *The W* (Sony/Columbia, 2000).

Is This the End
Words and music by Scott Stapp and Mark Tremonti.
Ensign Music, 2000.
Introduced by Creed on the soundtrack album *Scream 3* (BMG/Wind Up, 2000).

It Doesn't Matter
Words and music by Desmond Child, Mary Danoff, William Danoff, John Denver, Jerry Duplessis, Wyclef Jean, Andrew Long, Rob Rosa, and Ricky Walters.
Sony ATV Tunes LLC, Nashville, 2000/A Phantom Vox Music, Los Angeles, 2000/EMI-Blackwood Music Inc., 2000/Dreamworks Songs, 2000/Te Bass Music, 2000/Cherry Lane Music, 2000/Huss-Zwingli Publishing, 2000/Songs of Universal, 2000/Desmophobia, 2000/Warner-Tamerlane Music, 2000/Universal-Polygram Intl Tunes.
Introduced by Wyclef Jean featuring the Rock and Melky Sedeck on the album *The Ecleftic: 2 Sides II a Book* (Sony/Columbia, 2000).

It Feels So Good
Words by Sonique (pseudonym for Sonia Clarke), words and music by Simon Belofsky, Linus Burdick, and Graeme Pleeth.
Careers-BMG Music, Beverly Hills, 2000/BMG Songs Inc., 2000/Universal-Polygram Intl Tunes, 2000/Edition Kosmo, 2000/Sonia Clarke Publishing, 2000.
Best-selling record by Sonique from the album *Hear My Cry* (Uni/Universal, 2000).

It Must Be Love
Words and music by Robert McDill.
Ranger Bob Music, 1978/Universal-Polygram Intl Tunes, 1978.
Number one song as Revived by Alan Jackson on the album *Under the Influence* (BMG/Arista, 1999).

It Was
Words and music by Gary Burr and Mark Wright.
Universal-MCA Music Publishing, 1999/Marketwright Music, 1999/Songs of Universal, 1999/Gary Burr Music, 1999.
Introduced by Chely Wright on the album *Single White Female* (Uni/MCA Nashville, 1999).

It Wasn't Me
Words and music by Ricardo Ducent, Shaun Pizzonia, Shaggy (pseudonym for Orville Burrell), and Brian Thompson.
Livingsting Music, 2000/Far Out Music, 2000.
Best-selling record by Shaggy featuring Ricardo "Rikrok" Ducent from the album *Hotshot* (Uni/MCA, 2000).

It's Always Somethin'
Words and music by Marv Green and Aimee Mayo.
Careers-BMG Music, Beverly Hills, 1999/Golden Wheat Music, 1999/Warner-Tamerlane Music, 1999/New Haven Music, 1999.
Best-selling record by Joe Diffie from the album *A Night to Remember* (Sony/Epic, 1999).

It's Gonna Be Me
Words and music by Andreas Carlsson, Martin Sandberg, and Rami Yacoub.
Zomba Enterprises, 2000/Grantsville Publishing, 1999.
Number one song by 'N Sync from the album *No Strings Attached* (BMG/Jive/Silvertone, 2000).

It's My Life
Words and music by Bon Jovi (pseudonym for John Bongiovi), Max Martin (pseudonym for Martin Sandberg), and Richard Sambora.
Universal-Polygram Intl Tunes, 2000/Zomba Enterprises, 2000.
Best-selling record by Bon Jovi from the album *Crush* (Uni/Island/Def Jam, 2000).

It's Not a Game
Words and music by T. Birkett, D. Coward, J. Cummings, Chris Dewar, Michael Dewar, RZA (pseudonym for Robert Diggs), B. Mayfield, and Raekwon (pseudonym for Corey Woods).
Careers-BMG Music, Beverly Hills, 2000/Ayatollah Music Publishing, Yonkers, 2000/Cream Teamsters, New York, 2000/Wu-Tang Publishing, 2000.

Introduced by the American Cream Team featuring Raekwon in the film and on the soundtrack album *Black and White* (Sony/Columbia, 2000).

It's So Hard

Words and music by Big Punisher (pseudonym for Christopher Rios), Richard Frierson, and Julian Garfield.

Let Me Show You Music, New York, 2000/Young Lord Music, Baltimore, 2000/EMI-Blackwood Music Inc., 2000/Firm Body Music, 2000/Janice Combs Music, 2000.

Best-selling record by Big Punisher featuring Donell Jones from the album *Yeeeah Baby* (Sony/Columbia, 2000).

I've Seen It All

Words by Sigurjon Sigurdsson and Lars Von Trier, music by Bjork Gudmundsdottir.

Universal-Polygram Intl Tunes, 2000.

Introduced by Bjork featuring Thom Yorke in the film *Dancer in the Dark* and on the Bjork album *Selmasongs: Music from the Motion Picture Dancer in the Dark* (WEA/Elektra, 2000).Nominated for an Academy Award, Best Original Song of the Year, 2000.

J

Janie Runaway
Words and music by Walter Becker and Donald Fagen.
Freejunket Music, 1999/Len Freedman Music, 1999/Zeon Music, 1999/ EMI April Canada, 1999/Chase Chad Music, 1999.
Introduced by Steely Dan on the album *Two Against Nature* (WEA/ Warner Bros., 2000).

Judith
Words and music by William Howerdel and Maynard Keenan.
Transfixed Music, Los Angeles, 2000/EMI-Virgin Music, 2000/Toolshed Music, 2000.
Introduced by A Perfect Circle on the album *Mer de Noms* (EMD/ Virgin, 2000).

Jumpin, Jumpin
Words and music by Jovonn Alexander, Chad Elliot, Beyonce Knowles, and Rufus Moore.
Sony ATV Tunes LLC, Nashville, 1999/Beyonce Publishing, 1999/353 Music, 1999/Snook Life, 1999/Rufus T. Moore, 1999.
Best-selling record by Destiny's Child from the album *The Writing's on the Wall* (Sony/Columbia, 1999).

Just Another Day in Paradise
Words and music by Phillip Vassar and Craig Wiseman.
Daddy Rabbitt Music, Nashville, 2000/Almo Music Corp., 2000/EMI-April Music, 2000/Phil Vassar Music, 2000.
Number one song by Phil Vassar from the album *Phil Vassar* (BMG/ Arista, 2000).

Just Be a Man about It
Words and music by Johnta Austin, Teddy Bishop, Toni Braxton, and Bryan-Michael Cox.
Chrysalis Music Group, 2000/Naked Under My Clothes Music, 2000/ Babyboys Little Pub Co, 2000/October Eighth Music, 2000/Warner-Tamerlane Music, 2000/Braxtoni Music, 2000.

Introduced by Toni Braxton featuring Dr. Dre on the album *The Heat* (BMG/Arista/La Face, 2000).

K

Kenny Rogers-Pharoahe Monch Dub Plate
Words and music by Jerry Duplessis, Troy Jamerson, Wyclef Jean, and Donald Schlitz.
Sony ATV Tunes LLC, Nashville, 2000/Trescadecaphobia Music, Jamaica, 2000/Huss-Zwingli Publishing, 2000/EMI-Blackwood Music Inc., 2000/Te Bass Music, 2000/Cross Keys Publishing, 2000.
Introduced by Wyclef Jean featuring Kenny Rogers on the album *The Ecleftic: 2 Sides II a Book* (Sony/Columbia, 2000).

Kiss This
Words and music by Philip Douglas, Aaron Tippin, and Thea Tippin.
Curb Songs, Nashville, 2000/Nik's Place Publishing, Bowling Green, 2000/Mick Hits Music, Nashville, 2000/Charlie Monk Music, 2000/ Thea Later Music, 2000/Acuff Rose Music, 2000.
Number one song by Aaron Tippin from the album *People like Us* (Uni/ Lyric Street, 2000).

Kryptonite
Words and music by Brad Arnold, music by Robert Harrell and Matthew Roberts.
Escatawpa Songs, 2000/Songs of Universal, 2000.
Best-selling record by 3 Doors Down from the album *The Better Life* (Uni/Universal, 2000).Nominated for a Grammy Award, Best Rock Song, 2000.

L

L.A. Song
Words and music by Beth Hart.
Jezebel Blues Music, 1999.
Introduced by Beth Hart on the album *Screamin' for My Supper* (WEA/Atlantic/Lava, 1999).

Last Days of Disco
Words and music by Georgia Hubley, Ira Kaplan, and James McNew.
Roshashauna, Hoboken, 2000/Excellent Classical Songs, 2000.
Introduced by Yo La Tengo on the album *And Then Nothing Turned Itself Inside-Out* (Matador, 2000).

Last Resort
Words and music by David Buckner, Tobin Esperance, Jerry Horton, and Jacoby Shaddix.
Dreamworks Songs, 2000/Viva La Curcaracha Music, 2000.
Best-selling record by Papa Roach from the album *Infest* (Uni/DreamWorks, 2000). Also featured on the soundtrack album *Ready to Rumble* (WEA/Atlantic, 2000).

Leader of Men
Words and music by Chad Kroeger and Ryan Peake.
Warner-Tamerlane Music, 2000.
Best-selling record by Nickelback from the album *The State* (Uni/Roadrunner, 2000).

Left & Right
Words and music by D'Angelo (pseudonym for Michael Archer), Q-Tip (pseudonym for Kamaal Fareed), Redman (pseudonym for Reggie Noble), and Method Man (pseudonym for Clifford Smith).
Careers-BMG Music, Beverly Hills, 1999/Famous Music Corp., 1999/Universal-Polygram Intl Tunes, 1999/Zomba Enterprises, 1999/Wu-Tang Publishing, 1999/Funky Noble Productions, 1999.
Introduced by D'Angelo featuring Method Man and Redman on the album *Voodoo* (EMD/Virgin, 2000).

Left Right Left

Words and music by T. Cook, Alphonso Jordan, Lorenzo Jordan, and Demetrius Stewart.

Tight 2 Def Music, Atlanta, 2000/E One Music, 2000/E Two Music, 2000/EMI-April Music, 2000/Da Youngest and Da Crunkest, 2000/EMI-Blackwood Music Inc., 2000.

Best-selling record by Drama from the album *Causin' Drama* (WEA/Atlantic, 2000).

Lessons Learned

Words and music by Larry Boone, Tracy Lawrence, and Paul Nelson.

Sony ATV Songs LLC, Nashville, 1999/Sony ATV Tunes LLC, Nashville, 1999/Cross Keys Publishing, 1999/SLL Music, 1999/Asifits Music, 1999/Tree Publishing Co., Inc., 1999.

Best-selling record by Tracy Lawrence from the album *Lessons Learned* (WEA/Atlantic, 2000).

Let's Get It On

Words and music by Marvin Gaye and Edward Townsend.

Jobete Music Co., 1973/Stone Diamond Music, 1973.

Revived by Jack Black in the film and on the soundtrack album *High Fidelity* (Uni/Hollywood, 2000).

Let's Get Married

Words and music by Brandon Casey, Brian Casey, Bryan-Michael Cox, and Jermaine Dupri.

EMI-April Music, 2000/So So Def Music, 2000/Them Damn Twins Music, 2000/Babyboys Little Pub Co, 2000/EMI Music Publishing, 2000/Air Control Music, 2000.

Number one song by Jagged Edge from the album *J. E. Heartbreak* (Sony/Columbia, 1999).

Let's Make Love

Words and music by Marv Green, Christopher Lindsey, William Luther, and Aimee Mayo.

Careers-BMG Music, Beverly Hills, 1999/Cherry River Music, New York, 1999/Silverkiss Music, 1999/Songs of Nashville Dreamworks, 1999/Warner-Tamerlane Music, 1999/Golden Wheat Music, 1999/Dreamworks Songs, 1999.

Best-selling record by Faith Hill and Tim McGraw from the Faith Hill album *Breathe* (WEA/Warner, 1999). Later featured on the Tim McGraw album *Greatest Hits* (WEA/Atlantic/Curb, 2000).

Letting the Cables Sleep

Words and music by Gavin Rossdale.

Ensign Music, 1999/Mad Dog Winston Music, 1999.

Best-selling record by Bush from the album *The Science of Things* (Uni/Interscope, 1999).

Liar

Words and music by Tyrrell Bing, Ernest Dixon, and Roy Hamilton.

Platinum Firm Music, 2000/Zomba Enterprises, 2000.

Number one song by Profyle from the album *Nothin' but Drama* (Uni/Motown, 2000).

Lie Down

Words and music by Noah Bernardo, Marcos Curiel, Mark Daniels, and Paul Sandoval.

Famous Music Corp., 1999/Souljah Music, 1999.

Introduced by P.O.D. on the album *Fundamental Elements of Southtown* (WEA/Atlantic, 1999). Later featured on the soundtrack album *Blair Witch 2: Book of Shadows* (EMD/Priority, 2000).

Life Is Bad

Words and music by Bill Bottrell, Roger Fritz, Jay Joyce, Shelby Lynne, and Dorothy Overstreet.

Gumbo Woman Music, Pensacola, 1999/Sneaky Snake Music, Los Angeles, 1999/Magnasong, 1999/Ignorant, 1999/Irving Music Inc., 1999/Curb Magnasong Music Publishing, 1999.

Introduced by Shelby Lynne on the album *I Am Shelby Lynne* (Uni/Island, 2000).

The Light

Words and music by Robert Caldwell, Norman Harris, Lonnie Lynn, Bruce Malament, and James Yancey.

Bendan Music, North Hollywood, 2000/EMI-Blackwood Music Inc., 2000/Senseless Music, 2000/Sin Drome Music, 2000/Universal-Polygram Intl Tunes, 2000.

Best-selling record by Common from the album *Like Water for Chocolate* (Uni/MCA, 2000).

Little Black Backpack

Words and music by Luke Esterkyn, Greg Gueldner, and John McDermott.

King Nummy Publishing, 1999.

Introduced by Stroke 9 on the album *Nasty Little Thoughts* (Uni/Universal, 1999).

A Little Gasoline

Words and music by Roger Miller and Tammy Rogers.

Sony ATV Tunes LLC, Nashville, 2000/Cross Keys Publishing, 2000/Mighty Nice Music, 2000.

Introduced by Terri Clark on the album *Fearless* (Uni/Mercury Nashville, 2000).

The Little Girl

Words and music by Harley Allen.

Coburn Music, Nashville, 2000.
Number one song by John Michael Montgomery featuring Alison Krauss and Dan Tyminski from the album *Brand New Me* (WEA/ Atlantic, 2000).

Live, Laugh, Love
Words and music by Gary Nicholson and Allen Shamblin.
Famous Music Corp., 1999/Built on Rock Music, 1999/Song Matters Music, 1999/Gary Nicholson Music, 1999.
Introduced by Clay Walker on the album *Live, Laugh, Love* (WEA/ Warner Bros., 1999).

Lonely
Words and music by Robin Bruce and Roxie Dean.
Big Red Tractor Music, Nashville, 2000/WB Music Publishing, 2000.
Best-selling record by Tracy Lawrence from the album *Lessons Learned* (WEA/Atlantic, 2000).

Loser
Words and music by Brad Arnold, music by Robert Harrell and Matthew Roberts.
Escatawpa Songs, 2000/Songs of Universal, 2000.
Best-selling record by 3 Doors Down from the album *The Better Life* (Uni/Universal, 2000).

A Love Before Time
Words by James Schamus, music by Jorge Calandrelli and Tan Dun.
Introduced by Jorge Calandrelli and Tan Dun on the soundtrack album *Crouching Tiger Hidden Dragon* (Sony Classics, 2000).Nominated for an Academy Award, Best Original Song of the Year, 2001.

Love Calling Earth
Words and music by Kelvin Andrews, Guy Chambers, and Robbie Williams.
EMI-Virgin Songs, 2000/Hit & Run Music, 2000/EMI-Virgin Music, 2000/BMG Music Publishing Ltd., 2000.
Introduced by Robbie Williams on the album *Sing When You're Winning* (EMD/Capitol, 2000).

Love Is Blind
Words and music by Kasseem Dean and Eve Jeffers.
Ruff Ryders Entertainment, New York, 1999/Swizz Beats Publishing, Atlanta, 1999/Blondie Rockwell Music, 1999/Dead Game Publishing, 1999.
Introduced by Eve on the album *Let There Be Eve...Ruff Ryders' First Lady* (Uni/Interscope, 1999).

Love Life
Words and music by Fatboy Slim (pseudonym for Norman Cook), Macy

Gray (pseudonym for Natalie McIntyre), and Bill Withers.
Happy Mel Boopy's Cocktail Lounge, 2000/Universal Music Publishing Int. Ltd., 2000/Zomba Enterprises, 2000/Universal-Polygram Intl Tunes, 2000.
Introduced by Fatboy Slim featuring Macy Gray on the album *Halfway Between the Gutter and the Stars* (EMD/Astralwerks, 2000).

Love Sets You Free
Words and music by Aaron Philips, Kelly Price, Denise Rich, Edward Riley, and Charles Thompson.
Sony ATV Songs LLC, Nashville, 2000/Ninth Street Tunnel Music, Nashville, 2000/Dream Image IDG Publishing, New York, 2000/ Philmore Publishing, Portland, 2000/EMI-April Music, 2000/ Connotation Music, 2000/Tree Publishing Co., Inc., 2000/Warner-Tamerlane Music, 2000/EMI April Canada, 2000/Zomba Enterprises, 2000/Price is Right Music, 2000/Nine Street Songs, 2000.
Best-selling record by Kelly Price and Aaron Hall from the soundtrack album *The Hurricane* (Uni/MCA, 2000). Later featured on the Kelly Price album *Mirror Mirror* (Uni/Def Jam, 2000).

Love's the Only House
Words and music by James Cason and Tom Douglas.
Sony ATV Songs LLC, Nashville, 1999/Buzz Cason Publications, 1999/ Tree Publishing Co., Inc., 1999.
Best-selling record by Martina McBride from the album *Emotion* (BMG/ RCA, 1999).

Lucky
Words and music by Alexander Kronlund, Max Martin (pseudonym for Martin Sandberg), Jacob Schulze, and Rami Yacoub.
Universal-Polygram Intl Tunes, 2000/Zomba Enterprises, 2000/ Grantsville Publishing, 2000/MCA Music Publishing, 2000/MCA Music Canada, 2000.
Best-selling record by Britney Spears from the album *Oops!...I Did It Again* (BMG/Jive/Silvertone, 2000).

M

Mafia

Words by Markita, words and music by Chad Hugo and Pharrell Williams.

Waters of Nazareth Publishing, 1999/EMI-Blackwood Music Inc., 1999/EMI-April Music, 1999/Chase Chad Music, 1999/EMI Blackwood Music Canada Ltd., 1999.

Introduced by Kelis on the album *Kaleidoscope* (EMD/Virgin, 1999).

Magdalena

Words and music by William Howerdel and Maynard Keenan.

Transfixed Music, Los Angeles, 2000/EMI-Virgin Music, 2000/Toolshed Music, 2000.

Introduced by A Perfect Circle on the album *Mer de Noms* (EMD/Virgin, 2000).

Make Me Bad

Words by Jonathan Davis, music by Reginald Arvizu, James Shaffer, David Silveria, and Brian Welch.

Goathead Music, 1999.

Introduced by Korn on the album *Issues* (Sony/Epic, 1999).

Maria Maria

Words and music by Jerry Duplessis, Wyclef Jean, David McRae, Marvin Moore-Hough, Karl Perazzo, Raul Rekow, and Carlos Santana.

Sony ATV Tunes LLC, Nashville, 1999/Sony ATV Songs LLC, Nashville, 1999/EMI-April Music, 1999/Ghetto and Blues, 1999/Hempstead Live, 1999/Huss-Zwingli Publishing, 1999/EMI-Blackwood Music Inc., 1999/Stellabella Music, 1999/Te Bass Music, 1999.

Number one song by Santana featuring the Product G&B from the album *Supernatural* (BMG/Arista, 1999).

Me Neither

Words and music by Charles Dubois, Brad Paisley, and Frank Rogers.

EMI-April Music, 1999/Sea Gayle Music, 1999.
Introduced by Brad Paisley on the album *Who Needs Pictures* (BMG/Arista, 1999).

Meanwhile Back at the Ranch
Words and music by Gordon Kennedy and Wayne Kirkpatrick.
Universal-Polygram Intl Tunes, 2000/Warner-Tamerlane Music, 2000/Sell the Cow Music, 2000/Sondance Kid Music, 2000.
Best-selling single by the Clark Family Experience (WEA/Atlantic/Curb, 2000).

Minority
Words and music by Billie Armstrong, Mike Pritchard, and Frank Wright.
Green Daze Music, San Rafael, 2000/WB Music Publishing, 2000.
Best-selling record by Green Day from the album *Warning* (WEA/Warner Bros., 2000).

Mirror Mirror
Words and music by Dane DeViller, Sean Hosein, and Pamela Sheyne.
Careers-BMG Music, Beverly Hills, 2000/On Board Music, Santa Monica, 2000/Warner-Tamerlane Music, 2000/Bubalas Publishing, 2000/Appletree Songs, 2000/Warner-Chappell Music, 2000.
Introduced by M2M on the album *Shades of Purple* (WEA/Atlantic, 2000).

Miserable
Words and music by Kevin Baldes, Alan Popoff, Jeremy Popoff, and Allen Shellenberger.
EMI-April Music, 1999/Jagermaestro, 1999.
Introduced by Lit on the album *A Place in the Sun* (BMG/RCA, 1999).

Monica
Words and music by Marc Kinchen, Cynthia Loving, Carlos McKinney, and Jarret Washington.
WB Music Publishing, 1999/Ensign Music, 1999/Big on Blue Music, 1999/Penn State Urban Legends Music, 1999/Mo Lovin' Music, 1999.
Introduced by Before Dark on the album *Daydreamin'* (BMG/RCA, 1999).

More
Words and music by Del Gray and Thomas McHugh.
Volunteer Jam Music, Nashville, 1999/McHuge Music, 1999/Go to Del Music, 1999/Golden Wheat Music, 1999/Warner-Tamerlane Music, 1999.
Best-selling record by Trace Adkins from the album *More...* (EMD/Capitol, 1999).

Morning Bell
Words and music by Radiohead.
Warner-Chappell Music, 2000.
Introduced by Radiohead on the album *Kid A* (EMD/Capitol, 2000).

Most Girls
Words and music by Kenneth Edmonds and Damon Thomas.
Ecaf Music, Philadelphia, 2000/Sony ATV Songs LLC, Nashville, 2000/Demis Hot Songs, 2000/E Two Music, 2000/EMI-April Music, 2000.
Best-selling record by Pink from the album *Can't Take Me Home* (BMG/Arista/La Face, 2000).

Mr. E's Beautiful Blues
Words and music by Mark Everett and Michael Simpson.
420 Music, Pasadena, 2000/Almo Music Corp., 2000/Sexy Grandpa Music, 2000/Dinky B. Music, 2000.
Introduced by the Eels on the album *Daisies of the Galaxy* (Uni/DreamWorks, 2000). Later featured on the soundtrack album *Road Trip* (Uni/DreamWorks, 2000).

Mr. Too Damn Good
Words and music by Gerald Levert and Joe Little.
Divided Music, 2000/Warner-Tamerlane Music, 2000/Zomba Enterprises, 2000/Lil Mob Publishing, 2000.
Best-selling record by Gerald Levert from the album *G* (WEA/Elektra, 2000).

Ms. Jackson
Words and music by Andre Benjamin, Antwan Patton, and David Sheats.
Chrysalis Music Group, 2000/Dungeon Rat Music, 2000/EMI-April Music, 2000/Gnat Booty Music, 2000.
Number one song by Outkast from the album *Stankonia* (BMG/Arista, 2000).

MTV Get Off the Air, Part 2
Words and music by Paul Barman and Paul Huston.
Prinse Pawl Musick, 2000.
Introduced by MC Paul Barman on the album *It's Very Stimulating* (Wordsound, 2000).

Music
Words and music by Mirwais Ahmadzai and Madonna Ciccone.
Webo Girl, New York, 2000/WB Music Publishing, 2000/Warner-Tamerlane Music, 2000.
Number one song by Madonna from the album *Music* (WEA/Warner Bros., 2000).Nominated for a Grammy Award, Record of the Year, 2000.

My Back Pages
Words and music by Bob Dylan (pseudonym for Robert Zimmerman).
Special Rider Music, 1964/M. Witmark & Sons, 1964.
Revived by Joan Osborne and Jackson Browne on the soundtrack album *Steal This Movie* (Artemis, 2000).

My Best Friend
Words and music by William Luther and Aimee Mayo.
Careers-BMG Music, Beverly Hills, 1998.
Number one song by Tim McGraw from the album *A Place in the Sun* (WEA/Atlantic/Curb, 1999).

My Funny Friend and Me
Words and music by Sting (pseudonym for Gordon Sumner), music by David Hartley.
Wonderland Music, 2000.
Introduced by Sting in the film and on the soundtrack album *The Emperor's New Groove* (Uni/Disney/Duplicate Numbers, 2000) .Nominated for an Academy Award, Best Original Song, 2001.

My Heart's Saying Now
Words and music by Paul Barry and Mark Taylor.
Rive Droite Music, London Surrey, 2000.
Introduced by Jordan Knight on the soundtrack album *Snow Day* (Uni/Geffen, 2000).

My Love Goes On and On
Words and music by Christopher Cagle and Donald Pfrimmer.
Sony ATV Tunes LLC, Nashville, 2000/Caliber Music, Nashville, 2000/Platinum Plow, 2000/WB Music Publishing, 2000.
Best-selling record by Chris Cagle from the album *Play It Loud* (EMD/Capitol, 2000).

My Next Thirty Years
Words and music by Phillip Vassar.
EMI-April Music, 1999/Phil Vassar Music, 1999.
Number one song by Tim McGraw from the album *A Place in the Sun* (WEA/Atlantic/Curb, 1999).

My Winding Wheel
Words and music by Ryan Adams.
Barland Music, 2000.
Introduced by Ryan Adams on the album *Heartbreaker* (Bloodshot, 2000).

N

N 2gether Now

Words by Fred Durst and Method Man (pseudonym for Clifford Smith), music by Wesley Borland, DJ Lethal (pseudonym for Leor Dimant), DJ Premier (pseudonym for Chris Martin), John Otto, and Samuel Rivers.

Careers-BMG Music, Beverly Hills, 1999/EMI-April Music, 1999/ Zomba Enterprises, 1999/Wu-Tang Publishing, 1999/Gifted Pearl, 1999/Lethal Dose Music, 1999.

Introduced by Limp Bizkit featuring Method Man on the album *Significant Other* (Uni/Interscope, 1999).

The National Anthem

Words and music by Radiohead.

Warner-Chappell Music, 2000.

Introduced by Radiohead on the album *Kid A* (EMD/Capitol, 2000).

Natural Blues

Words and music by Moby (pseudonym for Richard Hall), Gabriel Jackson, and Bob Robinson.

Bobby Robinson Sweet Soul Music, New York, 1999/Warner-Tamerlane Music, 1999.

Introduced by Moby on the album *Play* (BMG/V2, 1999).

Need to Be Next to You

Words and music by Diane Warren.

Realsongs, 2000.

Introduced by Leigh Nash in the film and on the soundtrack album *Bounce* (BMG/Arista, 2000).

Never Let You Go

Words and music by Stephan Jenkins.

Three EB Publishing, Oakland, 1999/EMI-Blackwood Music Inc., 1999.

Best-selling record by Third Eye Blind from the album *Blue* (WEA/ Elektra, 1999).

The Next Episode
Words and music by David Axlerod, Brian Bailey, Melvin Bradford, Dr. Dre (pseudonym for Andre Young), and Snoop Dogg (pseudonym for Calvin Broadus).
Big Yacht Music, New York, 1999/Loot on Loose Leaf Music, Los Angeles, 2000/EMI-Blackwood Music Inc., 1999/Ain't Nothing but Funkin', 1999/WB Music Publishing, 1999/Beechwood Music, 1999/My Own Chit Publishing, 1999/Hard Working Black Folks, 1999.
Best-selling record by Dr. Dre featuring Snoop Dogg from the album *2001* (Uni/Interscope, 1999).

N.I.B.
Words and music by Terence Butler, Anthony Iommi, Ozzy Osbourne (pseudonym for John Osbourne), and William Ward.
Essex Music International, New York, 1970/TRO-Andover Music, Inc., 1970.
Revived by Primus featuring Ozzy Osbourne on the album *Nativity in Black II: A Tribute to Black Sabbath* (EMD/Priority/Divine, 2000).

911
Words and music by Mary Brown, Katia Cadet, Jerry Duplessis, and Wyclef Jean.
Sony ATV Tunes LLC, Nashville, 2000/Huss-Zwingli Publishing, 2000/EMI-Blackwood Music Inc., 2000/Ms. Mary's Music, 2000/Te Bass Music, 2000/Warner-Tamerlane Music, 2000.
Best-selling record by Wyclef Jean featuring Mary J. Blige from the album *The Ecleftic: 2 Sides II a Book* (Sony/Columbia, 2000).

No Fear
Words and music by Mary Chapin Carpenter and Terri Clark.
Why Walk Music, Nashville, 2000/Universal-Polygram Intl Tunes, 2000/Terri Ooo Tunes, 2000.
Introduced by Terri Clark on the album *Fearless* (Uni/Mercury Nashville, 2000).

No Love (I'm Not Used To)
Words and music by Daryl Simmons.
Boobie and DJ Songs, 1999/Warner-Tamerlane Music, 1999.
Best-selling record by Kevon Edmonds from the album *24/7* (BMG/RCA, 1999).

No Matter What They Say
Words and music by Edward Archer, Eric Barrier, Robert Beavers, Charles Bobbit, James Brown, Bobby Byrd, Bernard Edwards, Jose Feliciano, Darren Henson, Jack Hill, Peter Joyner, Lil' Kim (pseudonym for Kimberly Jones), and Rakim (pseudonym for William Griffin).

Undeas Music, Brooklyn, 2000/EMI-April Music, 2000/FAF Publishing, 2000/Notorious Kim Music, 2000/Bernard's Other Music, 2000/ Bridgeport Music, 2000/Crited Music, 2000/Sony Songs Inc., 2000/ Howie Tee Music, 2000/Special Ed Music, 2000/Promuse, 2000/ Touched by Jazz Music, 2000/No Gravity Music, 2000.
Best-selling record by Lil' Kim from the album *Notorious K.I.M.* (WEA/Atlantic, 2000).

No Me Dejes De Querer (Don't Stop Loving Me)
Words and music by Robert Blades, Emilio Estefan, and Gloria Estefan.
Foreign Imported Productions, 2000.
Introduced by Gloria Estefan on the album *Alma Caribena* (Sony/Epic, 2000).

No Mercy
Words and music by Todd Cerney, Stephen Davis, and Dennis Morgan.
Mighty Moe Music, Austin, 1999/Chrysalis Songs, 1999/Hamstein Cumberland Music, 1999/Screen Gems-EMI Music Inc., 1999/ Universal-MCA Music Publishing, 1999/Little Shop of Morgansongs, 1999/Tom Collins Music Corp., 1999/Red Brazos, 1999.
Best-selling record by Ty Herndon from the album *Steam* (Sony/Epic, 1999).

No More
Words and music by Edward Ferrell, Clifton Lighty, Darren Lighty, and Balewa Muhammad.
Eddie F. Music, Closter, 2000/WB Music Publishing, 2000/Universal-Polygram Intl Tunes, 2000/Jahque Joints, 2000.
Number one song by Ruff Endz from the album *Love Crimes* (Sony/ Epic, 2000).

None of Ur Friends Business
Words and music by Ginuwine (pseudonym for Elgin Lumpkin) and Timothy Mosley.
Black Fountain Music, 1999/Golddaddy Music, 1999/Virginia Beach Music, 1999/WB Music Publishing, 1999.
Introduced by Ginuwine on the album *100% Ginuwine* (Sony, 1999).

Nothing as It Seems
Words and music by Jeffrey Ament.
Scribing C-Ment Songs, Bellevue, 2000.
Introduced by Pearl Jam on the album *Binaural* (Sony/Epic, 2000).

O

One Day She'll Love Me
Words and music by David Hartley and Sting (pseudonym for Gordon Sumner).
Wonderland Music, 1999.
Introduced by Sting and Shawn Colvin in the film and on the soundtrack album *The Emperor's New Groove* (Uni/Disney/Duplicate Numbers, 2000).

One in a Million
Words and music by Staffan Olsson.
WB Music Publishing, 2000.
Introduced by Bosson on the album *One in a Million* (EMD/Capitol, 2000).

One Night Stand
Words and music by Charles Harrison, J-Shin (pseudonym for Jonathan Shinhoster), Leland Robinson, and LaTocha Scott.
1802 Music Publishing, Teaneck, 2000/First and Gold Publishing, 2000/Air Control Music, 2000/EMI-April Music, 2000/Juicy Time, 2000/EMI April Canada, 2000/Sugar Hill Music Publishing, Ltd., 2000.
Best-selling record by J-Shin from the album *My Soul, My Life* (WEA/Atlantic, 2000).

One Voice
Words and music by Don Cook and David Malloy.
Don Cook Music, Nashville, 2000/Sony ATV Songs LLC, Nashville, 2000/Malloy's Toys Music, 2000/Tree Publishing Co., Inc., 2000/Warner-Tamerlane Music, 2000/Starstruck Angel Music, 2000.
Best-selling record by Billy Gilman from the album *One Voice* (Sony/Epic, 2000).Nominated for a Grammy Award, Best Country Song, 2000.

Only God Knows Why
Words and music by Kid Rock (pseudonym for Robert Ritchie), Uncle Kracker (pseudonym for Matthew Shafer), and John Travis.

Cradle the Balls Music, Los Angeles, 1998/Gaje Music, 1998/Thirty Two Mile Music, 1998/Warner-Tamerlane Music, 1998.
Best-selling record by Kid Rock from the album *Devil Without a Cause* (WEA/Atlantic/Lava, 1998).

Oops!...I Did It Again
Words and music by Martin Sandberg and Rami Yacoub.
Zomba Enterprises, 2000.
Best-selling record by Britney Spears from the album *Oops!...I Did It Again* (BMG/Jive/Silvertone, 2000).

Open My Heart
Words and music by Yolanda Adams, James Harris, Terry Lewis, and James Wright.
EMI-April Music, 1999/Flyte Tyme Tunes, 1999/Jam Yo Music, 1999/Ji Branda Music Works, 1999/Minneapolis Guys Music, 1999.
Best-selling record by Yolanda Adams from the album *Mountain High Valley Low* (WEA/Elektra, 2000).

Optimistic
Words and music by Colin Greenwood, Jonathan Greenwood, Edward O'Brien, Philip Selway, and Thomas Yorke.
WB Music Publishing, 2000.
Introduced by Radiohead on the album *Kid A* (EMD/Capitol/Duplicate Numbers, 2000).

Otherside
Words and music by Flea (pseudonym for Michael Balzary), John Frusciante, Anthony Kiedis, and Chad Smith.
Moebetoblame Music, 1999.
Best-selling record by the Red Hot Chili Peppers from the album *Californication* (WEA/Warner Bros., 1999).

Out for the Count
Words and music by Eve Jeffers, Steven Jordan, Theodore Shapiro, and T. Turpin.
Steven A. Jordan Music, 2000.
Introduced by Stevie J. featuring Eve in the film and on the soundtrack album *Girlfight* (EMD/Capitol/Duplicate Numbers, 2000).

Outside
Words and music by Aaron Lewis.
Greenfund, 2000/WB Music Publishing, 2000.
Best-selling record by Staind featuring Fred Durst from the album *The Family Values Tour '99* (Uni/Interscope, 2000).

Over My Head
Words and music by Jeremy Popoff.
TCF Music Publishing, 2000.

Introduced by Lit in the film and on the soundtrack album *Titan A.E.* (EMD/Capitol, 2000).

P

Painted on My Heart
Words and music by Diane Warren.
Realsongs, 2000.
Introduced by Cult in the film and on the soundtrack album *Gone in 60 Seconds* (Uni/Island, 2000).

Paranoia Key of E
Words and music by Lou Reed.
Lou Reed Music, New York, 2000/EMI-Blackwood Music Inc., 2000.
Introduced by Lou Reed on the album *Ecstasy* (WEA/Warner Bros., 2000).

Pardon Me
Words and music by Brandon Boyd, Michael Einziger, Alex Katunich, Chris Kilmore, and Jose Pasillas.
EMI-April Music, 1999/Hunglikeyora, 1999.
Introduced by Incubus on the album *Make Yourself* (Sony/Epic, 1999).

Party Up (Up in Here)
Words and music by Kasseem Dean and DMX (pseudonym for Earl Simmons).
Boomer X Publishing, New York, 1999/Ruff Ryders Entertainment, New York, 1999/Swizz Beats Publishing, Atlanta, 1999.
Best-selling record by DMX from the album *And Then There Was X* (Uni/Def Jam, 1999).

Perfect World
Words and music by David Hartley and Sting (pseudonym for Gordon Sumner).
Wonderland Music, 2000.
Introduced by Tom Jones in the film and on the soundtrack album *The Emperor's New Groove* (Uni/Disney/Duplicate Numbers, 2000).

Picture of You
Words and music by Ronan Keating, Eliot Kennedy, Andrew Watkins,

and Paul Wilson.
BMG Songs Inc., 1997/Universal Songs of Polygram Intl., 1997/BMG Music Publishing Ltd., 1997/19 Music, 1997.
Performed by Boyzone on the soundtrack album *Snow Day* (Uni/Geffen, 2000).

Pinch Me
Words and music by Steven Page and Lloyd Robertson.
WB Music Publishing, 2000.
Best-selling record by the Barenaked Ladies from the album *Maroon* (WEA/Warner Bros., 2000).

Playmate of the Year
Words and music by Gregory Bergdorf, Justin Mauriello, Ben Osmundson, Ali Tabatabaee, and Edwin Udhus.
Bust a Nut in Your Eye Music, Los Angeles, 2000/Butt Nugget and the Squirrels Music, Los Angeles, 2000/Grand Master Chimp and Da Cronies Music, Los Angeles, 2000/Kamakaze Zero Music, Los Angeles, 2000/Plagiarism Publishing, Los Angeles, 2000/Ensign Music, 2000.
Introduced by Zebrahead on the album *Playmate of the Year* (Sony/Columbia, 2000). Later featured in the film and on the soundtrack album *Dude, Where's My Car?* (WEA/London/Sire, 2000).

Plenty
Words and music by Erykah Badu (pseudonym for Erica Wright), Guru (pseudonym for Keith Elam), Braylon Lacy, and Harold Martin.
Ill Kid Music, New York, 2000/BMG Songs Inc., 2000/EMI-April Music, 2000/Divine Pimp Music, 2000.
Introduced by Guru's Jazzmatazz featuring Erykah Badu on the album *Streetsoul* (EMD/Virgin, 2000).

Poor Girl
Words and music by Exene Cervenka (pseudonym for Christine Cervenka) and John Doe (pseudonym for John Duchac).
Cherry River Music, New York, 1983/Warner-Tamerlane Music, 1983/Eight/Twelve Music, 1983.
Revived by the Supersuckers featuring Eddie Vedder on the benefit album *Free the West Memphis 3* (Koch, 2000).

Pop Ya Collar
Words and music by Kevin Briggs, Kandi Buruss, and Raymond Usher.
Air Control Music, 2000/EMI-April Music, 2000/Kandacy Music, 2000/Shek' Em Down Music, 2000.
Best-selling record by Usher from the album *All about U* (La Face, 2000).

The Powerpuff Girls (End Theme)
Words and music by Thomas Chase, John Clark, Steven Clark, Amanda MacKinnon, Stephen Rucker, and James Venable.
Techwood Music, Atlanta, 2000/Ten Fifty Music, Atlanta, 2000.
Introduced by Bis in the cartoon *The Powerpuff Girls* and on the soundtrack album *Heroes & Villains: Music Inspired by the Powerpuff Girls* (WEA/Rhino, 2000).

The Powerpuff Girls (Main Theme)
Words and music by Thomas Chase, Stephen Rucker, and James Venable.
Ten Fifty Music, Atlanta, 2000.
Introduced by Chemical X in the cartoon *The Powerpuff Girls* and on the soundtrack album *Heroes & Villains: Music Inspired by the Powerpuff Girls* (WEA/Rhino, 2000).

Prayin' for Daylight
Words and music by Steve Bogard and Rick Giles.
Careers-BMG Music, Beverly Hills, 2000/Tanner Music, Hales Corners, 2000/Sontanner Music, 2000/Warner-Tamerlane Music, 2000.
Best-selling record by Rascal Flatts from the album *Rascal Flatts* (Hollywood, 2000).

Private Emotion
Words and music by Eric Bazilian and Robert Hyman.
WB Music Publishing, 1999/Dub Notes, 1999/Human Boy Music, 1999.
Introduced by Ricky Martin featuring Meja on the album *Ricky Martin* (Sony/Columbia, 1999).

Promise
Words and music by James Collins, Anthony Fagenson, and Jonathan Siebels.
Southfield Road Music, Los Angeles, 2000/Fake and Jaded Music, 2000/Less Than Zero, 2000.
Best-selling record by Eve 6 from the album *Horrorscope* (BMG/RCA, 2000).

Proud to Be Your Old Man
Words and music by Merle Haggard and Abe Manuel.
Merle Haggard Music, 2000.
Introduced by Merle Haggard on the album *If I Could Only Fly* (Anti/Epitaph, 2000).

Pull Over
Words and music by Adam Duggins, Maurice Marshall, Lasana Smith, and Katrina Taylor.
Funk So Righteous Music, Miami, 2000/First and Gold Publishing, 2000.

Introduced by Trina featuring Trick Daddy on the single *Pull Over* (WEA/Atlantic, 2000).

Pumping on Your Stereo
Words and music by Gareth Coombes, Robert Coombes, Daniel Goffey, and Michael Quinn.
EMI-April Music, 1999.
Introduced by Supergrass on the album *Supergrass* (Uni/Island, 1999). Later featured in the film and on the soundtrack album *Road Trip* (Uni/DreamWorks, 2000).

Pure Shores (English)
Words and music by Tricia Lewis and William Orbit (pseudonym for William Wainwright).
Almo Music Corp., 2000/Universal-MCA Music Publishing, 2000/Rondor Music, 2000/TCF Music Publishing, 2000.
Introduced by All Saints on the album *Saints and Sinners* (London Recordings, 2000).

A Puro Dolor (Purest of Pain)
Words and music by Omar Alfano and Maria Llord.
EMOA Music Publishing, Miami Beach, 2000/EMI April Canada, 2000.
Best-selling record by Son by Four from the album *Son by Four* (Sony Discos, 2000). Englishlanguage version, "Purest of Pain," featured on the album *Purest of Pain* (Sony/Columbia, 2000).

Put Your Hand in Mine
Words and music by Jimmy Barber and Skip Ewing.
Milene Music, 1999/Acuff Rose Music, 1999/Write on Music, 1999.
Introduced by Tracy Byrd on the album *It's About Time* (BMG/RCA, 1999).

Q

Quarantined
Words and music by Cedric Bixler, Antoine Hajjar, Paul Hinojos, Omar Rodriguez, and James Ward.
Air Station Seven, 2000/Alto Chroma, 2000/Dystopia, 2000/Imposto, 2000/Lopsided, 2000.
Introduced by At the Drive-In on the album *Relationship of Command* (EMD/Virgin, 2000).

R

(Rap) Superstar
Words and music by Louis Freeze and Lawrence Muggerud.
Soul Assassin Music, Los Angeles, 2000/Hits from Da Bong Music, Seattle, 2000/BMG Songs Inc., 2000.
Introduced by Cypress Hill on the album *Skull & Bones* (Sony/Columbia, 2000).

Razor Love
Words and music by Neil Young.
Silver Fiddle Music, 1987.
Introduced by Neil Young on the album *Silver & Gold* (WEA/Warner Bros., 2000).

Real Live Woman
Words and music by Bobbie Cryner.
Lonesome Dove Music, 2000/Child Bride Music, 2000/Cryn'er Way to the Bank Music, 2000.
Best-selling record by Trisha Yearwood from the album *Real Live Woman* (Uni/MCA Nashville, 2000).

The Real Slim Shady
Words and music by Thomas Coster and Dr. Dre (pseudonym for Andre Young), words by Michael Elizondo and Eminem (pseudonym for Marshall Mathers).
Eight Mile Style Music, 2000/Strawberry Blonde Music, 2000/Elvis Mambo Music, 2000/Five Card Music, 2000/Ensign Music, 2000/Music of Windswept, 2000/Famous Music Corp., 2000/WB Music Publishing, 2000/Ain't Nothin' Goin on But F****n Music, 2000/Bug Music, 2000.
Best-selling record by Eminem from the album *The Marshall Mathers LP* (Uni/Interscope, 2000).

The Reckoning
Words and music by Ullrich Hepperlin, Jason Miller, Michael Miller, and James O'Connor.

Trinity of Relative Evil Music, Los Angeles, 2000/Warner-Tamerlane Music, 2000.
Introduced by Godhead on the soundtrack album *Blair Witch 2: Book of Shadows* (EMD/Priority, 2000).

Red Alert
Words and music by Felix Buxton and Simon Ratcliffe.
Universal-MCA Music Publishing, 1999.
Introduced by Basement Jaxx on the album *Remedy* (XL Recordings/Astralwerks, 1999). Later featured on the soundtrack album *Whatever It Takes* (Uni/Hollywood, 2000).

Renegades of Funk
Words and music by Bambaataa Aasim, Arthur Baker, John Miller, and John Robie.
Bambaataa Music, 1984/Shakin Baker Music, Inc., 1984/T Girl Music LLC, 1984/Tommy Boy Music, 1984.
Revived by Rage Against the Machine on the album *Renegades* (Sony/Epic, 2000).

Riddle
Words and music by Terry Ellis, Denzil Foster, Cindy Herron, Maxine Jones, and Thomas McElroy.
Two Tuff-Enuff Publishing, Oakland, 2000/EV Music Publishing, Los Angeles, 2000/EMI-Blackwood Music Inc., 2000/EMI Blackwood Music Canada Ltd., 2000.
Introduced by En Vogue on the album *Masterpiece Theatre* (WEA/Elektra, 2000).

Riding with the King
Words and music by John Hiatt.
Queen Isabella's Subjects, 1983.
Revived by Eric Clapton and B.B. King on the album *Riding with the King* (WEA/Warner Bros., 2000).

Right Now
Words and music by Mitchell Scherr and Bradley Walker.
EMI-April Music, 2000/Scorpiorock Tunes, 2000/WB Music Publishing, 2000.
Introduced by SR-71 on the album *Now You See Inside* (BMG/RCA, 2000).

Righteous Love
Words and music by Joseph Arthur and Joan Osborne.
Womanly Hips Music, Chicago, 2000/Radio Legs Music, New York, 2000/Ellipsis Music, 2000/EMI Virgin Music Ltd., 2000.
Introduced by Joan Osborne in the television show and on the soundtrack album *Sex and the City* (WEA/London/Sire, 2000). Later

featured on the Joan Osborne album *Righteous Love* (Uni/Interscope, 2000).

Rock DJ

Words and music by Kelvin Andrews, Guy Chambers, Ekundayo Paris, Nelson Pigford, and Robbie Williams.

EMI-Virgin Songs, 2000/Hit & Run Music, 2000/BMG Songs Inc., 2000/EMI-April Music, 2000/EMI-Virgin Music, 2000/Ba-Dake Music, 2000/BMG Music Publishing Ltd., 2000.

Introduced by Robbie Williams on the album *Sing When You're Winning* (EMD/Capitol, 2000).

(Rock) Superstar

Words and music by Louis Freeze, Lawrence Muggerud, and Senen Reyes.

Soul Assassin Music, Los Angeles, 2000/Phreakas Ada Phunk, Cypress, 2000/Hits from Da Bong Music, Seattle, 2000/BMG Songs Inc., 2000.

Introduced by Cypress Hill on the album *Skull & Bones* (Sony/Columbia, 2000).

Rock Wit U

Words and music by K. Brothers, Alicia Keys, and T. Smith.

EMI-April Music, 2000/Famous Music Corp., 2000.

Introduced by Alicia Keys on the soundtrack album *Shaft (2000)* (BMG/Arista/La Face, 2000).

Ryde or Die, Chick

Words and music by Sean Jacobs, Brian Kidd, Jason Phillips, David Styles, and Timbaland (pseudonym for Timothy Mosley).

Swizz Beats Publishing, Atlanta, 1999/Dead Game Publishing, 1999/Virginia Beach Music, 1999.

Best-selling record by the Lox featuring Timbaland and Eve from the various-artists album *Ryde or Die, Vol. 1* (Uni/Interscope, 1999). Later featured on the Lox album *We Are the Streets* (Uni/Interscope, 2000).

S

Sailing to Philadelphia
Words and music by Mark Knopfler.
Straitjacket Songs, 2000/Rondor Music, 2000/Almo Music Corp., 2000.
Introduced by Mark Knopfler featuring James Taylor on the album *Sailing to Philadelphia* (WEA/Warner Bros., 2000).

Same Script, Different Cast
Words and music by Anthony Crawford, Stacey Daniels, Shae Jones, and Montell Jordan.
Hudson Jordan Music, Tarzana, 2000/Shae Shae Music, Charlotte, 2000/Wixen Music, Calabasas, 2000/Almo Music Corp., 2000/Famous Music Corp., 2000/Montel Jordan Music, 2000/Dove Daniels Music, 2000.
Best-selling record by Whitney Houston featuring Deborah Cox from the album *The Greatest Hits* (BMG/Arista, 2000).

Samurai Showdown
Words and music by RZA (pseudonym for Robert Diggs).
Careers-BMG Music, Beverly Hills, 2000/Wu-Tang Publishing, 2000/Ramecca Publishing, 2000.
Introduced by the RZA on the soundtrack album *Ghost Dog: The Way of the Samurai* (Sony/Epic, 2000).

Satellite Blues
Words and music by Angus Young and Malcolm Young.
J. Albert & Son Music, 2000.
Introduced by AC/DC on the album *Stiff Upper Lip* (WEA/Elektra, 2000).

Save Me
Words and music by Aimee Mann.
Aimee Mann, Boston, 2000.
Introduced by Aimee Mann in the film and on the soundtrack album *Magnolia* (WEA/Warner Bros., 1999).Nominated for a Grammy Award, Best Song Written for a Movie, 2000.

Say It Isn't So
Words and music by Bon Jovi (pseudonym for John Bongiovi) and William Falcone.
Pretty Blue Songs, Nashville, 2000/Universal-Polygram Intl Tunes, 2000/Warner-Tamerlane Music, 2000/Bon Jovi Publishing, 2000.
Introduced by Bon Jovi on the album *Crush* (Uni/Island/Def Jam, 2000).

Say My Name
Words and music by Lashawn Daniels, Fred Jerkins, Rodney Jerkins, Beyonce Knowles, Letoya Luckett, Latavia Roberson, and Kelendria Rowland.
Sony ATV Tunes LLC, Nashville, 1999/Beyonce Publishing, 1999/EMI-April Music, 1999/Kelendria Music, 1999/Latavia Music Publishing, 1999/Letoya Music Publishing, 1999/EMI-Blackwood Music Inc., 1999/Ensign Music, 1999/Fred Jerkins Publishing, 1999/Rodney Jerkins Music, 1999/Famous Music Corp., 1999/Lashawn Daniels Productions, 1999.
Number one song by Destiny's Child from the album *The Writing's on the Wall* (Sony/Columbia, 1999).Won a Grammy Award for Best R&B Song of the Year 2000. Nominated for Grammy Awards, Record of the Year, 2000 and Song of the Year, 2000.

Scum of the Earth
Words and music by Scott Humphrey and Rob Zombie (pseudonym for Robert Cummings).
WB Music Publishing, 2000/Gimme Back My Publishing, 2000/Demonoid Deluxe Music, 2000.
Introduced by Rob Zombie on the soundtrack album *Music from and Inspired by M:I-2* (Uni/Hollywood, 2000).

Separated
Words and music by Myron Avant and Stephen Huff.
Grindtime Publishing, 1999/Tuff Huff Music, 1999/Zomba Enterprises, 1999.
Number one song by Avant from the album *My Thoughts* (Uni/MCA, 2000).

Sex and the City Theme
Words and music by Andrew Cocup, Douglas Cuomo, and Thomas Findlay.
Universal-Polygram Intl Tunes, 2000/LT Music Publishing, 2000/Warner/Chappell Music Canada Ltd., 2000.
Introduced by Groove Armada in the television show and on the soundtrack album *Sex and the City* (WEA/London/Sire, 2000).

Shackles (Praise You)
Words and music by Erica Atkins, Trecina Atkins, and Warryn Campbell.

EMI-April Music, 2000/It's Tea Time, 2000/Nyrraw Music, 2000/That's Plum Song, 2000.
Best-selling record by Mary Mary from the album *Thankful* (Sony/Columbia, 2000).

Shake Ya Ass
Words and music by Charles Hugo, Mystikal (pseudonym for Michael Tyler), and Pharrell Williams.
Chase Chad Music, 2000/EMI-April Music, 2000/Zomba Enterprises, 2000/EMI-Blackwood Music Inc., 2000/Waters of Nazareth Publishing, 2000.
Best-selling record by Mystikal from the album *Let's Get Ready* (BMG/Jive/Silvertone, 2000).

Shame
Words and music by Ghostface Killah (pseudonym for Dennis Coles), Genius (pseudonym for Gary Grice), Inspectah Deck (pseudonym for Jason Hunter), Method Man (pseudonym for Clifford Smith), Ol' Dirty Bastard (pseudonym for Russell Jones), Raekwon (pseudonym for Corey Woods), RZA (pseudonym for Robert Diggs), and U-God (pseudonym for Lamont Hawkins).
Careers-BMG Music, Beverly Hills, 1993/Wu-Tang Publishing, 1993/BMG Songs Inc., 1993/Screen Gems-EMI Music Inc., 1993.
Introduced by the Wu-Tang Clan featuring System of a Down on the various-artists album *Loud Rocks* (Sony/Columbia, 2000). Based on the song "Shame on a Nigga" from the Wu-Tang Clan album *Enter the Wu-Tang (36 Chambers)* (Loud/RCA, 1993).

Shape of My Heart
Words and music by Max Martin (pseudonym for Martin Sandberg), Lisa Miskovsky, and Rami Yacoub.
Zomba Enterprises, 2000/Universal Songs of Polygram Intl., 2000/SODRAC, 2000.
Best-selling record by the Backstreet Boys from the album *Black & Blue* (BMG/Jive/Silvertone, 2000).

She Bangs
Words and music by Walter Afanasieff, Desmond Child, and Rob Rosa.
Sony ATV Tunes LLC, Nashville, 2000/A Phantom Vox Music, Los Angeles, 2000/WB Music Publishing, 2000/Warner-Tamerlane Music, 2000/Wally World Music, 2000.
Introduced by Ricky Martin on the album *Sound Loaded* (Sony/Columbia, 2000).

She's More
Words and music by Rob Crosby and Elizabeth Hengber.
Glen Nikki Music, 1999/WB Music Publishing, 1999/Crutchfield Music, 1999/Warner-Tamerlane Music, 1999/Starstruck Writers Group, 1999.

Best-selling record by Andy Griggs from the album *You Won't Ever Be Lonely* (BMG/RCA, 1999).

Show Me Heaven
Words and music by Maria McKee, Alan Rackin, and Jay Rifkin.
Famous Music Corp., 2000/Ensign Music, 2000/Little Diva Music, 2000.
Introduced by Jessica Andrews on the soundtrack album *Songs from Dawson's Creek, Volume 2* (Sony/Columbia, 2000).

Show Me the Meaning of Being Lonely
Words and music by Herbert Crichlow and Martin Sandberg.
Sony ATV Tunes LLC, Nashville, 1999/Zomba Enterprises, 1999/Grantsville Publishing, 1999/Megasong Publishing, 1999.
Best-selling record by the Backstreet Boys from the album *Millennium* (BMG/Jive/Silvertone, 1999).

Shut Up
Words and music by Deuce of 24 Karatz, Tre +6, Trick Daddy (pseudonym for Maurice Young), and Trina.
First and Gold Publishing, 2000/Trick N Rick, 2000/Ms Trina Music Publishing, 2000.
Best-selling record by Trick Daddy from the album *Book of Thugs: AK Versus 47* (WEA/Atlantic, 2000).

Silver & Gold
Words and music by Neil Young.
Silver Fiddle Music, 1982.
Introduced by Neil Young on the album *Silver & Gold* (WEA/Warner Bros., 2000).

Simple Kind of Life
Words and music by Gwen Stefani.
Universal-MCA Music Publishing, 2000/World of the Dolphin Music, 2000.
Best-selling record by No Doubt from the album *Return of Saturn* (Uni/Interscope, 2000).

Sleep Now in the Fire
Words and music by Timothy Commerford, Zack de la Rocha, Tom Morello, and Brad Wilk.
Retribution Music, Philadelphia, 1999/Sony ATV Songs LLC, Nashville, 1999.
Introduced by Rage Against the Machine on the album *The Battle of Los Angeles* (Sony/Epic, 1999).

Sleepwalker
Words and music by Jakob Dylan.
WB Music Publishing, 2000/Brother Jumbo Music, 2000.

Introduced by the Wallflowers on the album *Breach* (Uni/Interscope, 2000).

Smile
Words and music by Keith Follese and Christopher Lindsey.
Bud Dog Music, Beverly Hills, 1999/Songs of Nashville Dreamworks, 1999/WB Music Publishing, 1999/Music of Windswept, 1999/ Follazoo Crew Music, 1999/Songs of Dreamworks, 1999.
Number one song by Lonestar from the album *Lonely Grill* (BMG/BNA Entertainment, 1999).

Smoke Rings in the Dark
Words and music by Boyd Robert and Melvern Rutherford.
Universal-MCA Music Publishing, 1999/Bar R Music, 1999/Universal-Polygram Intl Tunes, 1999.
Introduced by Gary Allan on the album *Smoke Rings in the Dark* (Uni/ MCA Nashville, 1999).

Snow
Words and music by Mark Greaney.
Warner/Chappell Music Canada Ltd., 2000.
Introduced by JJ72 on the album *JJ72* (Sony/Columbia, 2000).

Some Things Never Change
Words and music by James Aldridge and Truman Crisler.
House of Fame, Muscle Shoals, 1999/EMI-April Music, 1999/Waltz Time Music, 1999.
Best-selling record by Tim McGraw from the album *A Place in the Sun* (WEA/Atlantic/Curb, 1999).

Someday Out of the Blue
Words and music by Elton John, Patrick Leonard, and Timothy Rice.
Cherry River Music, New York, 2000/SKG Music Publishing LLC, 2000.
Introduced by Elton John in the film and on the soundtrack album *The Road to El Dorado* (Uni/ DreamWorks, 2000).

Son of Sam
Words and music by Elliott Smith.
Careers-BMG Music, Beverly Hills, 2000/Spent Bullets Music, 2000/ SKG Music Publishing LLC, 2000.
Introduced by Elliott Smith on the album *Figure 8* (Uni/DreamWorks, 2000).

A Song for Assata
Words and music by Thomas Burton, Common (pseudonym for Rashid Lynn), and James Poyser.
Senseless Music, 2000/Universal-Polygram Intl Tunes, 2000/Songs of Universal, 2000/EPHCY Music, 2000.

Introduced by Common on the album *Like Water for Chocolate* (Uni/MCA, 2000).

A Song for the Lovers
Words and music by Richard Ashcroft.
EMI-Virgin Songs, 2000/EMI Virgin Music Ltd., 2000.
Introduced by Richard Ashcroft on the album *Alone with Everybody* (EMD/Virgin, 2000).

Sour Girl
Words and music by Dean Deleo, Robert Deleo, Eric Kretz, and Scott Weiland.
EMI-April Music, 1999/Foxy Dead Girl Music, 1999/WB Music Publishing, 1999.
Introduced by Stone Temple Pilots on the album *No. 4* (WEA/Atlantic, 1999).

Stan
Words and music by Dido Armstrong, Eminem (pseudonym for Marshall Mathers), and Paul Herman.
WB Music Publishing, 2000/Eight Mile Style Music, 2000/EMI-Blackwood Music Inc., 2000/Ensign Music, 2000/Warner-Chappell Music, 2000/Champion Music UK, 2000.
Introduced by Eminem featuring Dido on the album *The Marshall Mathers LP* (Uni/Interscope, 2000).

Stand Inside Your Love
Words and music by Billy Corgan.
Faust's Haus Music, 1999.
Introduced by Smashing Pumpkins on the album *MACHINA/The Machines of the God* (EMD/Virgin, 2000).

Stay the Night
Words and music by Donald Davis, Marques Houston, Tony Isaac, Jerome Jones, Kelton Kessee, Tony Oliver, Harvey Scales, Lawrence Stephans, and Albert Vance.
EMI-Full Keel Music, 1999/Blue Khakis Music, 1999/Demolition Man Music, 1999/Put It Down Music, 1999/T. Scott Style Music, 1999/Young Fiano Music, 1999.
Introduced by IMx on the album *Introducing IMx* (Uni/MCA, 1999).

Steal My Kisses
Words and music by Ben Harper.
EMI-Virgin Music, 1999/Innocent Criminal, 1999.
Introduced by Ben Harper on the album *Burn to Shine* (EMD/Virgin, 1999).

Stellar
Words and music by Brandon Boyd, Michael Einziger, Alex Katunich,

Chris Kilmore, and Jose Pasillas.
EMI April Canada, 1999/Hunglikeyora, 1999.
Introduced by Incubus on the album *Make Yourself* (Sony/Epic, 1999).

Stiff Upper Lip
Words and music by Angus Young and Malcolm Young.
J. Albert & Son Music, 2000.
Best-selling record by AC/DC from the album *Stiff Upper Lip* (WEA/Elektra, 2000).

Still D.R.E.
Words and music by Jay-Z (pseudonym for Shawn Carter), Dr. Dre (pseudonym for Andre Young), Snoop Dogg (pseudonym for Calvin Broadus), and Scott Storch.
TVT Music, NYC, 1999/Ain't Nothin' Goin on But F****n Music, 1999/EMI-Blackwood Music Inc., 1999/Lil Lu Lu Publishing, 1999/WB Music Publishing, 1999/Hard Working Black Folks, 1999/Scott Storch Music, 1999/Wee Small Hours Music, 1999.
Introduced by Dr. Dre featuring Snoop Dogg on the album *2001* (Uni/Interscope, 1999).

Still in My Heart
Words by Andrea Martin and Ivan Matias, music by Kenneth Karlin and Soulshock (pseudonym for Carsten Schack).
Ghetto Fabulous Entertainment, Brooklyn, 1999/Almo Music Corp., 1999/WB Music Publishing, 1999/EMI-Blackwood Music Inc., 1999/One Ol' Ghetto Hoe Music, 1999/EMI Blackwood Music Canada Ltd., 1999/Sailandra Publishing, 1999/Casadida Publishing, 1999/Soulvang Music, 1999/Jungle Fever Music, 1999/GC Publishing, 1999/Full of Soul Music, 1999.
Introduced by Tracie Spencer on the album *Tracie* (EMD/Capitol, 1999).

Still Not a Player
Words and music by Big Punisher (pseudonym for Christopher Rios), Jerome Foster, Rodney Jerkins, Brenda Russell, Jolyon Skinner, Japhe Tejeda, Joe Thomas, and Michele Williams.
Let Me Show You Music, New York, 1998/Rutland Road, Encino, 1998/Sounds of Da Red Drum, Bronx, 1998/EMI-Blackwood Music Inc., 1998/Rodney Jerkins Music, 1998/Almo Music Corp., 1998/Conversation Tree Entertainment, 1998/EMI-April Music, 1998/Foray Music, 1998/Zomba Enterprises, 1998/Black Hand Music, 1998/Henchi Music, 1998/1972 Music, 1998.
Introduced by Incubus and Big Punisher on the various-artists album *Loud Rocks* (Sony/Columbia, 2000).

Stoopid Ass
Words and music by Ralph Jezzard, James Butler, and Richard

Battersby.
Universal-Polygram Intl Tunes, 2000.
Introduced by Grand Theft Audio on the album *Blame Everyone* (WEA/London/Sire, 2000).

Straight Up
Words and music by Bryan-Michael Cox, Cynthia Loving, and Jermaine Dupri.
EMI-April Music, 2000/So So Def Music, 2000/EMI April Canada, 2000.
Best-selling record by Chante Moore from the album *Exposed* (Uni/MCA, 2000).

Stronger
Words and music by Martin Sandberg and Rami Yacoub.
Zomba Enterprises, 2000/Grantsville Publishing, 2000.
Best-selling record by Britney Spears from the album *Oops!...I Did It Again* (BMG/Jive/Silvertone, 2000).

Stupify
Words and music by Dan Donegan, David Draiman, Steve Kmak, and Michael Wengren.
Mother Culture Publishing, 2000/WB Music Publishing, 2000.
Introduced by Disturbed on the album *The Sickness* (WEA/Warner Bros., 2000). Later featured on the soundtrack album *Little Nicky* (WEA/Warner Bros., 2000).

Summer Rain
Words and music by Dwight Myers, Dewayne Rogers, and Stevie Wonder (pseudonym for Steveland Morris).
Sounds from the Soul, Woodland, 2000/Black Bull Music, 2000/EMI-April Music, 2000/Jobete Music Co., 2000/Soul on Soul Music, 2000.
Best-selling record by Carl Thomas from the album *Emotional* (BMG/Arista/Bad Boy, 2000). Later featured on the soundtrack album *Shaft (2000)* (BMG/Arista/La Face, 2000).

Summerfling
Words and music by K. D. Lang and David Piltch.
Pulling Teeth Music, 2000/Thumb Print Music, 2000/Universal Songs of Polygram Intl., 2000.
Introduced by K. D. Lang on the album *Invincible Summer* (WEA/Warner Bros., 2000).

Sundown
Words and music by Gordon Lightfoot.
Moose Music Ltd., 1973.
Revived by Elwood on the album *The Parlance of Our Time* (Palm Pictures, 2000).

Sunset (Bird of Prey)
Words and music by Robert Densmore, Fatboy Slim (pseudonym for Norman Cook), Robbie Krieger, Raymond Manzarek, and Jim Morrison.
Universal-Polygram Intl Tunes, 2000/Doors Music Co., 2000.
Introduced by Fatboy Slim on the album *Halfway Between the Gutter and the Stars* (EMD/Astralwerks, 2000).

Superman
Words and music by John Ondrasik.
EMI-Blackwood Music Inc., 2000/EMI Blackwood Music Canada Ltd., 2000/Five for Fighting Music, 2000.
Introduced by Five for Fighting on the album *America Town* (Sony/Columbia, 2000). Later featured on the soundtrack album *Songs from Dawson's Creek, Volume 2* (Sony/Columbia, 2000).

Supreme
Words and music by Guy Chambers, Dino Fekaris, Frederick Perren, and Robbie Williams.
EMI-Virgin Songs, 2000/Hit & Run Music, 2000/EMI-Virgin Music, 2000/Universal-Polygram Intl Tunes, 2000/Perren Vibes Music, Inc., 2000/BMG Music Publishing Ltd., 2000.
Introduced by Robbie Williams on the album *Sing When You're Winning* (EMD/Capitol, 2000).

Swear It Again
Words and music by Wayne Hector and Steve Mac.
Irving Music Inc., 1999/Rondor Music, 1999/Songs of Windswept Pacific, 1999/Rokstone Music, 1999.
Best-selling record by Westlife from the album *Westlife* (BMG/Arista, 1999).

T

Ta Da

Words and music by Anthony Crawford, Stacey Daniels, and Montell Jordan.

Hudson Jordan Music, Tarzana, 1999/Wixen Music, Calabasas, 1999/ Almo Music Corp., 1999/Famous Music Corp., 1999/Montel Jordan Music, 1999/Dove Daniels Music, 1999/Shep and Shep Publishing, 1999.

Best-selling single by Lil' Mo (WEA/Elektra, 2000).

Take It Back

Words and music by Nathan Cox, Jonathan Davis, Michael Doling, and John Fahnestock.

Goathead Music, 2000.

Introduced by Strait Up featuring Jonathan Davis on the album *Strait Up* (EMD/Virgin, 2000).

Take a Look Around

Words and music by Fred Durst and Lalo Schifrin.

Famous Music Corp., 2000/Bruin Music Co., 2000.

Introduced by Limp Bizkit on the soundtrack album *Music from and Inspired by M:I-2* (Uni/Hollywood, 2000). Later featured on the Limp Bizkit album *Chocolate Starfish and the Hot Dog Flavored Water* (Uni/Interscope, 2000).

Take That

Words and music by Henri Charlemagne, Melissa Elliott, Howard Hewett, and Dana Meyers.

Sony ATV Tunes LLC, Nashville, 2000/Sony ATV Songs LLC, Nashville, 2000/Johnny Handsome Music, New York, 2000/WB Music Publishing, 2000/LFS III Music, 2000/Mass Confusion Productions, 2000.

Best-selling single by Torrey Carter featuring Missy "Misdemeanor" Elliott (WEA/Elektra, 2000).

Taking You Home
Words and music by Stuart Brawley, Don Henley, and Stanley Lynch.
Matanzas Music, St. Augustine, 1999/WB Music Publishing, 1999/Warner-Tamerlane Music, 1999/Wishart Songs, 1999/Wisteria Music, 1999.
Best-selling record by Don Henley from the album *Inside Job* (WEA/Warner Bros., 2000).

Teenage Dirtbag
Words and music by Brendan Brown.
EMI-Blackwood Music Inc., 2000/Montauk Mantis Production, 2000.
Introduced by Wheatus in the film *Loser*. Later featured on the Wheatus album *Wheatus* (Sony/Columbia, 2000) and on the soundtrack album *Songs from Dawson's Creek, Volume 2* (Sony/Columbia, 2000).

Tell Her
Words and music by Mark Cornell and Craig Wiseman.
Daddy Rabbitt Music, Nashville, 1999/Almo Music Corp., 1999/Rondor Music, 1999.
Best-selling record by Lonestar from the album *Lonely Grill* (BMG/BNA Entertainment, 1999).

Tell Me Why (The Riddle)
Words and music by Sarah Cracknell, Robert Stanley, Paul Van Dyk, and Peter Wiggs.
BMG Songs Inc., 2000/Warner/Chappell Music Canada Ltd., 2000.
Introduced by Paul van Dyk featuring St. Etienne on the album *Out There and Back* (Mute, 2000).

Thank God I Found You
Words and music by Mariah Carey, James Harris, and Terry Lewis.
Rye Songs, Philadelphia, 1999/Sony ATV Songs LLC, Nashville, 1999/EMI-April Music, 1999/Flyte Tyme Tunes, 1999.
Number one song by Mariah Carey featuring Joe and 98 Degrees from the album *Rainbow* (Sony/Columbia, 1999).

Thank You
Words and music by Dido Armstrong and Paul Herman.
WB Music Publishing, 1998/EMI-Blackwood Music Inc., 1998/Champion Music, 1998.
Best-selling record by Dido from the album *No Angel* (BMG/Arista, 1999).

That Other Woman
Words and music by Joe Thomas and Joshua Thompson.
563 Music Publishing, 2000/Tallest Tree Music, 2000/Zomba Enterprises, 2000.

Introduced by Changing Faces on the album *Visit Me* (WEA/Atlantic, 2000).

That's the Beat of a Heart
Words and music by Tena Clark and Timothy Heintz.
Kodeko Music, Pasadena, 2000/Fifty-Seven Varieties Music, 2000/TCF Music Publishing, 2000/Fox Film Music Corp., 2000/Songs of Universal, 2000/Group Productions, 2000.
Best-selling record by Warren Brothers featuring Sara Evans from the soundtrack album *Where the Heart Is* (BMG/RCA, 2000). Later featured on the Warren Brothers album *King of Nothing* (BMG/BNA Entertainment, 2000).

That's the Kind of Mood I'm In
Words and music by Rick Giles, Gilles Godard, and Tim Nichols.
Diamond Storm Music, Nashville, 2000/Ty Land Music, Old Hickory, 2000/Buzz Cut Music, 2000/EMI-Blackwood Music Inc., 2000/Mike Curb Music, 2000/EMI Blackwood Music Canada Ltd., 2000.
Best-selling record by Patty Loveless from the album *Strong Heart* (Sony/Epic, 2000).

That's the Way
Words and music by Mary Lamar and Annie Roboff.
Almo Music Corp., 2000/Anwa Music, 2000/Platinum Plow, 2000/WB Music Publishing, 2000.
Number one song by Jo Dee Messina from the album *Burn* (WEA/Atlantic/Curb, 2000).

That's What I'm Looking For
Words and music by Da Brat (pseudonym for Shawntae Harris) and Jermaine Dupri.
Air Control Music, 2000/EMI-April Music, 2000/So So Def Music, 2000/Throwin' Tantrums Music, 2000.
Best-selling record by Da Brat from the album *Unrestricted* (So Def/Sony, 2000).

Theme from Shaft
Words and music by Isaac Hayes.
Irving Music Inc.-East Memphis, 1971.
Revived by Isaac Hayes in the film and on the soundtrack album *Shaft (2000)* (BMG/Arista/La Face, 2000).

There You Are
Words and music by Robert DiPiero, Edward Hill, and Mark Sanders.
Careers-BMG Music, Beverly Hills, 1999/Sony ATV Songs LLC, Nashville, 1999/Soda Creek Songs, 1999/Universal-MCA Music Publishing, 1999/Love Monkey Music, 1999/Music Hill Music, 1999/Tree Publishing Co., Inc., 1999/Sony ATV Tree Publishing, 1999.

Introduced by Martina McBride on the album *Emotion* (BMG/RCA, 1999).

There You Go

Words and music by Kevin Briggs, Kandi Burruss, and Alecia Moore.

Air Control Music, 1999/EMI-April Music, 1999/Kandacy Music, 1999/ Pink Panther Music, 1999/Shek' Em Down Music, 1999/Hitco Music, 1999.

Best-selling record by Pink from the album *Can't Take Me Home* (BMG/Arista/ La Face, 2000).

Things Have Changed

Words and music by Bob Dylan (pseudonym for Robert Zimmerman).

Special Rider Music, 2000.

Introduced by Bob Dylan in the film and on the soundtrack album *Wonder Boys* (Sony/Columbia, 2000). Later featured on the Bob Dylan album *Essential Bob Dylan* (Sony/Columbia, 2000).Won an Academy Award for Best Original Song of the Year 2001. Nominated for a Grammy Award, Best Song Written for a Movie, 2000.

This Can't Be Life

Words and music by Kenneth Gamble, Dwight Grant, Leon Huff, Jay-Z (pseudonym for Shawn Carter), Brad Jordan, and Kaye West.

EMI-Blackwood Music Inc., 2000/Lil Lu Lu Publishing, 2000/Warner-Tamerlane Music, 2000/Music of Windswept, 2000/N-The Water Publishing, 2000/EMI Blackwood Music Canada Ltd., 2000.

Introduced by Jay-Z featuring Scarface on the album *The Dynasty: Roc la Familia* (Uni/Def Jam, 2000).

This Could Be Heaven

Words and music by Guy Gersoni, Henry Jackman, David Palmer, and Seal (pseudonym for Sealhenry Samuel).

SPZ Music, New York, 2000.

Introduced by Seal in the film and on the soundtrack album *The Family Man* (WEA/London/Sire, 2000).

This Is Love

Words and music by Polly Harvey.

EMI-Blackwood Music Inc., 2000.

Introduced by PJ Harvey on the album *Stories from the City, Stories from the Sea* (Uni/Island, 2000).

This Time Around

Words and music by Clarke Hanson, Jordan Hanson, and Zachary Hanson.

Jam N' Bread Music, 2000.

Best-selling record by Hanson from the album *This Time Around* (Uni/ Island, 2000).

This Woman Needs
Words and music by Bonnie Baker, Connie Harrington, and Kristyn Osborn.
Without Anna Music, Nashville, 1999/Songs of Hamstein Cumberland, Austin, 1999/EMI-April Music, 1999/Little Cricket Music, 1999/ Songs of Otis Barker, 1999/Howlin' Hits Music, 1999.
Introduced by SHeDAISY on the album *The Whole Shebang* (Uni/Lyric Street, 1999).

Thong Song
Words and music by Desmond Child, Marquis Collins, Tim Kelley, Joseph Longo, Bob Robinson, Rob Rosa, and Sisqo (pseudonym for Mark Andrews).
A Phantom Vox Music, Los Angeles, 1999/Cherry River Music, New York, 1999/Time for Flytes Music, Dunwoody, 1999/Warner-Tamerlane Music, 1999/Warner-Chappell Music, 1999/Sugar Hill Music Publishing, Ltd., 1999.
Best-selling record by Sisqo from the album *Unleash the Dragon* (Uni/ Def Jam, 1999).Nominated for a Grammy Award, Best R&B Song, 2000.

3 Little Words
Words and music by Gary St. Clair.
Hit Boy Music, 1999.
Introduced by Nu Flavor on the album *It's On* (WEA/Warner Bros., 1999).

'Til I Say So
Words and music by Michele Williams, Vito Colapietro, Noah Porter, Neely Dinkins, Gregory Crapps, and James Glasco.
Foray Music, 2000/1972 Music, 2000.
Introduced by 3LW on the soundtrack album *Bring It On* (Sony/Epic, 2000). Later featured on the 3LW album *3LW* (Sony/Epic, 2000).

Time Has Come Today
Words and music by Joseph Chambers and Willie Chambers.
Careers-BMG Music, Beverly Hills, 1967/Spinnaker Music, 1967.
Revived by Steve Earle and Sheryl Crow on the soundtrack album *Steal This Movie* (Artemis, 2000).

Too Sick to Pray
Words and music by John Black, Simon Edwards, Mark Sams, and Robert Spragg.
Chrysalis Music Group, 2000.
Introduced by A3 on the album *La Peste* (Sony/Columbia, 2000).

Took the Bait
Words and music by Dangerous (pseudonym for Damon Williams),

Vada Nobles, Rasheen Pugh, and Scarface (pseudonym for Brad Jordan).
Kilosheem Publishing, Orange, 2000/N-The Water Publishing, 2000/ Jermaine Music, 2000.
Introduced by Scarface featuring Dangerous on the soundtrack album *Bait* (WEA/Warner Bros., 2000).

Tough Guy
Words and music by Andre Benjamin, Chad Butler, Bernard Freeman, Antwan Patton, and David Sheats.
Chrysalis Music Group, 2000/Zomba Enterprises, 2000/Dungeon Rat Music, 2000/Gnat Booty Music, 2000/Pimp My Pen International, 2000.
Introduced by Outkast on the soundtrack album *Shaft (2000)* (BMG/ Arista/La Face, 2000).

Train Song
Words and music by Eliza Carthy, Ben Ivitsky, Barnaby Stradling, and Sam Thomas.
Happy Valley Music, 2000.
Introduced by Eliza Carthy on the album *Angels & Cigarettes* (WEA/ Warner Bros., 2000).

Transcendental Blues
Words and music by Stephen Earle.
Sarangel Music, Nashville, 2000/Bughouse, 2000.
Introduced by Steve Earle on the album *Transcendental Blues* (Artemis, 2000).

Treat Her like a Lady
Words and music by Isaac Hayes and Stephen Huff.
Almo Music Corp., 2000/Zomba Enterprises, 2000/Tuff Huff Music, 2000/Rondor Music, 2000.
Best-selling record by Joe from the album *My Name Is Joe* (BMG/Jive/ Silvertone, 2000).

Tricky, Tricky
Words and music by Achim Kleist, Lou Bega (pseudonym for David Lubega), Christian Pletschacher, and Wolfgang Von Webenau.
Unicade Music, New York, 1999/BMG Songs Inc., 1999/Edition Syndicate Songs, 1999.
Best-selling record by Lou Bega from the album *A Little Bit of Mambo* (BMG/RCA, 1999).

Try Again
Words and music by Stephen Garrett and Timothy Mosley.
Black Fountain Music, 2000/Herbalicious Music, 2000/Virginia Beach Music, 2000/WB Music Publishing, 2000.

Number one song by Aaliyah from the soundtrack album *Romeo Must Die* (EMD/Virgin, 2000).

Try Try Try
Words and music by Billy Corgan.
Faust's Haus Music, 2000.
Introduced by the Smashing Pumpkins on the album *MACHINA/The Machines of God* (EMD/Virgin, 2000).

Turn (English)
Words and music by Francis Healy.
Sony ATV Songs LLC, Nashville, 1999.
Introduced by Travis on the album *The Man Who* (Sony International, 1999).

Turn Me on "Mr. Deadman"
Words and music by Patrick Kennison and Bryan Scott.
Superman Music, 2000/WB Music Publishing, 2000.
Introduced by the Union Underground on the album *An Education in Rebellion* (Sony, 2000).

Turning Time Around
Words and music by Lou Reed.
Lou Reed Music, New York, 2000/EMI-Blackwood Music Inc., 2000.
Introduced by Lou Reed on the album *Ecstasy* (WEA/Warner Bros., 2000).

24/7
Words and music by Angelo Ray, David Scott, and Anthony Smith.
C Town Music, Cincinnati, 1999/Sounds Heard Everywhere Music, 1999/White Rhino Music, 1999.
Best-selling record by Kevon Edmonds from the album *24/7* (BMG/RCA, 1999).

Two Against Nature
Words and music by Walter Becker and Donald Fagen.
Freejunket Music, 1999/Len Freedman Music, 1999/Zeon Music, 1999.
Introduced by Steely Dan on the album *Two Against Nature* (WEA/Warner Bros., 2000).

U

U Don't Love Me
Words and music by John Dunson and Sean Dunson.
Dunson Twin Music, Davenport, 1999.
Introduced by the Kumbia Kings featuring A. B. Quintanilla on the album *Amor, Familia y Respeto* (EMD/EMI Latin, 2000).

U Understand
Words and music by Juvenile (pseudonym for Terius Gray) and Byron Thomas.
Money Mack Music, 1999.
Introduced by Juvenile on the album *Tha G-Code* (Uni/Universal/Cash Money, 1999).

Ultra Mega
Words and music by Michael Cummings, Dorian Heartsong, Allan Pahanish, Michael Tempesta, and Adam Williams.
Dreamworks Songs, 2000/Soulsuck Music, 2000.
Introduced by Powerman 5000 on the soundtrack album *Dracula 2000* (Sony/Columbia, 2000).

Unconditional
Words and music by Nancy Bryant, Elizabeth Hengber, and Melvern Rutherford.
Glen Nikki Music, 1999/WB Music Publishing, 1999/Songs of Universal, 1999.
Best-selling record by Clay Davidson from the album *Unconditional* (EMD/Virgin, 2000).

Untitled (How Does It Feel)
Words and music by D'Angelo (pseudonym for Michael Archer) and Raphael Saadiq.
Ah Choo Music, 2000/Universal-Polygram Intl Tunes, 2000/Tony! Toni! Tone! Music, 2000.
Best-selling record by D'Angelo from the album *Voodoo* (EMD/Virgin, 2000).Nominated for a Grammy Award, Best R&B Song, 2000.

Up with People
Words and music by Kurt Wagner.
Pathetic Hindsight Music, 2000.
Introduced by Lambchop on the album *Nixon* (Merge, 2000).

V

V.I.P

Words and music by Alex Gifford, Nathaniel Hall, Buddy Kaye, Hugo Montenegro, and Michael Small.

Universal Songs of Polygram Intl., 2000/Screen Gems-EMI Music Inc., 2000/Chrysalis Music Group, 2000/Colgems-EMI Music, 2000/Jungle Brothers Music, 2000.

Introduced by the Jungle Brothers on the album *V. I. P.* (Gee Street/V2, 2000). Later featured on the soundtrack album *Whatever It Takes* (Uni/Hollywood, 2000).

Voodoo

Words and music by Salvatore Erna and Robert Merrill.

Meeengya Music, 1998/Universal-MCA Music Publishing, 1998/MCA Music Publishing, 1998/Mick Dog, 1998.

Re-introduced by Godsmack on the album *Godsmack* (Uni/Universal, 1999).

W

The Way I Am
Words and music by Eminem (pseudonym for Marshall Mathers).
Ensign Music, 2000/Eight Mile Style Music, 2000.
Best-selling record by Eminem from the album *The Marshall Mathers LP* (Uni/Interscope, 2000).

The Way You Love Me
Words and music by Michael Delaney and Keith Follese.
Encore Entertainment LLC, Nashville, 1999/Airstream Dreams Music, 1999/Coyote House Music, 1999/Famous Music Corp., 1999/Follazoo Crew Music, 1999/Scott & Soda, 1999.
Number one song by Faith Hill from the album *Breathe* (WEA/Warner Bros., 1999).Nominated for a Grammy Award, Best Country Song, 2000.

We Danced
Words and music by Charles Dubois and Brad Paisley.
EMI-April Music, 1999/Sea Gayle Music, 1999.
Number one song by Brad Paisley from the album *Who Needs Pictures* (BMG/Arista, 1999).

West Side Story
Words and music by Dow Brain, Rich Cronin, and Bradley Young.
BMG Songs Inc., 1999/Zomba Enterprises, 1999/BKY Music, 1999/Trans Continental Music, 1999/Trans Con Publishing, 1999/Dow Tone Music, 1999.
Introduced by LFO on the album *LFO* (BMG/Arista, 1999). Live version featured on the album *Power of 3* (BMG/Arista, 2000).

What About Now
Words and music by Aaron Barker, Ronald Harbin, and Anthony Smith.
Ron Harbin Music, Nashville, 1999/Sony ATV Tunes LLC, Nashville, 1999/Blind Sparrow Music, Brentwood, 1999/O Tex Music, Nashville, 1999/Sony ATV Songs LLC, Nashville, 1999/Notes to Music, 1999/WB Music Publishing, 1999/Warner-Chappell Music,

1999/Muy Bueno Music, 1999.
Number one song by Lonestar from the album *Lonely Grill* (BMG/BNA Entertainment, 1999).

What a Girl Wants
Words and music by Shelly Peiken and Guy Roche.
Manuiti LA Music, Encino, 1999/Hidden Pun Music, 1999/Sushi Too Music, 1999.
Number one song by Christina Aguilera from the album *Christina Aguilera* (BMG/RCA, 1999). Spanish-language version, "Una Mujer," featured on the album *Mi Reflejo* (BMG/U.S. Latin, 2000).

What I Need to Do
Words and music by Thomas Damphier and William Luther.
Cut Out Music, Nashville, 1999/Two Guys Who Are Publishers, Nashville, 1999/Careers-BMG Music, Beverly Hills, 1999.
Best-selling record by Kenny Chesney from the album *Greatest Hits* (BMG/BNA Entertainment, 2000).

What If
Words and music by Scott Stapp and Mark Tremonti.
Dwight Frye Music, New York, 1999/Tremonti Stapp Music, New York, 1999.
Introduced by Creed on the album *Human Clay* (BMG/Wind Up, 1999). Later featured on the soundtrack album *Scream 3* (BMG/Wind Up, 2000).

What Means the World to You
Words and music by Sting (pseudonym for Gordon Sumner).
EMI-Blackwood Music Inc., 2000/Magnetic Music Publishing Co., 2000.
Introduced by Cam'ron on the album *S. D. E.* (Sony, 2000).

What You Want
Words and music by DMX (pseudonym for Earl Simmons), Tamir Ruffin, Sisqo (pseudonym for Mark Andrews), and Phillip Weatherspoon.
Reach Music International, New York, 1999.
Best-selling record by DMX featuring Sisqo from the various-artists album *Ryde or Die, Vol. 1* (Uni/Interscope, 1999).

What'chu Like
Words and music by Da Brat (pseudonym for Shawntae Harris), Jermaine Dupri, Joerg Evers, and Juergen Korduletsch.
Air Control Music, 2000/EMI-April Music, 2000/So So Def Music, 2000/Throwin' Tantrums Music, 2000/Warner-Tamerlane Music, 2000/EMI April Canada, 2000.

Best-selling record by Da Brat featuring Tyrese from the album *Unrestricted* (So Def/Sony, 2000).

Whatever
Words and music by Edward Berkeley, Kobie Brown, Oliver Cheatam, Keir Gist, Robert Huggar, and Kevin McCord.
Proceed Music, 1999/Famous Music Corp., 1999/Universal Duchess Music, 1999/Uh-Oh Entertainment, 1999/WB Music Publishing, 1999/Perk's Music, Inc., 1999/Divine Mill Music, 1999/Fingaz Goal Music, 1999.
Best-selling record by Ideal from the album *Ideal* (EMD/Virgin, 1999).

What's My Name
Words and music by DMX (pseudonym for Earl Simmons), Edward Hinson, and Irving Lorenzo.
Boomer X Publishing, New York, 1999/Ruff Ryders Entertainment, New York, 1999/DJ Irv, 1999/Ensign Music, 1999/Songs of Universal, 1999/Tiarra's Daddy Music, 1999.
Best-selling record by DMX from the album *And Then There Was X* (Uni/Def Jam, 1999).

What's Your Fantasy
Words and music by Christopher Bridges and Shondrae Crawford.
EMI-April Music, 2000/Ludacris Music, 2000.
Introduced by Ludacris on the album *Back for the First Time* (Uni/ Def Jam, 2000).

When She Loved Me
Words and music by Randy Newman.
Pixar Talking Pictures, Richmond, 1999/Walt Disney Music, 1999.
Introduced by Sarah McLachlan in the film and on the soundtrack album *Toy Story 2* (Uni/Disney, 1999).Won a Grammy Award for Best Song Written for a Movie 2000.

When You Come Back to Me Again
Words and music by Garth Brooks and Jenny Yates.
In My Dreams, Los Angeles, 2000/No Fences Music, Nashville, 2000/Major Bob Music, 2000.
Introduced by Garth Brooks in the film *Frequency.*

When You Need My Love
Words and music by Wynn Varble and Darryl Worley.
EMI-Blackwood Music Inc., 2000/Warner-Tamerlane Music, 2000/Starstruck Angel Music, 2000.
Best-selling record by Darryl Worley from the album *Hard Rain Don't Last* (Uni/DreamWorks, 2000).

Where the Birds Always Sing
Words and music by Jason Cooper and Robert Smith, music by Perry

Bamonte, Simon Gallup, and Roger O'Donnell.
Fiction Songs Ltd., 2000.
Introduced by the Cure on the album *Bloodflowers* (WEA/Elektra, 2000).

Where I Wanna Be
Words and music by Donell Jones and Kyle West.
Checkman Music, 1999/EMI-April Music, 1999/NNC Publishing, 1999/WB Music Publishing, 1999/Willarie Publishing Co., 1999.
Best-selling record by Donell Jones from the album *Where I Wanna Be* (BMG/Arista/La Face, 1999).

Where I Wanna Be
Words and music by Edward Berkeley, Keir Gist, Robert Huggar, Robert Kimball, Kurupt (pseudonym for Ricardo Brown), Nate Dogg (pseudonym for Nathaniel Hale), David Paich, Shisty, and Tramayne Thompson.
Antraphil Music, 2000/Nate Dogg Music, 2000/WB Music Publishing, 2000/EMI April Canada, 2000/Divine Mill Music, 2000/Fingaz Goal Music, 2000.
Introduced by Shade Sheist featuring Nate Dogg and Kurupt on the album *Damizza Presents: Where I Wanna Be* (WEA/London/Sire, 2000).

Where You Are
Words and music by Louis Biancaniello, Nick Lachey, Adamancia Stamapoulou, and Samuel Watters.
Sony ATV Tunes LLC, Nashville, 1999/Sony ATV Songs LLC, Nashville, 1999/EMI-April Music, 1999/SMY Music, 1999/EMI April Canada, 1999/27th and May Music, 1999/98 Degrees and Rising, 1999/Breakthrough Creations, 1999.
Introduced by Jessica Simpson featuring Nick Lachey on the album *Sweet Kisses* (Sony, 1999). Later featured on the soundtrack album *Here on Earth* (Sony/Columbia, 2000).

Whistle While You Twurk
Words and music by Michael Crooms, Deongelo Holmes, and Eric Jackson.
Collipark, 2000/Da Crippler Publishing, 2000/E W C Publishing Co, 2000.
Best-selling record by the Ying Yang Twins from the album *Thug Walkin'* (Uni/Universal, 2000).

Who Let the Dogs Out
Words and music by Anslem Douglas, words by Marvin Prosper.
Sony ATV Songs LLC, Nashville, 2000/Desmone Music, 2000.
Best-selling record by the Baha Men from the album *Who Let the Dogs Out* (S-Curve, 2000).

Whoa!
Words and music by Anthony Best, Black Rob (pseudonym for Robert Ross), and Harve Pierre.
Harve Pierre Publishing, Laurelton, 1999/BMG Songs Inc., 1999/ Diamond Rob Music, 1999/EMI-April Music, 1999/Justin Combs Publishing, 1999/Still Digging Music, 1999.
Best-selling record by Black Rob from the album *Life Story* (BMG/ Arista/Bad Boy, 1999).

Why Does It Always Rain on Me?
Words and music by Francis Healy.
Sony ATV Songs LLC, Nashville, 1999/Sony ATV Tunes LLC, Nashville, 1999.
Introduced by Travis on the album *The Man Who* (Sony, 1999).

Why Pt. 2
Words and music by Ed Roland.
Sugarfuzz Music, 2000/Warner-Tamerlane Music, 2000.
Introduced by Collective Soul on the album *Blender* (WEA/Atlantic, 2000).

Wifey
Words and music by Edward Berkeley, Keir Gist, and Robert Huggar.
Divine Mill Music, 2000/EMI-April Music, 2000/Famous Music Corp., 2000/Fingaz Goal Music, 2000/Uh-Oh Entertainment, 2000/WB Music Publishing, 2000.
Number one song by Next from the album *Welcome II Nextasy* (BMG/ Arista, 2000).

Wild Child
Words and music by Enya (pseudonym for Eithne Ni Bhraonain), Nicky Ryan, and Roma Ryan.
EMI Songs Ltd., 2000/EMI-Blackwood Music Inc., 2000/EMI Blackwood Music Canada Ltd., 2000.
Introduced by Enya on the album *A Day Without Rain* (WEA/Warner Bros., 2000).

Wishin' All These Old Things Were New
Words and music by Merle Haggard.
Merle Haggard Music, 1999.
Introduced by Merle Haggard on the album *If I Could Only Fly* (Anti/ Epitaph, 2000).

With Arms Wide Open
Words and music by Scott Stapp and Mark Tremonti.
Dwight Frye Music, New York, 1999/Tremonti Stapp Music, New York, 1999.

Number one song by Creed from the album *Human Clay* (BMG/Wind Up, 1999).Won a Grammy Award for Best Rock Song 2000.

Without You

Words and music by Eric Silver and Natalie Maines.

703 Music, 1999/EMI-April Music, 1999/Scrapin' Toast Music, 1999.

Number one song by the Dixie Chicks from the album *Fly* (Sony/ Monument, 1999).

Wobble Wobble

Words and music by Darin Black and Marc D'Andrea.

Black at Cha Publishing, West Covina, 2000/Marc 'n Tha Dark Music, 2000.

Best-selling record by the 504 Boyz from the album *Goodfellas* (EMD/ Priority, 2000).

Wonderful

Words and music by Arthur Alexakis, Greg Eklund, and Craig Montoya.

Common Green Music, 2000/Evergleam Music, 2000/Irving Music Inc., 2000/Montalupis Music, 2000.

Best-selling record by Everclear from the album *Songs from an American Movie, Vol. One: Learning How to Smile* (EMD/Capitol, 2000).

World Looking In

Words and music by Skye Edwards, Paul Godfrey, and Ross Godfrey.

Chrysalis Songs, 2000/Chrysalis Music Group, 2000.

Introduced by Morcheeba on the album *Fragments of Freedom* (WEA/ London/Sire, 2000). Later featured in the film and on the soundtrack album *The Family Man* (WEA/London/Sire, 2000).

Y

Ya Mama

Words and music by Frankie Cutlass, Fatboy Slim (pseudonym for Norman Cook), Gene Finley, Richard Heckstall-Smith, John Hiseman, and Charles Smith.

Cutlass Music, New York, 2000/Twenty Three West Music, New York, 2000/Fede Yon Music, Philadelphia, 2000/Universal-MCA Music Publishing, 2000/Universal Songs of Polygram Intl., 2000/Warner-Tamerlane Music, 2000/Cotillion Music Inc., 2000/Connor Ryan Music, 2000/Jessica Michael Music, 2000.

Introduced by Fatboy Slim on the album *Halfway Between the Gutter and the Stars* (EMD/Astralwerks, 2000). Also featured on the soundtrack album *Charlie's Angels* (Sony/Columbia, 2000).

Yeah Yeah Yeah

Words and music by Kid Rock (pseudonym for Robert Ritchie), James Trombly, and Uncle Kracker (pseudonym for Matthew Shafer).

Gaje Music, 2000/Squamosal Music, 2000/Thirty Two Mile Music, 2000/Warner-Tamerlane Music, 2000.

Introduced by Uncle Kracker on the album *Double Wide* (WEA/Atlantic/Lava, 2000).

Year 2000

Words and music by Melvin Bradford and Xzibit (pseudonym for Alvin Joiner).

Hennesy for Everyone, Sherman Oaks, 2000/Hard Working Black Folks, 2000/WB Music Publishing, 2000/Voco Music, 2000.

Introduced by Xzibit featuring Jonathan Davis on the soundtrack album *Black and White* (Sony/Columbia, 2000).

Yellow

Words and music by Guy Berryman, Jonathan Buckland, William Champion, and DJ Premier (pseudonym for Chris Martin).

BMG Songs Inc., 2000.

Introduced by Coldplay on the album *Parachutes* (EMD/Capitol, 2000).

Yes!

Words and music by Chad Brock, James Collins, and Stephony Smith.

Single's Only Music, Brentwood, 2000/Cuts R Us Songs, 2000/EMI-Blackwood Music Inc., 2000/Lehsem Songs, 2000/Warner-Tamerlane Music, 2000/Make Shift Music, 2000/Starstruck Angel Music, 2000.

Number one song by Chad Brock from the album *Yes!* (WEA/Warner Bros., 2000).

Y.O.U.

Words and music by Redman (pseudonym for Reggie Noble), Erick Sermon, and Clifford Smith.

Careers-BMG Music, Beverly Hills, 1999/Zomba Enterprises, 1999/Wu-Tang Publishing, 1999/Famous Music Corp., 1999/EMI United Catalogue, 1999/Funky Noble Productions, 1999/Jazz Merchant Music, 1999/Erick Sermon Enterprises, 1999.

Introduced by Method Man and Redman on the album *Blackout!* (Uni/Island, 1999).

You All Dat

Words and music by Imani Coppola, Luigi Creatore, Steve Greenberg, Nehemia Hield, Mark Hudson, Michael Mangini, Hugo Peretti, Herschel Small, and George Weiss.

The Songwriters Guild, Weehawken, 2000/Riddum Music, Nashville, 2000/EMI-Blackwood Music Inc., 2000/Ensign Music, 2000/Universal Songs of Polygram Intl., 2000/Famous Music Corp., 2000/Tsanoddnos Music, 2000/MCA Music Publishing, 2000/Abilene Music Inc., 2000/Beef Puppet, 2000/Gee Street Sounds, 2000/Godchildren Music, 2000/Ahe Belle Music, 2000.

Introduced by the Baha Men on the album *Who Let the Dogs Out* (Artemis/S-Curve, 2000).

You Can Do It

Words and music by R. Allen, Arthur Baker, Aasim Bambaataa, Robert Fogleman, John Gentile, Ice Cube (pseudonym for O'Shea Jackson), Mack 10 (pseudonym for Dedrick Rolison), John Miller, One Eye (pseudonym for Donald Saunders), J. Robie, and Ellis Williams.

No Hassle, New York, 2000/Gangsta Boogie Music, 2000/Kohaw Music, 2000/Real an Ruff Muzik, 2000/Universal-MCA Music Publishing, 2000/WB Music Publishing, 2000/Shakin Baker Music, Inc., 2000/T Girl Music LLC, 2000.

Introduced by Ice Cube featuring Mack 10 and Ms. Toi on the album *War & Peace, Vol. 2 (The Peace Disc)* (EMD/Priority, 2000).

You Owe Me

Words and music by Stephen Garrett, Timothy Mosley, Nas (pseudonym for Nasir Jones), and Ralph Rice.

Black Fountain Music, 1999/Herbalicious Music, 1999/Ill Will, 1999/Virginia Beach Music, 1999/WB Music Publishing, 1999/Alva Music,

1999/Arrival Music, 1999/Pokey Dog Music, 1999/St. Swithin's Songs, 1999.
Best-selling record by Nas featuring Ginuwine from the album *Nastradamus* (Sony/Columbia,1999).

You Sang to Me
Words and music by Marc Anthony and Mark Rooney.
Sony ATV Tunes LLC, Nashville, 1999/Cori Tiffani Music, Great Neck, 1999/Sony ATV Songs LLC, Nashville, 1999.
Best-selling record by Marc Anthony from the album *Marc Anthony* (Sony/Columbia, 1999).

You Should've Told Me
Words and music by James Moss.
Llerol Music, 2000.
Best-selling record by Kelly Price from the album *Mirror Mirror* (Uni/Def Jam, 2000).

You Spin Me 'Round (Like a Record)
Words and music by Peter Burns, Stephen Coy, Timothy Lever, and Michael Percy.
Chappell & Co., Inc., 1985/Burning Music Ltd., 1985/Mat Music, 1985/Chappell Music Publishers Ltd., 1985.
Revived by Dope on the soundtrack album *American Psycho* (Koch, 2000).

You Stole My Bell
Words and music by Declan McManus and Cait O'Riordan.
Plangent Visions Music, Inc., London, England, 2000.
Introduced by Elvis Costello in the film and on the soundtrack album *The Family Man* (WEA/London/Sire, 2000).

You Won't Be Lonely Now
Words and music by John Bettis and Brett James.
Big Red Tractor Music, Nashville, 2000/Songs of Teracel, 2000/Hay Wagon Music, 2000/Tree Publishing Co., Inc., 2000.
Best-selling record by Billy Ray Cyrus from the album *Southern Rain* (Sony/Monument, 2000).

You'll Always Be Loved by Me
Words and music by Ronnie Dunn and Terry McBride.
Showbilly Music, Nashville, 1999/Sony ATV Songs LLC, Nashville, 1999/Tree Publishing Co., Inc., 1999.
Best-selling record by Brooks and Dunn from the album *Tight Rope* (BMG/Arista, 1999).

Your Everything
Words and music by Christopher Lindsey and Robert Regan.
BMG Songs Inc., 1999/Songs of Nashville Dreamworks, 1999/Yessiree

Bob Music, 1999.
Best-selling record by Keith Urban from the album *Keith Urban* (EMD/Capitol, 1999).

Your Lies
Words and music by Bill Bottrell, Roger Fritz, Jay Joyce, Shelby Lynne, and Dorothy Overstreet.
Magnasong, 1999/Ignorant, 1999/Irving Music Inc., 1999/Curb Magnasong Music Publishing, 1999.
Introduced by Shelby Lynne on the album *I Am Shelby Lynne* (Uni/Island, 2000).

You're a God
Words and music by Matthew Scannell.
WB Music Publishing, 1999/Mascan Music, 1999.
Best-selling record by Vertical Horizon from the album *Everything You Want* (BMG/RCA, 1999).

You're the One
Words and music by Paul Simon.
Paul Simon Music, 2000.
Introduced by Paul Simon on the album *You're the One* (WEA/Warner Bros., 2000).

Lyricists & Composers Index

Aasim, Bambaataa
Renegades of Funk
Abbott, Darrel
Immortally Insane
Abbott, Vincent
Immortally Insane
Aberg, Johan
Come On Over Baby (All I Want Is You)
Adams, Bryan
Don't Give Up
Adams, Ryan
My Winding Wheel
Adams, Yolanda
Open My Heart
Adler, Richard
Dance with Me
Adu, Helen *see* Sade
Afanasieff, Walter
She Bangs
Aguilar, R.
Dramacide
Aguilera, Christina
Come On Over Baby (All I Want Is You)
Ahmadzai, Mirwais
Music
Albro, Shawn
Godless
Aldridge, James
Some Things Never Change
Alexakis, Arthur
A.M. Radio
Wonderful
Alexander, Jovonn
Jumpin, Jumpin
Alexander, Phalon
I Don't Wanna
Alfano, Omar
A Puro Dolor (Purest of Pain)
Allen, Harley
The Little Girl
Allen, R.
You Can Do It
Allen, Sara
Can't Go for That
Ament, Jeffrey
Nothing as It Seems
Anderson, Stig
Dancing Queen
Andersson, Benny
Dancing Queen
Andrews, Kelvin
Love Calling Earth
Rock DJ
Andrews, Mark *see* Sisqo
Anselmo, Philip
Immortally Insane
Anthony, Marc
You Sang to Me
April, John
Home
Arbuckle, Tiffany
I Wanna Be with You

Archer, Edward
No Matter What They Say
Archer, Michael *see* D'Angelo
Armato, Antonina
Another Dumb Blonde
Armstrong, Billie
Minority
Armstrong, Dido
Stan
Thank You
Arnold, Brad
Kryptonite
Loser
Arnold, Monica
I Still Got to Have It
Arthur, Joseph
Righteous Love
Arvizu, Reginald
Make Me Bad
Ashcroft, Richard
C'mon People (We're Making It Now)
A Song for the Lovers
Atkins, Erica
Shackles (Praise You)
Atkins, Jeffrey *see* Ja Rule
Atkins, Trecina
Shackles (Praise You)
Attewell, Benjamin
Bring Your Lovin' Back Here
Austin, Dallas
I Like It
Austin, Johnta
I Don't Wanna
Just Be a Man about It
Avant, Myron
Separated
Axlerod, David
The Next Episode
Babyface
Dear Lie
Badu, Erykah
Bag Lady
Plenty
Bagge, Anders
Give Me Just One Night (Una Noche)
Gotta Tell You
Bailey, Brian
Bag Lady
The Next Episode
Bailey, K.
Dramacide
Baker, Arthur
Renegades of Funk
You Can Do It
Baker, Bonnie
This Woman Needs
Baldes, Kevin
Miserable
Ball, Ian
Bring Your Lovin' Back Here
Balzary, Michael *see* Flea
Bambaataa, Aasim
You Can Do It
Bamonte, Perry
Bloodflowers
Where the Birds Always Sing
Barber, Jimmy
Put Your Hand in Mine
Barker, Aaron
What About Now
Barker, Paul
Burning Inside
Barman, Paul
MTV Get Off the Air, Part 2
Barnes, Samuel
Freakin' It
Independent Women Part I
Barnett, Jonathan
The Chain of Love
Barrier, Eric
No Matter What They Say
Barrow, Jamaal *see* Shyne
Barry, Mark
Back Here
Barry, Paul
Be with You
I Will Love Again
My Heart's Saying Now
Battersby, Richard
Stoopid Ass
Bazilian, Eric
Private Emotion
Beal, Teron
The Best of Me

Beavers, Robert
No Matter What They Say
Beck, Billy
As We Lay
Becker, Walter
Bodhisattva
Cousin Dupree
Janie Runaway
Two Against Nature
Beenie Man
Girls Dem Sugar
Bega, Lou
Tricky, Tricky
Bell, Carl
Hemorrhage (In My Hands)
Bell, Robert
Breathe and Stop
Do You
Bell, Ronald
Breathe and Stop
Do You
Belmaati, Joseph
Can I Get Your Number (A Girl like You)
Belofsky, Simon
It Feels So Good
Benjamin, Andre
Ms. Jackson
Tough Guy
Bennett, Lennie
Freakin' It
Bentley, Stephanie
Breathe
Beres, Jeff
Change Your Mind
Bergdorf, Gregory
Playmate of the Year
Berkeley, Edward
Whatever
Where I Wanna Be
Wifey
Bernardo, Noah
Lie Down
Berryman, Guy
Yellow
Best, Anthony
Whoa!
Bettis, John
You Won't Be Lonely Now
Bhraonain, Eithne Ni *see* Enya
Biancaniello, Louis
I'm Outta Love
Where You Are
Big Punisher
Dramacide
Feelin' So Good
It's So Hard
Still Not a Player
Bing, Tyrrell
Liar
Binzer, Seth
Butterfly
Birgisson, Arnthor
Give Me Just One Night (Una Noche)
Gotta Tell You
Birkett, T.
It's Not a Game
Bishop, Teddy
Just Be a Man about It
Bixler, Cedric
Quarantined
Black, Charles
Carlene
Black, Clint
Been There
Black, Darin
Wobble Wobble
Black, John
Too Sick to Pray
Black Rob
Whoa!
Blackburn, Paul
Bring Your Lovin' Back Here
Blackmon, Chaka
Come On Over Baby (All I Want Is You)
Blades, Robert
No Me Dejes De Querer (Don't Stop Loving Me)
Blige, Mary
Deep Inside
Block, Ken
Change Your Mind
Bobbit, Charles
No Matter What They Say

Bogard, Steve
Prayin' for Daylight
Bolton, Stefanie
Green Grass Vapors
Bon Jovi
It's My Life
Say It Isn't So
Bongiovi, John *see* Bon Jovi
Bono
Beautiful Day
The Ground Beneath Her Feet
Boone, Larry
Lessons Learned
Boone, Waymon
I Think God Can Explain
Boots
Good Life
Borland, Wesley
Break Stuff
N 2gether Now
Bottrell, Bill
Black Light Blue
Life Is Bad
Your Lies
Bourke, Rory
Carlene
Boyce, Donald
Do You
Boyd, Brandon
Drive
Pardon Me
Stellar
Bracegirdle, Nicholas *see* Chicane
Bradford, Melvin
Forgot about Dre
The Next Episode
Year 2000
Brain, Dow
West Side Story
Bralower, James
Don't Say You Love Me
Branda, Robin
Daddy Won't Sell the Farm
Brawley, Stuart
Taking You Home
Braxton, Toni
Just Be a Man about It
Bridges, Christopher
What's Your Fantasy
Briggs, Kevin
Beautiful Women
Don't Think I'm Not
Pop Ya Collar
There You Go
Broadus, Calvin *see also* Snoop Dogg
Can't Go for That
Brock, Chad
Yes!
Brooks, Garth
When You Come Back to Me Again
Brothers, K.
Rock Wit U
Broussard, Joseph
A.M. Radio
Browder, Stony
Cherchez Laghost
Brown, Brendan
Teenage Dirtbag
Brown, George
Breathe and Stop
Do You
Brown, James
No Matter What They Say
Brown, Kobie
Whatever
Brown, Mary
911
Brown, Rex
Immortally Insane
Brown, Ricardo *see also* Kurupt
Bag Lady
Bruce, Joseph
Dirt Ball
Bruce, Robin
Lonely
Bryant, Nancy
Unconditional
Buck, Peter
The Great Beyond
Buckland, Jonathan
Yellow
Buckner, David
Last Resort
Buppert, Timothy
Another Nine Minutes

Burdick, Linus
It Feels So Good
Burns, Christian
Back Here
Burns, Peter
You Spin Me 'Round (Like a Record)
Burr, Gary
It Was
Burrell, Orville *see* Shaggy
Burruss, Kandi
Beautiful Women
There You Go
Burton, Thomas
A Song for Assata
Buruss, Kandi
Don't Think I'm Not
Pop Ya Collar
Busta Rhymes
Grinch 2000
Butler, Chad
Tough Guy
Butler, James
Stoopid Ass
Butler, Terence
N.I.B.
Buxton, Felix
Red Alert
Byrd, Bobby
No Matter What They Say
Cadet, Katia
911
Cadogan, Kevin
Deep Inside of You
Cagle, Christopher
My Love Goes On and On
Calandrelli, Jorge
A Love Before Time
Caldwell, Robert
The Light
Camp, Gregory
Come On, Come On
Campbell, Warryn
Shackles (Praise You)
Cannon, Chuck
How Do You Like Me Now?!
Carey, Mariah
Crybaby
Thank God I Found You
Carlsson, Andreas
Bye Bye Bye
It's Gonna Be Me
Carpenter, Mary Chapin
No Fear
Carpenter, Stephen
Change (In the House of Flies)
Elite
Cartagena, Joseph *see* Fat Joe
Carter, D'Wayne *see* Lil' Wayne
Carter, Shawn *see* Jay-Z
Carthy, Eliza
Train Song
Casale, Gerald
Go Monkey Go
Casey, Brandon
Let's Get Married
Casey, Brian
Let's Get Married
Cash, John
I'm Leavin' Now
Cason, James
Love's the Only House
Cerney, Todd
No Mercy
Cervenka, Christine *see* Cervenka, Exene
Cervenka, Exene
Poor Girl
Cham, Raymond
Come On Over Baby (All I Want Is You)
Chamberlain, Carson
The Best Day
Chambers, Guy
Love Calling Earth
Rock DJ
Supreme
Chambers, Joseph
Time Has Come Today
Chambers, Kasey
The Captain
Cry Like a Baby
Chambers, Willie
Time Has Come Today
Champion, William
Yellow
Charlemagne, Henri
Take That

Chase, Thomas
The Powerpuff Girls (Main Theme)
The Powerpuff Girls (End Theme)
Cheatam, Oliver
Whatever
Cheng, Chi
Change (In the House of Flies)
Elite
Chicane
Don't Give Up
Chierchia, Giuseppe
Don't Call Me Baby
Child, Desmond
It Doesn't Matter
She Bangs
Thong Song
Chisolm, Melanie
Go!
Christensen, Alex
Around the World (La La La La La)
Ciccone, Madonna
Music
City, Mike
I Wish
Clark, Guy
Bang the Drum Slowly
Clark, John
The Powerpuff Girls (End Theme)
Clark, Steven
The Powerpuff Girls (End Theme)
Clark, Tena
That's the Beat of a Heart
Clark, Terri
No Fear
Clarke, Sonia *see* Sonique
Clayton, Adam
Beautiful Day
The Ground Beneath Her Feet
Coates, April
Don't Call Me Baby
Cocup, Andrew
Sex and the City Theme
Cohen, Jeff
Crazy for This Girl
Cohen, Jerry
Don't Call Me Baby
Colapietro, Vito
'Til I Say So
Coles, Dennis *see also* Ghostface Killah
For Heaven's Sake 2000
Gravel Pit
Intro (Shaolin Finger Jab)/Chamber Music
Collins, James
Promise
Yes!
Collins, Marquis
Got to Get It
Thong Song
Combs, Sean *see* Puff Daddy
Commerford, Timothy
Sleep Now in the Fire
Common
A Song for Assata
Connelly, Christopher
Burning Inside
Cook, Don
One Voice
Cook, Norman *see* Fatboy Slim
Cook, T.
Left Right Left
Coombes, Gareth
Pumping on Your Stereo
Coombes, Robert
Pumping on Your Stereo
Cooper, Craig
Baby U Are
Cooper, Jason
Bloodflowers
Where the Birds Always Sing
Cooper, Jemma
I Want to Be a Millionaire
Cooper, Rufus
Baby Don't Cry (Keep Ya Head Up II)
Copeland, Andrew
Change Your Mind
Copeland, Zane
Callin' Me
Coppola, Imani
You All Dat
Corgan, Billy
Heavy Metal Machine
Stand Inside Your Love
Try Try Try
Cornell, Mark
Tell Her

Corr, Andrea
Breathless
Corr, Caroline
Breathless
Corr, James
Breathless
Corr, Sharon
Breathless
Coster, Thomas
The Real Slim Shady
Coward, D.
It's Not a Game
Cox, Bryan-Michael
Bounce with Me
I Still Got to Have It
Just Be a Man about It
Let's Get Married
Straight Up
Cox, Malik *see* Memphis Bleek
Cox, Nathan
Take It Back
Coy, Stephen
You Spin Me 'Round (Like a Record)
Cozier, Jimmy
The Best of Me
Cracknell, Sarah
Tell Me Why (The Riddle)
Crago, Scott
Everything Is Different Now
Crain, William
Another Nine Minutes
Crapps, Gregory
'Til I Say So
Crawford, Anthony
Incomplete
Same Script, Different Cast
Ta Da
Crawford, Shondrae
What's Your Fantasy
Creatore, Luigi
You All Dat
Crichlow, Herbert
Show Me the Meaning of Being Lonely
Crisler, Truman
Some Things Never Change
Cronin, Rich
West Side Story
Crooms, Michael
Whistle While You Twurk
Crosby, Rob
She's More
Cross, Christopher
Best Friend
Crowe, Cameron
Fever Dog
Cryner, Bobbie
Real Live Woman
Cummings, J.
It's Not a Game
Cummings, Michael
Ultra Mega
Cummings, Robert *see* Rob Zombie
Cunningham, Abran
Change (In the House of Flies)
Elite
Cuomo, Douglas
Sex and the City Theme
Curiel, Marcos
Lie Down
Cutlass, Frankie
Ya Mama
Da Brat
Bounce with Me
That's What I'm Looking For
What'chu Like
Damon, Delvis
Dancin'
Damphier, Thomas
What I Need to Do
D'Andrea, Marc
Wobble Wobble
D'Angelo
Devil's Pie
Left & Right
Untitled (How Does It Feel)
Dangerous
Took the Bait
Daniels, Lashawn
He Wasn't Man Enough
Say My Name
Daniels, Mark
Lie Down
Daniels, Stacey
Same Script, Different Cast
Ta Da

Danoff, Mary
It Doesn't Matter
Danoff, William
It Doesn't Matter
Darnell, August
Cherchez Laghost
Daugherty, Jay Dee
Gung Ho
Davis, Donald
Stay the Night
Davis, Jonathan
Make Me Bad
Take It Back
Davis, Moses *see* Beenie Man
Davis, Stephen
No Mercy
Davis, Tracey
G'd Up
Davis, Vidal
Gettin' in the Way
Dawkins, Eric
Come On Over Baby (All I Want Is You)
de la Rocha, Zack
Sleep Now in the Fire
Dean, Kasseem
The Best of Me
Love Is Blind
Party Up (Up in Here)
Dean, Roxie
Lonely
Deane, Kevin
Deep Inside
Deere, Jason
I Will...But
Delaney, Michael
The Way You Love Me
Deleo, Dean
Sour Girl
Deleo, Robert
Sour Girl
Delisle, Paul
Come On, Come On
Delonge, Thomas
Adam's Song
Denman, Paul
By Your Side
Densmore, Robert
Sunset (Bird of Prey)
Denver, John
It Doesn't Matter
Deuce of 24 Karatz
Shut Up
Deutsch, Josh
Graduation (Friends Forever)
DeViller, Dane
I Don't Wanna Kiss You Goodnight
Mirror Mirror
Dewar, Chris
It's Not a Game
Dewar, Michael
It's Not a Game
DeWitt, Lewis
Flowers on the Wall
Diggs, Mitchell
For Heaven's Sake 2000
Diggs, Robert *see also* RZA
Careful (Click, Click)
For Heaven's Sake 2000
Gravel Pit
Intro (Shaolin Finger Jab)/Chamber Music
Dillon, Dean
The Best Day
Dimant, Leor *see* DJ Lethal
Dinkins, Neely
'Til I Say So
DiPiero, Robert
There You Are
Dixon, Ernest
Liar
DJ Hurricane
Connect
DJ Lethal
N 2gether Now
DJ Premier
Devil's Pie
N 2gether Now
Yellow
DJ Soulshock
Baby Don't Cry (Keep Ya Head Up II)
DMX
Do You
Party Up (Up in Here)

What You Want
What's My Name
Dr. Dre
Forgot about Dre
The Next Episode
The Real Slim Shady
Still D.R.E.
Doe, John
Poor Girl
Doling, Michael
Funeral Flights
Take It Back
Donegan, Dan
Down with the Sickness
Stupify
Dorsey, Chris
I Need a Hot Girl
Douglas, Anslem
Who Let the Dogs Out
Douglas, Philip
Kiss This
Douglas, Tom
Another Nine Minutes
Love's the Only House
Draiman, David
Down with the Sickness
Stupify
Drury, Timothy
Everything Is Different Now
Dubois, Charles
Me Neither
We Danced
Ducent, Ricardo
It Wasn't Me
Duchac, John *see* Doe, John
Duffy, Martin
Exterminator
Duggins, Adam
Pull Over
Dumont, Thomas
Ex-Girlfriend
Dun, Tan
A Love Before Time
Dunn, Ronnie
You'll Always Be Loved by Me
Dunson, John
U Don't Love Me
Dunson, Sean
U Don't Love Me
Duplessis, Jerry
It Doesn't Matter
Kenny Rogers-Pharoahe Monch Dub Plate
Maria Maria
911
Dupri, Jermaine
Bounce with Me
I Still Got to Have It
Let's Get Married
Straight Up
That's What I'm Looking For
What'chu Like
Durst, Fred
Break Stuff
N 2gether Now
Take a Look Around
Dylan, Bob
Hurricane
My Back Pages
Things Have Changed
Dylan, Jakob
Sleepwalker
Earle, Stephen
Transcendental Blues
The Edge
Beautiful Day
The Ground Beneath Her Feet
Edmonds, Kenneth *see also* Babyface
Most Girls
Edwards, Bernard
Don't Think I'm Not
Freakin' It
No Matter What They Say
Edwards, Simon
Too Sick to Pray
Edwards, Skye
Be Yourself
World Looking In
Einziger, Michael
Drive
Pardon Me
Stellar
Eklund, Greg
A.M. Radio
Wonderful

Elam, Keith *see* Guru
Elizondo, Michael
The Real Slim Shady
Elliot, Chad
Jumpin, Jumpin
Elliot, Jack
I Want to Be a Millionaire
Elliott, Melissa
Can't Go for That
Take That
Ellis, Terry
Riddle
Eminem
Forgot about Dre
The Real Slim Shady
Stan
The Way I Am
Enya
Wild Child
Epperson, Jason
Country Grammar (Hot Shit)
Erna, Salvatore
Bad Religion
Voodoo
Esperance, Tobin
Last Resort
Estefan, Emilio
No Me Dejes De Querer (Don't Stop Loving Me)
Estefan, Gloria
No Me Dejes De Querer (Don't Stop Loving Me)
Esterkyn, Luke
Little Black Backpack
Evans, Brycyn
Can't Go for That
Evans, David *see* The Edge
Evans, Sara
Born to Fly
Everett, Mark
Grace Kelly Blues
Mr. E's Beautiful Blues
Evers, Joerg
What'chu Like
Ewing, Skip
Put Your Hand in Mine
Fafara, B. Dez
Funeral Flights
Fagen, Donald
Bodhisattva
Cousin Dupree
Janie Runaway
Two Against Nature
Fagenson, Anthony
Promise
Fahnestock, John
Funeral Flights
Take It Back
Fair, Ronald
Come On Over Baby (All I Want Is You)
Falcone, William
Say It Isn't So
Fareed, Kamaal *see* Q-Tip
Fat Joe
Feelin' So Good
Fatboy Slim
Demons
Love Life
Sunset (Bird of Prey)
Ya Mama
Feek, Rory
The Chain of Love
Fekaris, Dino
Supreme
Feliciano, Jose
No Matter What They Say
Ferrell, Edward
Dancin'
No More
Findlay, Thomas
Sex and the City Theme
Finley, Gene
Ya Mama
Fite, Wendell *see* DJ Hurricane
Fitzpatrick, Colleen
Graduation (Friends Forever)
Flansburgh, John
Boss of Me
Flea
Butterfly
Californication
Otherside
Fogleman, Robert
You Can Do It

Follese, Keith
Smile
The Way You Love Me
Folmar, Irving
Callin' Me
Ford-Payne, Sherree
All or Nothing
Foster, Denzil
Riddle
Foster, Jerome
Still Not a Player
Fox, Steve
Daddy Won't Sell the Farm
Franks, James
The Bad Touch
Frederiksen, Martin
Angel's Eye
Freeman, Bernard
Tough Guy
Freeze, Louis
Deadly Assassins
Highlife
(Rap) Superstar
(Rock) Superstar
Friedman, Marty
Breadline
Frierson, Richard
It's So Hard
Frierson, Shante
All or Nothing
Fritz, Roger
Black Light Blue
Life Is Bad
Your Lies
Frusciante, John
Butterfly
Californication
Otherside
Funk, Jim
Buy Me a Rose
Furtado, Nelly
I'm like a Bird
Gabriel, Peter
I Still Got to Have It
Gaither, Todd
Best Friend
Gallagher, Noel
Go Let It Out
Gallup, Simon
Bloodflowers
Where the Birds Always Sing
Gamble, Kenneth
This Can't Be Life
Gardner, Adam
Fa Fa (Never Be the Same Again)
Garfield, Julian
It's So Hard
Garrett, Stephen
Try Again
You Owe Me
Gatling, Timothy
Crybaby
Gaye, Marvin
Let's Get It On
Geisel, Theo
Grinch 2000
Genius
Shame
Gentile, John
You Can Do It
Gersoni, Guy
This Could Be Heaven
Geter, Tara
Deep Inside
Ghostface Killah
Cherchez Laghost
Shame
Gifford, Alex
V.I.P
Giles, Rick
Prayin' for Daylight
That's the Kind of Mood I'm In
Gill, Vince
Feels like Love
Gillespie, Bobby
Exterminator
Gilliam, Kevin
G'd Up
Ginuwine
None of Ur Friends Business
Gipp, Cameron
Connect
Gist, Keir
Whatever
Where I Wanna Be
Wifey

Glasco, James
'Til I Say So
Godard, Gilles
That's the Kind of Mood I'm In
Godfrey, Paul
Be Yourself
World Looking In
Godfrey, Ross
Be Yourself
World Looking In
Goffey, Daniel
Pumping on Your Stereo
Grant, Dwight
Do It Again (Put Ya Hands Up)
This Can't Be Life
Grant, Oli
For Heaven's Sake 2000
Gray, David
Babylon
Gray, Del
More
Gray, Macy
Demons
I Try
Gray, Terius *see also* Juvenile
I Need a Hot Girl
Gray, William
Bring Your Lovin' Back Here
Greaney, Mark
Snow
Green, Marv
It's Always Somethin'
Let's Make Love
Greenberg, Steve
You All Dat
Greenidge, Malcolm
Baby Don't Cry (Keep Ya Head Up II)
Greenwood, Colin
Optimistic
Greenwood, Jonathan
Optimistic
Grice, Gary *see also* Genius
Intro (Shaolin Finger Jab)/Chamber Music
Griffin, Gene
Crybaby
Griffin, Warren
Can't Go for That
Griffin, William *see* Rakim
Groff, Benjamin
I Don't Wanna Kiss You Goodnight
Grohl, David
Breakout
Goodbye Lament
Gross, Martin
Early Mornin' Stoned Pimp
Gudmundsdottir, Bjork
I've Seen It All
Gueldner, Greg
Little Black Backpack
Guru
Plenty
Guthrie, Trevor
Faded
Haggard, Merle
I'm Still Your Daddy
Proud to Be Your Old Man
Wishin' All These Old Things Were New
Hague, Albert
Grinch 2000
Hajjar, Antoine
Quarantined
Hale, Andrew
By Your Side
Hale, N.
Can't Go for That
Hale, Nathaniel *see also* Nate Dogg
Bag Lady
Hale, Traci
Case of the Ex (Watcha Gonna Do)
Hall, Aaron
Crybaby
Hall, Daryl
Can't Go for That
Hall, Nathaniel
V.I.P
Hall, Richard *see* Moby
Hamilton, Roy
Liar
Hammond, Russell
Fever Dog
Hampson, John
Absolutely (Story of a Girl)
If I Am

Handy, Roy
Breathe and Stop
Hansen, Mich
Can I Get Your Number (A Girl like You)
Hanson, Clarke
This Time Around
Hanson, Jordan
This Time Around
Hanson, Zachary
This Time Around
Harbin, Ronald
What About Now
Harper, Ben
Steal My Kisses
Harrel, Roosevelt
Can't Go for That
Harrell, Robert
Kryptonite
Loser
Harrington, Connie
This Woman Needs
Harris, Emmylou
Bang the Drum Slowly
Harris, James
The Best Man I Can Be
Doesn't Really Matter
Free
Open My Heart
Thank God I Found You
Harris, Norman
The Light
Harris, Shawntae *see* Da Brat
Harris, Sheldon
Got It All
Harrison, Charles
One Night Stand
Harrison, Mya
The Best of Me
Free
Hart, Beth
L.A. Song
Hartley, David
My Funny Friend and Me
One Day She'll Love Me
Perfect World
Harvey, Polly
This Is Love
Harwell, Steven
Come On, Come On
Hathaway, Lalah
All This Time
Hawkins, Lamont *see also* U-God
Careful (Click, Click)
Gravel Pit
Intro (Shaolin Finger Jab)/Chamber Music
Hawkins, Oliver
Breakout
Hayes, Darren
Crash and Burn
I Knew I Loved You
Hayes, Isaac
Bag Lady
Theme from Shaft
Treat Her like a Lady
Haynes, Cornell *see* Nelly
Haynes, Ontario
All or Nothing
Healy, Francis
Turn
Why Does It Always Rain on Me?
Heartsong, Dorian
Ultra Mega
Heckstall-Smith, Richard
Ya Mama
Hector, Wayne
Swear It Again
Hedges, Raymond
Don't Give Up
Heintz, Timothy
That's the Beat of a Heart
Hengber, Elizabeth
She's More
Unconditional
Henley, Don
Everything Is Different Now
Taking You Home
Henson, Darren
No Matter What They Say
Hepperlin, Ullrich
Break You Down
The Reckoning
Herman, Paul
Stan
Thank You

Herron, Cindy
Riddle
Hersh, Howie
Crybaby
Hetfield, James
American Bad Ass
I Disappear
Hewett, Howard
Take That
Hewson, Paul *see* Bono
Hiatt, John
Riding with the King
Hickenlooper, Erik
Buy Me a Rose
Hicks, Kevin
I Don't Wanna
Hield, Nehemia
You All Dat
Hill, Darryl
Careful (Click, Click)
For Heaven's Sake 2000
Intro (Shaolin Finger Jab)/Chamber Music
Hill, Edward
There You Are
Hill, Jack
No Matter What They Say
Hinds, Natalie
Demons
Hinojos, Paul
Quarantined
Hinson, Edward
What's My Name
Hiseman, John
Ya Mama
Hollister, David
Can't Stay
Holmes, Deongelo
Whistle While You Twurk
Hoppus, Mark
Adam's Song
Horne, Cleveland
Breathe and Stop
Horton, Jerry
Last Resort
Hosein, Sean
I Don't Wanna Kiss You Goodnight
Mirror Mirror
Houston, Marques
Stay the Night
Howerdel, William
Judith
Magdalena
Hubley, Georgia
Last Days of Disco
Hudson, Kristin
Incomplete
Hudson, Mark
You All Dat
Huff, Leon
This Can't Be Life
Huff, Stephen
Separated
Treat Her like a Lady
Huggar, Robert
Whatever
Where I Wanna Be
Wifey
Hugo, Chad
Girls Dem Sugar
Mafia
Hugo, Charles
Shake Ya Ass
Hummon, Marcus
Born to Fly
Cowboy Take Me Away
Humphrey, Scott
Scum of the Earth
Hunt, Jim
Exterminator
Hunter, Jason *see also* Inspectah Deck
Careful (Click, Click)
For Heaven's Sake 2000
Intro (Shaolin Finger Jab)/Chamber Music
Hurley, Steven
I'll Go
Huston, Paul
MTV Get Off the Air, Part 2
Hyman, Robert
Private Emotion
Iannello, Kevin
Come On, Come On
Ice Cube
You Can Do It

Iglesias, Enrique
Be with You
Innes, Andrew
Exterminator
Inspectah Deck
Shame
Iommi, Anthony
Goodbye Lament
N.I.B.
Iommi, Tommy
For Heaven's Sake 2000
Isaac, Tony
Stay the Night
Ivitsky, Ben
Train Song
J-Shin
One Night Stand
Ja Rule
Between Me and You
Jackman, Henry
This Could Be Heaven
Jackson, Eric
Whistle While You Twurk
Jackson, Gabriel
Natural Blues
Jackson, Janet
Doesn't Really Matter
Jackson, O'Shea *see* Ice Cube
Jackson, R.
Demons
Jacobs, Sean
Ryde or Die, Chick
Jadakiss
Got It All
Jagger, Michael
(I Can't Get No) Satisfaction
Jamerson, Troy
Kenny Rogers-Pharoahe Monch Dub Plate
James, Brett
You Won't Be Lonely Now
James, Timothy
Another Dumb Blonde
Jay-Z
Big Pimpin'
Do It Again (Put Ya Hands Up)
Hey Papi
Still D.R.E.
This Can't Be Life
Jean, Wyclef
It Doesn't Matter
Kenny Rogers-Pharoahe Monch Dub Plate
Maria Maria
911
Jeffers, Eve
Got It All
Love Is Blind
Out for the Count
Jenkins, Stephan
Deep Inside of You
Never Let You Go
Jerkins, Fred
He Wasn't Man Enough
Say My Name
Jerkins, Rodney
He Wasn't Man Enough
Say My Name
Still Not a Player
Jezzard, Ralph
Stoopid Ass
John, Elton
Deep Inside
Every Story Is a Love Story
Someday Out of the Blue
Joiner, Alvin *see* Xzibit
Jolicoeur, David
Hemorrhage (In My Hands)
Jones, Daniel
Crash and Burn
I Knew I Loved You
Jones, David
Bad Boyz
Jones, Donell
Where I Wanna Be
Jones, Jerome
Stay the Night
Jones, Kenneth
Callin' Me
Jones, Kimberly *see* Lil' Kim
Jones, Maxine
Riddle
Jones-Muhammad, Ali
Dance Tonight

Jones-Muhammed, Ali
Don't Mess with My Man
Jones, Nasir *see* Nas
Jones, Russell *see* Ol' Dirty Bastard
Jones, Shae
Same Script, Different Cast
Jordan, Alphonso
Left Right Left
Jordan, Brad *see also* Scarface
This Can't Be Life
Jordan, Lorenzo
Left Right Left
Jordan, Montell
Incomplete
Same Script, Different Cast
Ta Da
Jordan, Steven
Out for the Count
Joshua, Kyambo
Big Pimpin'
Do It Again (Put Ya Hands Up)
Jourgensen, Allen
Burning Inside
Joyce, Jay
Black Light Blue
Life Is Bad
Your Lies
Joyner, Peter
No Matter What They Say
Juvenile
U Understand
Kalberg, Eelke *see* Kalmani
Kalmani
Better Off Alone
Kanal, Tony
Ex-Girlfriend
Kaplan, Ira
Last Days of Disco
Karlin, Kenneth
Baby Don't Cry (Keep Ya Head Up II)
Still in My Heart
Katunich, Alex
Drive
Pardon Me
Stellar
Kaye, Buddy
V.I.P
Kaye, Lenny
Gung Ho
Keating, Ronan
Picture of You
Keenan, Maynard
Judith
Magdalena
Keith, Toby
Country Comes to Town
How Do You Like Me Now?!
Kelley, Tim
Thong Song
Kelly, Robert
Bad Man
I Wish
Kelly, Sherman
Dancing in the Moonlight
Kennedy, Eliot
Picture of You
Kennedy, Gordon
Meanwhile Back at the Ranch
Kennison, Patrick
Turn Me on "Mr. Deadman"
Kessee, Kelton
Stay the Night
Keys, Alicia
Rock Wit U
Kid Rock
American Bad Ass
Early Mornin' Stoned Pimp
Only God Knows Why
Yeah Yeah Yeah
Kidd, Brian
Ryde or Die, Chick
Kiedis, Anthony
Butterfly
Californication
Otherside
Kierulf, Brian
Aaron's Party (Come Get It)
The Hardest Part of Breaking Up (Is Getting Back Your Stuff)
Kilmore, Chris
Drive
Pardon Me
Stellar
Kimball, Robert
Where I Wanna Be

Kinchen, Marc
Monica
Kipner, Stephen
I Don't Wanna Kiss You Goodnight
Kirkpatrick, Wayne
Meanwhile Back at the Ranch
Kleist, Achim
Tricky, Tricky
Kmak, Steve
Down with the Sickness
Stupify
Knopfler, Mark
Sailing to Philadelphia
Knowles, Beyonce
Independent Women Part I
Jumpin, Jumpin
Say My Name
Koenemann, Peter
Around the World (La La La La La)
Kool G Rap
Dramacide
Korduletsch, Juergen
What'chu Like
Kravitz, Leonard
Again
Kretz, Eric
Sour Girl
Krieger, Robbie
Sunset (Bird of Prey)
Kroeger, Chad
Leader of Men
Kronlund, Alexander
Lucky
Kurupt
Where I Wanna Be
Lachey, Nick
Where You Are
Lacy, Braylon
Plenty
Lacy, Ty
I Need You
Lamar, Holly
Breathe
Lamar, Mary
That's the Way
Lang, K. D.
Summerfling
Lange, Robert
Breathless
Larsen, Marit
Don't Say You Love Me
Lassiter, Sean
Got It All
Lawrence, Tracy
Lessons Learned
Lazarides, Kostas
Because You Love Me
Leach, Gary
Blue Moon
Leigh, Richard
Cold Day in July
Leonard, Patrick
Someday Out of the Blue
Leor, Dimant
Break Stuff
Lever, Timothy
You Spin Me 'Round (Like a Record)
Levert, Gerald
Baby U Are
Mr. Too Damn Good
Levy, Barrington
Bad Boyz
Levy, Jacques
Hurricane
Lewis, Aaron
Home
Outside
Lewis, Terry
The Best Man I Can Be
Doesn't Really Matter
Free
Open My Heart
Thank God I Found You
Lewis, Tricia
Pure Shores
Lightfoot, Gordon
Sundown
Lighty, Clifton
Dancin'
No More
Lighty, Darren
Dancin'
No More

Lil' Kim
How Many Licks?
No Matter What They Say
Lil' Mac
He Did That
Lil' Wayne
I Need a Hot Girl
Lim, Jinsoo
I Try
Linde, Dennis
Goodbye Earl
Lindsey, Christopher
Let's Make Love
Smile
Your Everything
Linnel, John
Boss of Me
Little, Joe
Mr. Too Damn Good
Llord, Maria
A Puro Dolor (Purest of Pain)
Logios, George
Feelin' So Good
Long, Andrew
It Doesn't Matter
Longmiles, Craig
Bag Lady
Longo, Joseph
Thong Song
Lopez, Jennifer
Feelin' So Good
Lorenz, Trey
Crybaby
Lorenzo, Irving
Between Me and You
Do You
What's My Name
Louris, Gary
I'm Gonna Make You Love Me
Loving, Cynthia
Monica
Straight Up
Lowenstein, Jaron
Crazy for This Girl
Lubega, David *see* Bega, Lou
Luckett, Letoya
Say My Name
Lumpkin, Elgin *see* Ginuwine
Lundin, Kristian
Bye Bye Bye
Luther, William
Let's Make Love
My Best Friend
What I Need to Do
Lyles, Aaron
Green Grass Vapors
Lynch, Stanley
Taking You Home
Lynn, Lonnie
The Light
Lynn, Rashid *see* Common
Lynne, Jeffrey
I Won't Back Down
Lynne, Shelby
Black Light Blue
Life Is Bad
Your Lies
Mac, Steve
Swear It Again
Mack 10
You Can Do It
Mackay, Duncan
Exterminator
MacKinnon, Amanda
The Powerpuff Girls (End Theme)
Macy Gray
Love Life
Maines, Natalie
Without You
Malament, Bruce
The Light
Malloy, David
One Voice
Maman, Alan
Deadly Assassins
Mangini, Michael
You All Dat
Mann, Aimee
Save Me
Manuel, Abe
Proud to Be Your Old Man
Manzarek, Raymond
Sunset (Bird of Prey)
Markita
Mafia

Marlette, Robert
For Heaven's Sake 2000
Goodbye Lament
Marshall, Maurice
Pull Over
Martin, Andrea
Still in My Heart
Martin, Anthony
Go On
Martin, Chris *see* DJ Premier
Martin, Harold
Bag Lady
Plenty
Martin, Max
It's My Life
Lucky
Shape of My Heart
Mason, Harvey
He Wasn't Man Enough
Master P
He Did That
Mathers, Marshall *see* Eminem
Matias, Ivan
Still in My Heart
Matkosky, Dennis
I Need You
Matthewman, Stuart
By Your Side
Matthews, D.
Dramacide
Matthias, Paul
Another Way
Mauriello, Justin
Playmate of the Year
Mayfield, B.
It's Not a Game
Mayo, Aimee
It's Always Somethin'
Let's Make Love
My Best Friend
Mays, Robert
Between Me and You
Mazur, Bret
Butterfly
McBride, Terry
You'll Always Be Loved by Me
McCary, Michael
Beautiful Women
McCord, Kevin
Whatever
McDermott, John
Little Black Backpack
McDill, Robert
It Must Be Love
McElroy, Thomas
Riddle
McFadden, Gene
Don't Call Me Baby
McHugh, Thomas
More
McIntyre, Natalie *see also* Macy Gray
Demons
I Try
McKee, Maria
Show Me Heaven
McKinney, Carlos
Monica
McLean, Don
American Pie
McLeod, Marilyn
Freakin' It
McManus, Declan
You Stole My Bell
Mcnair, T. *see* Monch, Pharoahe
McNally, Stephen
Back Here
McNew, James
Last Days of Disco
McRae, David
Maria Maria
Means, Danny
G'd Up
Mellencamp, John
I Think I'm in Love with You
Memphis Bleek
Hey Papi
Mendel, Nate
Breakout
Merrill, Robert
Voodoo
Method Man
Left & Right
N 2gether Now
Shame
Meyers, Dana
Take That

Mickens, Robert
Breathe and Stop
Do You
Migliore, Stephen
Can I Get Your Number (A Girl like You)
Miller, Jason
Break You Down
The Reckoning
Miller, John
Renegades of Funk
You Can Do It
Miller, Marcus
All This Time
Miller, Michael
Break You Down
The Reckoning
Miller, Percy *see* Master P
Miller, Roger
A Little Gasoline
Miller, Ryan
Fa Fa (Never Be the Same Again)
Miller, Zyshonne *see* Silkk the Shocker
Mills, Michael
The Great Beyond
Minor, Enchante
All or Nothing
Miskovsky, Lisa
Shape of My Heart
Moby
Natural Blues
Molijn, Sebastian *see* Pronti
Monch, Pharoahe
Connect
Montenegro, Hugo
V.I.P
Montoya, Craig
A.M. Radio
Wonderful
Mooney, Darrin
Exterminator
Moore, Alecia
There You Go
Moore-Hough, Marvin
Maria Maria
Moore, Rufus
Jumpin, Jumpin
Moorman, Paulisa
Gravel Pit
Morello, Tom
Sleep Now in the Fire
Moreno, Camilo
Change (In the House of Flies)
Elite
Morgan, Dennis
No Mercy
Morris, Nathan
Beautiful Women
Morris, Steveland *see* Wonder, Stevie
Morris, Wanya
Beautiful Women
Morrison, Duane
Don't Call Me Baby
Morrison, Jim
Sunset (Bird of Prey)
Mosley, Timothy *see also* Timbaland
Big Pimpin'
Hey Papi
None of Ur Friends Business
Try Again
You Owe Me
Moss, James
You Should've Told Me
Mothersbaugh, Robert
Go Monkey Go
Mounfield, Gary
Exterminator
Muggerud, Lawrence
Highlife
(Rap) Superstar
(Rock) Superstar
Muhammad, Balewa
Dancin'
No More
Mullen, Larry
Beautiful Day
The Ground Beneath Her Feet
Mumba, Samantha
Gotta Tell You
Mushok, Michael
Home
Mustaine, Dave
Breadline
Myers, Dwight
Summer Rain

Mystikal
Shake Ya Ass
Nas
I Still Got to Have It
You Owe Me
Nate Dogg
Where I Wanna Be
Nelly
Country Grammar (Hot Shit)
Nelson, Paul
Lessons Learned
Nesler, Mark
Go On
Newell, Ryan
Change Your Mind
Newkirk, Anastacia
I'm Outta Love
Newman, Randy
A Fool in Love
When She Loved Me
Nichols, Tim
That's the Kind of Mood I'm In
Nicholson, Gary
Live, Laugh, Love
Nkhereanye, Thabiso
Case of the Ex (Watcha Gonna Do)
Noble, Reggie *see* Redman
Nobles, Vada
Took the Bait
Oates, John
Can't Go for That
O'Brien, Brendan
Break Stuff
O'Brien, Edward
Optimistic
O'Connor, James
Break You Down
The Reckoning
O'Donnell, Roger
Bloodflowers
Where the Birds Always Sing
Ogalde, Huentenau
Give Me Just One Night (Una Noche)
Ogletree, Larry
Do You
Ol' Dirty Bastard
Shame
Olander, James
I Lost It
Oliver, Tony
Stay the Night
Olivier, Jean
Freakin' It
Independent Women Part I
Olsson, Staffan
One in a Million
Ondrasik, John
Superman
One Eye
You Can Do It
Orbit, William
Pure Shores
O'Riordan, Cait
You Stole My Bell
Osborn, Kristyn
Deck the Halls
I Will...But
This Woman Needs
Osborne, Joan
Righteous Love
Osbourne, John *see* Ozzy Osbourne
Osmundson, Ben
Playmate of the Year
Osterberg, James *see* Pop, Iggy
Otto, John
Break Stuff
N 2gether Now
Overstreet, Dorothy
Black Light Blue
Life Is Bad
Your Lies
Owens, Conesha
Don't Mess with My Man
Ozzy Osbourne
For Heaven's Sake 2000
N.I.B.
Page, Steven
Pinch Me
Pahanish, Allan
Ultra Mega
Paich, David
Where I Wanna Be
Paisley, Brad
Me Neither
We Danced

Palm, Michael
Bloodstains
Palmer, David
This Could Be Heaven
Paris, Ekundayo
Rock DJ
Parker, Lawrence
Cherchez Laghost
Pasillas, Jose
Drive
Pardon Me
Stellar
Patterson, Rahsaan
I'll Go
Patton, Antwan
Ms. Jackson
Tough Guy
Peacock, Oliver
Bring Your Lovin' Back Here
Peake, Ryan
Leader of Men
Peiken, Shelly
As If
Come On Over Baby (All I Want Is You)
I Wanna Be with You
What a Girl Wants
Peoples, Eugene
Can't Stay
Perazzo, Karl
Maria Maria
Percy, Michael
You Spin Me 'Round (Like a Record)
Peretti, Hugo
You All Dat
Perren, Frederick
Supreme
Perry, Anthony
Angel's Eye
Petty, Thomas
I Won't Back Down
Pfrimmer, Donald
My Love Goes On and On
Philips, Aaron
Love Sets You Free
Phillips, J.
The Best of Me
Phillips, Jason *see also* Jadakiss
Ryde or Die, Chick
Pierre, Harve
Whoa!
Pigford, Nelson
Rock DJ
Piltch, David
Summerfling
Pizzonia, Shaun
It Wasn't Me
Pleeth, Graeme
It Feels So Good
Pletschacher, Christian
Tricky, Tricky
Pop, Iggy
Bad Boyz
Popoff, Alan
Miserable
Popoff, Jeremy
Miserable
Over My Head
Porter, Lamont
Bad Boyz
Porter, Noah
'Til I Say So
Potekhin, Aleksei
Around the World (La La La La La)
Poyser, James
A Song for Assata
Prager, Bud
Breadline
Price, Kelly
Love Sets You Free
Pritchard, Mike
Minority
Pronti
Better Off Alone
Prosper, Marvin
Who Let the Dogs Out
Puff Daddy
Best Friend
Feelin' So Good
Pugh, Rasheen
Took the Bait
Q-Tip
Breathe and Stop
Left & Right

Quinn, Michael
Pumping on Your Stereo
Rackin, Alan
Show Me Heaven
Radiohead
Everything in Its Right Place
Morning Bell
The National Anthem
Raekwon
Intro (Shaolin Finger Jab)/Chamber Music
It's Not a Game
Shame
Rakim
No Matter What They Say
Ratcliffe, Simon
Red Alert
Ravn, Marion
Don't Say You Love Me
Ray, Angelo
24/7
Ray, Oliver
Glitter in Their Eyes
Gung Ho
Redd, Clarence
Breathe and Stop
Redd, Gene
Breathe and Stop
Redman
Left & Right
Y.O.U.
Reed, Lou
Paranoia Key of E
Turning Time Around
Reese, Barry
Got It All
Regan, Robert
Your Everything
Reinikainen, Pauli
Come On Over Baby (All I Want Is You)
Rekow, Raul
Maria Maria
Reyes, Senen
Highlife
(Rock) Superstar
Reznor, Michael
Into the Void
Rhodes, Taylor
I'm Gonna Make You Love Me
Rhone, John
All or Nothing
Rice, Ralph
You Owe Me
Rice, Timothy
Every Story Is a Love Story
Someday Out of the Blue
Rich, Denise
Love Sets You Free
Richards, Keith
(I Can't Get No) Satisfaction
Richbourg, Alexander
Free
Rieflin, William
Burning Inside
Rifkin, Jay
Show Me Heaven
Riley, Edward
Crybaby
Dancin'
Love Sets You Free
Rios, Christopher *see* Big Punisher
Ritchie, Robert *see* Kid Rock
Rivers, Samuel
Break Stuff
N 2gether Now
Rob Zombie
Scum of the Earth
Roberson, Latavia
Say My Name
Robert, Boyd
Smoke Rings in the Dark
Roberts, Matthew
Kryptonite
Loser
Robertson, Donald
He Did That
Robertson, Lloyd
Pinch Me
Robie, J.
You Can Do It
Robie, John
Renegades of Funk
Robinson, Bob
Natural Blues
Thong Song

Robinson, Dawn
Dance Tonight
Don't Mess with My Man
Robinson, Leland
One Night Stand
Robinson, William
Cruisin'
Roboff, Annie
That's the Way
Roche, Guy
As If
Come On Over Baby (All I Want Is You)
What a Girl Wants
Rodgers, Nile
Freakin' It
Rodriguez, Omar
Quarantined
Rogers, Dewayne
Summer Rain
Rogers, Frank
Me Neither
Rogers, Tammy
A Little Gasoline
Roland, Ed
Why Pt. 2
Rolison, Dedrick *see* Mack 10
Rooney, Cory
Feelin' So Good
I Think I'm in Love with You
Rooney, Mark
Independent Women Part I
You Sang to Me
Rosa, Rob
It Doesn't Matter
She Bangs
Thong Song
Rosenworcel, Brian
Fa Fa (Never Be the Same Again)
Ross, Jerry
Dance with Me
Ross, Robert *see* Black Rob
Rossdale, Gavin
Letting the Cables Sleep
Rowland, Kelendria
Say My Name
Rucker, Stephen
The Powerpuff Girls (Main Theme)
The Powerpuff Girls (End Theme)
Ruffin, Tamir
What You Want
Rushdie, Salman
The Ground Beneath Her Feet
Russell, Brenda
Still Not a Player
Rutherford, Melvern
Smoke Rings in the Dark
Unconditional
Ruzumna, Jeremy
I Try
Ryan, Nicky
Wild Child
Ryan, Roma
Wild Child
RZA
4 Sho Sho
It's Not a Game
Samurai Showdown
Shame
Rzeznik, John
Broadway
Saadiq, Raphael
Dance Tonight
Don't Mess with My Man
Untitled (How Does It Feel)
Sade
By Your Side
St. Clair, Gary
3 Little Words
Sambora, Richard
It's My Life
Sams, Mark
Too Sick to Pray
Samuel, Sealhenry *see* Seal
Sandberg, Martin *see also* Martin, Max
It's Gonna Be Me
Oops!...I Did It Again
Show Me the Meaning of Being Lonely
Stronger
Sanders, Mark
I Hope You Dance
There You Are

Sandoval, Paul
Lie Down
Santana, Carlos
Maria Maria
Saunders, Donald *see* One Eye
Sawyer, Pamela
Freakin' It
Scales, Harvey
Stay the Night
Scannell, Matthew
Everything You Want
You're a God
Scantlebury, Darnley
I Don't Wanna
Scarface
Took the Bait
Schack, Carsten *see also* Soulshock
Baby Don't Cry (Keep Ya Head Up II)
Schamus, James
A Love Before Time
Scherr, Mitchell
Right Now
Schifrin, Lalo
Take a Look Around
Schlitz, Donald
Kenny Rogers-Pharoahe Monch Dub Plate
Schneider, Robert
Blue Skies for Everyone
Schrody, Eric
Deadly Assassins
Schulze, Jacob
Bye Bye Bye
Lucky
Schwartz, Joshua
Aaron's Party (Come Get It)
The Hardest Part of Breaking Up (Is Getting Back Your Stuff)
Scott, Bryan
Turn Me on "Mr. Deadman"
Scott, Darrell
Born to Fly
Scott, David
24/7
Scott, Jill
Gettin' in the Way
Scott, LaTocha
If You Don't Wanna Love Me
One Night Stand
Seal
This Could Be Heaven
Seidel, Martie
Cowboy Take Me Away
Selway, Philip
Optimistic
Sermon, Erick
Y.O.U.
Shaddix, Jacoby
Last Resort
Shafer, Matthew *see* Uncle Kracker
Shaffer, James
Make Me Bad
Shaggy
It Wasn't Me
Shakur, Tupac
Baby Don't Cry (Keep Ya Head Up II)
Shamblin, Allen
Live, Laugh, Love
Shanahan, Tony
Gung Ho
Shapiro, Theodore
Out for the Count
Shea, Daniel
I Think I'm in Love with You
Sheats, David
Ms. Jackson
Tough Guy
Shellenberger, Allen
Miserable
Sherrill, John
Because You Love Me
Sheyne, Pamela
Mirror Mirror
Shinhoster, Jonathan *see* J-Shin
Shisty
Where I Wanna Be
Shyne
Bad Boyz
Siebels, Jonathan
Promise
Sigurdsson, Sigurjon
I've Seen It All
Silkk the Shocker
He Did That

Sillers, Tia
I Hope You Dance
Silver, Eric
Without You
Silveria, David
Make Me Bad
Simmons, Aleese
All or Nothing
Simmons, Daryl
No Love (I'm Not Used To)
Simmons, Earl *see* DMX
Simmons, Latrelle
All or Nothing
Simon, Paul
You're the One
Simpson, Michael
Mr. E's Beautiful Blues
Sisqo
Got to Get It
How Many Licks?
Thong Song
What You Want
Skinner, Jolyon
I Wanna Know
Still Not a Player
Small, Herschel
You All Dat
Small, Michael
V.I.P
Smith, Anthony
24/7
What About Now
Smith, Chad
Butterfly
Californication
Otherside
Smith, Charles
Ya Mama
Smith, Claydes
Breathe and Stop
Do You
Smith, Clifford *see also* Method Man
Gravel Pit
Intro (Shaolin Finger Jab)/Chamber Music
Y.O.U.
Smith, Elliott
Son of Sam
Smith, Lasana
Pull Over
Smith, Lloyd
Crybaby
Smith, Patti
Glitter in Their Eyes
Gung Ho
Smith, Robert
Bloodflowers
Where the Birds Always Sing
Smith, Stephony
Yes!
Smith, T.
Rock Wit U
Smith, Trevor *see* Busta Rhymes
Smith, Willard
Freakin' It
Snoop Dogg
Crybaby
G'd Up
The Next Episode
Still D.R.E.
Sonique
It Feels So Good
Soulshock
Still in My Heart
Spillman, Keiwan
G'd Up
Spragg, Robert
Too Sick to Pray
Stamapoulou, Adamancia
Where You Are
Standard, Steven
Feelin' So Good
Stanley, Robert
Tell Me Why (The Riddle)
Stapp, Scott
Is This the End
What If
With Arms Wide Open
Steele, Jeffrey
Couldn't Last a Moment
Stefani, Gwen
Ex-Girlfriend
Simple Kind of Life
Stephans, Lawrence
Stay the Night

Stewart, Christopher
Case of the Ex (Watcha Gonna Do)
If You Don't Wanna Love Me
Stewart, Demetrius
Left Right Left
Stewart, John
Daydream Believer
Stewart, Tommy
Bad Religion
Sting
Desert Rose
My Funny Friend and Me
One Day She'll Love Me
Perfect World
What Means the World to You
Stinson, Dana
Do It Again (Put Ya Hands Up)
Stipe, Michael
The Great Beyond
Stockman, Shawn
Beautiful Women
Storch, Scott
Still D.R.E.
Strachan, Keith
I Want to Be a Millionaire
Strachan, Matthew
I Want to Be a Millionaire
Stradling, Barnaby
Train Song
Styles, David
Ryde or Die, Chick
Sumner, Gordon *see* Sting
Symonds, Philip
Deck the Halls
T-Boz
Dear Lie
Tabatabaee, Ali
Playmate of the Year
Tallarico, Steven *see* Tyler, Steven
Tarplin, Marvin
Cruisin'
Taupin, Bernard
Deep Inside
Taylor, Courtney
Bohemian like You
Taylor, Katrina
Pull Over
Taylor, Mark
Be with You
I Will Love Again
My Heart's Saying Now
Taylor, Roderick
Beat from Underground
Tejeda, Japhe
Still Not a Player
Tempesta, Michael
Ultra Mega
Thomas, B. W.
I Need a Hot Girl
Thomas, Byron
Get Your Roll On
U Understand
Thomas, Damon
Most Girls
Thomas, Dennis
Breathe and Stop
Do You
Thomas, Joe
I Wanna Know
Still Not a Player
That Other Woman
Thomas, Keith
I Wanna Be with You
Thomas, Robert
Bent
If You're Gone
Thomas, Sam
Train Song
Thompson, Brian
It Wasn't Me
Thompson, Charles
Love Sets You Free
Thompson, Joshua
That Other Woman
Thompson, Tramayne
Where I Wanna Be
Thornalley, Philip
Back Here
Thrasher, Joe
I Lost It
Tifrere, Mashonda
The Best of Me
Timbaland
Ryde or Die, Chick

Tinney, Mark
Blue Moon
Tippin, Aaron
Kiss This
Tippin, Thea
Kiss This
Tolbert, Tony
Free
Townsend, Edward
Let's Get It On
Travis, James
Got to Get It
Travis, John
Only God Knows Why
Tre +6
Shut Up
Tremonti, Mark
Is This the End
What If
With Arms Wide Open
Trick Daddy
Shut Up
Trina
Shut Up
Tritt, Travis
Best of Intentions
Trojanowski, Mark
Change Your Mind
Trombly, James
Yeah Yeah Yeah
Troutman, Larry
As We Lay
Turner, Elgin
Careful (Click, Click)
For Heaven's Sake 2000
Intro (Shaolin Finger Jab)/Chamber Music
Turpin, T.
Out for the Count
Tyler, Michael *see* Mystikal
Tyler, Steven
Angel's Eye
U-God
Shame
Udhus, Edwin
Playmate of the Year
Ulrich, Lars
American Bad Ass
I Disappear
Ulvaeus, Bjoern
Dancing Queen
Uncle Kracker
Only God Knows Why
Yeah Yeah Yeah
Usher, Raymond
Pop Ya Collar
Van Dorsselaer, Andrew
Don't Call Me Baby
Van Dyk, Paul
Tell Me Why (The Riddle)
Vance, Albert
Stay the Night
Varble, Wynn
When You Need My Love
Vassar, Phillip
Carlene
Just Another Day in Paradise
My Next Thirty Years
Venable, James
The Powerpuff Girls (Main Theme)
The Powerpuff Girls (End Theme)
Virgil
I Need a Hot Girl
Von Trier, Lars
I've Seen It All
Von Webenau, Wolfgang
Tricky, Tricky
Wagner, Kurt
Up with People
Wainwright, William *see also* Orbit, William
Go!
Walker, Bradley
Right Now
Walters, Ricky
It Doesn't Matter
Ward, James
Quarantined
Ward, William
N.I.B.
Wariner, Steven
Been There
Warren, Diane
Can't Fight the Moonlight

Could I Have This Kiss Forever
Give Me You
I Turn to You
If I Don't Tell You Now
I'll Be
Need to Be Next to You
Painted on My Heart
Warren, Dominick
Callin' Me
Washington, Carol
A.M. Radio
Washington, Jarret
Monica
Waters, Roger
Have a Cigar
Watkins, Andrew
Picture of You
Watkins, Tionne *see* T-Boz
Watters, Samuel
I'm Outta Love
Where You Are
Weatherspoon, Phillip
What You Want
Weber, Christopher
Godless
Weiland, Scott
Sour Girl
Weiss, George
You All Dat
Welch, Brian
Make Me Bad
Wells, Danny
Couldn't Last a Moment
Wengren, Michael
Down with the Sickness
Stupify
West, Alvin
Got to Get It
West, Kaye
This Can't Be Life
West, Kyle
Where I Wanna Be
Westfield, Richard
Breathe and Stop
Do You
White, Eric
From the Bottom of My Broken Heart
White, Gary
I Like It
Whitehead, John
Don't Call Me Baby
Wiggs, Peter
Tell Me Why (The Riddle)
Wilder, David
I Try
Wilk, Brad
Sleep Now in the Fire
Williams, A.
Dramacide
Williams, Adam
Ultra Mega
Williams, Bryan
Get Your Roll On
I Need a Hot Girl
Williams, Damon *see* Dangerous
Williams, Ellis
You Can Do It
Williams, Hank, Jr.
A Country Boy Can Survive
Williams, Michele
Still Not a Player
'Til I Say So
Williams, Pharrell
Girls Dem Sugar
Mafia
Shake Ya Ass
Williams, Ralph
A.M. Radio
Williams, Robbie
Love Calling Earth
Rock DJ
Supreme
Williams, Victoria
Gladys and Lucy
Willis, Katrina
Don't Think I'm Not
Wilson, Nancy
Fever Dog
Wilson, Nathaniel *see* Kool G Rap
Wilson, Paul
Picture of You
Winans, Mario
Best Friend
How Many Licks?

Wiseman, Craig
Just Another Day in Paradise
Tell Her
Withers, Bill
Demons
Love Life
Wonder, Stevie
Summer Rain
Woods, Corey *see* Raekwon
Worley, Darryl
When You Need My Love
Wright, Erica *see* Badu, Erykah
Wright, Frank
Minority
Wright, J.
Dramacide
Wright, James
The Best Man I Can Be
Open My Heart
Wright, Mark
It Was
Wysocki, Jonathan
Home
Xzibit
Connect
Year 2000
Yacoub, Rami
It's Gonna Be Me
Lucky
Oops!...I Did It Again
Shape of My Heart
Stronger
Yancey, James
Breathe and Stop
The Light
Yates, Jenny
When You Come Back to Me Again
Yorke, Thomas
Optimistic
Young, Andre *see also* Dr. Dre
Bag Lady
Young, Angus
Satellite Blues
Stiff Upper Lip
Young, Bradley
West Side Story
Young, Malcolm
Satellite Blues
Stiff Upper Lip
Young, Maurice *see* Trick Daddy
Young, Neil
Buffalo Springfield Again
Razor Love
Silver & Gold
Young, Robert
Exterminator
Zero, Darryl
I Don't Wanna Kiss You Goodnight
Zhukov, Sergei
Around the World (La La La La La)
Zimmerman, Robert *see* Dylan, Bob
Zizzo, Peter
Don't Say You Love Me

Important Performances Index

Songs are listed under the works in which they were introduced or given significant renditions. The index is organized into major sections by performance medium: Album, Movie, Musical, Performer, Revue, Television Show.

Album

Aaron's Party (Come Get It)
  Aaron's Party (Come Get It)
Abandoned Shopping Trolley Hotline
  Bring Your Lovin' Back Here
The Abba Generation
  Dancing Queen
Affirmation
  Crash and Burn
  I Knew I Loved You
All about U
  Pop Ya Collar
All That You Can't Leave Behind
  Beautiful Day
Alma Caribena
  No Me Dejes De Querer (Don't Stop Loving Me)
Almost Famous
  Fever Dog
Alone with Everybody
  C'mon People (We're Making It Now)
  A Song for the Lovers
America Town
  Superman
American III: Solitary Man
  I Won't Back Down
  I'm Leavin' Now
American Psycho
  You Spin Me 'Round (Like a Record)
Amor, Familia y Respeto
  U Don't Love Me
Amplified
  Breathe and Stop
And Then Nothing Turned Itself Inside-Out
  Last Days of Disco
And Then There Was X
  Party Up (Up in Here)
  What's My Name
Angels & Cigarettes
  Train Song
Around the World (La La La La La)
  Around the World (La La La La La)
Art and Life
  Girls Dem Sugar
Astro Lounge
  Come On, Come On
At Any Cost
  Beat from Underground
...Baby One More Time
  From the Bottom of My Broken Heart
Back for the First Time
  What's Your Fantasy

Bait
Took the Bait
The Battle of Los Angeles
Sleep Now in the Fire
Behind the Sun
Don't Give Up
Belly
Devil's Pie
The Best Man
The Best Man I Can Be
The Better Life
Kryptonite
Loser
Beware of Dog
Bounce with Me
Big Momma's House
Bounce with Me
I Still Got to Have It
Binaural
Nothing as It Seems
Black & Blue
Shape of My Heart
Black and White
Dramacide
It's Not a Game
Year 2000
Black Diamond
Green Grass Vapors
Blackout!
Y.O.U.
Blair Witch 2: Book of Shadows
Goodbye Lament
Lie Down
The Reckoning
Blame Everyone
Stoopid Ass
Blender
Why Pt. 2
Bloodflowers
Bloodflowers
Where the Birds Always Sing
Blue
Deep Inside of You
Never Let You Go
Blue Moon
Blue Moon
The Bocephus Box: 1979-1999
A Country Boy Can Survive
Book of Thugs: AK Versus 47
Shut Up
Born to Fly
Born to Fly
Bounce
Need to Be Next to You
Brand New Day
Desert Rose
Brand New Me
The Little Girl
Brand New Year
Deck the Halls
Breach
Sleepwalker
Breathe
Breathe
Let's Make Love
The Way You Love Me
Bring It On
As If
'Til I Say So
Burn
That's the Way
Burn to Shine
Steal My Kisses
Californication
Californication
Otherside
Can't Take Me Home
Most Girls
There You Go
The Captain
The Captain
Cry Like a Baby
Causin' Drama
Left Right Left
Charlie's Angels
Angel's Eye
Independent Women Part I
Ya Mama
Chocolate Starfish and the Hot Dog
Flavored Water
Take a Look Around
Christina Aguilera
Come On Over Baby (All I Want Is You)
I Turn to You
What a Girl Wants

Country Grammar
Country Grammar (Hot Shit)
Coyote Ugly
Can't Fight the Moonlight
Crouching Tiger Hidden Dragon
A Love Before Time
The Crow: Salvation
Burning Inside
Crush
It's My Life
Say It Isn't So
Daisies of the Galaxy
Grace Kelly Blues
Mr. E's Beautiful Blues
Damizza Presents: Where I Wanna Be
Where I Wanna Be
Dance with Me
Dance with Me
A Day Without Rain
Wild Child
Daydreamin'
Monica
Devil Without a Cause
Only God Knows Why
Dizzy Up the Girl
Broadway
D'lectrified
Been There
Don't Sleep
Connect
Double Wide
Yeah Yeah Yeah
Down the Road I Go
Best of Intentions
Dracula 2000
Break You Down
Ultra Mega
Dude, Where's My Car
Playmate of the Year
Duets
Cruisin'
The Dynasty: Roc la Familia
This Can't Be Life
Dysfunction
Home
Eat at Whitey's
Deadly Assassins
The Ecleftic: 2 Sides II a Book
It Doesn't Matter
Kenny Rogers-Pharoahe Monch Dub Plate
911
Ecstasy
Paranoia Key of E
Turning Time Around
An Education in Rebellion
Turn Me on 'Mr. Deadman'
Emotion
Love's the Only House
There You Are
Emotional
I Wish
Summer Rain
The Emperor's New Groove
My Funny Friend and Me
One Day She'll Love Me
Perfect World
Enema of the State
Adam's Song
Enrique
Be with You
Could I Have This Kiss Forever
Essential Bob Dylan
Things Have Changed
Evan and Jaron
Crazy for This Girl
Everything You Want
Everything You Want
You're a God
Exposed
Straight Up
Faith in You
Been There
Familiar to Millions
Go Let It Out
The Family Man
This Could Be Heaven
World Looking In
You Stole My Bell
The Family Values Tour '99
Outside
Fanmail
Dear Lie
Fear of Flying
The Best of Me

Case of the Ex (Watcha Gonna Do)
Free
Fearless
A Little Gasoline
No Fear
Figure 8
Son of Sam
Fly
Cold Day in July
Cowboy Take Me Away
Goodbye Earl
Without You
Forever
Best Friend
Fortress
Change Your Mind
The Fragile
Into the Void
Fragments of Freedom
Be Yourself
World Looking In
Free the West Memphis 3
Poor Girl
From the Bottom to the Top
I Like It
Fundamental Elements of Southtown
Lie Down
G
Baby U Are
Mr. Too Damn Good
George Strait
Go On
Ghetto Hymns
Can't Stay
Ghost Dog: The Way of the Samurai
4 Sho Sho
Samurai Showdown
The Gift
I'm Still Your Daddy
The Gift of Game
Butterfly
Girlfight
Out for the Count
Godsmack
Bad Religion
Voodoo
Gone in 60 Seconds
Painted on My Heart
Goodfellas
Wobble Wobble
Gotta Tell You
Gotta Tell You
Greatest Hits (Lenny Kravitz)
Again
The Greatest Hits
Could I Have This Kiss Forever
Greatest Hits (Kenny Chesney)
I Lost It
Greatest Hits (Tim McGraw)
Let's Make Love
The Greatest Hits
Same Script, Different Cast
Greatest Hits (Kenny Chesney)
What I Need to Do
Guerilla Warfare
I Need a Hot Girl
Gun Shy
Blue Skies for Everyone
Gung Ho
Glitter in Their Eyes
Gung Ho
Halfway Between the Gutter and the Stars
Demons
Love Life
Sunset (Bird of Prey)
Ya Mama
Halfway down the Sky
I Think God Can Explain
Hard Rain Don't Last
When You Need My Love
He Did That
He Did That
Hear My Cry
It Feels So Good
Heartbreaker
My Winding Wheel
The Heat
He Wasn't Man Enough
Just Be a Man about It
Heavy Metal 2000
Dirt Ball
Immortally Insane
Here on Earth
Where You Are

Heroes & Villains: Music Inspired by the Powerpuff Girls
Go Monkey Go
The Powerpuff Girls (Main Theme)
The Powerpuff Girls (End Theme)
Hey Kandi
Don't Think I'm Not
High Fidelity
Let's Get It On
The History of Rock
American Bad Ass
Early Mornin' Stoned Pimp
Hoku
Another Dumb Blonde
Hooray for Boobies
The Bad Touch
Horrorscope
Promise
Hotshot
It Wasn't Me
How Do You Like Me Now?!
Country Comes to Town
How Do You Like Me Now?!
How the Grinch Stole Christmas
Grinch 2000
Human Clay
What If
With Arms Wide Open
The Hurricane
Hurricane
Love Sets You Free
I Am Shelby Lynne
Black Light Blue
Life Is Bad
Your Lies
I Got That Work
Get Your Roll On
I Hope You Dance
I Hope You Dance
I Wanna Be with You
I Wanna Be with You
Ideal
Whatever
If I Could Only Fly
I'm Still Your Daddy
Proud to Be Your Old Man
Wishin' All These Old Things Were New
III
Dancin'
I'm Alright
Because You Love Me
I'm Outta Love
I'm Outta Love
In Blue
Breathless
Infest
Last Resort
Inside Job
Everything Is Different Now
Taking You Home
Introducing IMx
Stay the Night
Invincible Summer
Summerfling
Iommi
Goodbye Lament
Issues
Make Me Bad
It's About Time
Put Your Hand in Mine
It's On
3 Little Words
It's Very Stimulating
MTV Get Off the Air, Part 2
J. E. Heartbreak
Let's Get Married
JJ72
Snow
Kaleidoscope
Mafia
Keith Urban
Your Everything
Kid A
Everything in Its Right Place
Morning Bell
The National Anthem
Optimistic
King of Nothing
That's the Beat of a Heart
La Peste
Too Sick to Pray
The Ladies Man
All This Time
Lara Fabian
I Will Love Again

Latest Greatest Straitest Hits
The Best Day
Lessons Learned
Lessons Learned
Lonely
Let There Be Eve...Ruff Ryders' First
Lady
Love Is Blind
Let's Get Ready
Shake Ya Ass
Let's Make Sure We Kiss Goodbye
Feels like Love
LFO
I Don't Wanna Kiss You Goodnight
West Side Story
Life Story
Whoa!
Like Water for Chocolate
The Light
A Song for Assata
A Little Bit of Mambo
Tricky, Tricky
Little Nicky
Change (In the House of Flies)
Stupify
Live, Laugh, Love
The Chain of Love
Live, Laugh, Love
Lonely Grill
Smile
Tell Her
What About Now
Lost and Gone Forever
Fa Fa (Never Be the Same Again)
Loud Rocks
For Heaven's Sake 2000
Shame
Still Not a Player
Love & Basketball
I'll Go
Love Crimes
No More
Lovers Rock
By Your Side
Lucy Pearl
Dance Tonight
Don't Mess with My Man
MACHINA/The Machines of God
Heavy Metal Machine
Stand Inside Your Love
Try Try Try
Mad Season
Bent
If You're Gone
The Madding Crowd
Absolutely (Story of a Girl)
If I Am
Magnolia
Save Me
Make Yourself
Drive
Pardon Me
Stellar
Malcolm in the Middle
Boss of Me
Mama's Gun
Bag Lady
Man on the Moon
The Great Beyond
The Man Who
Turn
Why Does It Always Rain on Me?
Marc Anthony
You Sang to Me
Maroon
Pinch Me
The Marshall Mathers LP
The Real Slim Shady
Stan
The Way I Am
Mary
Deep Inside
Give Me You
Masterpiece Theatre
Riddle
Me, Myself & Irene
Bodhisattva
Deep Inside of You
Meanwhile Back at the Ranch
Meanwhile Back at the Ranch
Meet the Parents
A Fool in Love
Mer de Noms
Judith
Magdalena

Mi Reflejo
Come On Over Baby (All I Want Is You)
I Turn to You
What a Girl Wants
Millennium
Show Me the Meaning of Being Lonely
Million Dollar Hotel
The Ground Beneath Her Feet
Mirror Mirror
As We Lay
Love Sets You Free
You Should've Told Me
Miss Congeniality
Dancing Queen
Mix Tape, Volume 4: 60 Minutes of Funk
Do You
More...
More
Mountain High Valley Low
Open My Heart
Music
Music
Music from and Inspired by M:I-2
Have a Cigar
I Disappear
Scum of the Earth
Take a Look Around
My Name Is Joe
I Wanna Know
Treat Her like a Lady
My Soul, My Life
One Night Stand
My Thoughts
Separated
Nastradamus
You Owe Me
Nasty Little Thoughts
Little Black Backpack
Nathan Michael Shawn Wayna
Beautiful Women
Nativity in Black II: A Tribute to Black Sabbath
N.I.B.
The Next Best Thing
American Pie
A Night to Remember
It's Always Somethin'
Nixon
Up with People
No Angel
Thank You
No Authority
Can I Get Your Number (A Girl like You)
No. 4
Sour Girl
No One Does It Better
Faded
No Pleasantries
Godless
No Strings Attached
Bye Bye Bye
It's Gonna Be Me
Northern Star
Go!
Nothin' but Drama
Liar
Notorious K.I.M.
How Many Licks?
No Matter What They Say
Now You See Inside
Right Now
A Nu Day
Can't Go for That
Nutty Professor II: The Klumps
Doesn't Really Matter
Hey Papi
On How Life Is
I Try
On the 6
Feelin' So Good
100% Ginuwine
None of Ur Friends Business
One in a Million
One in a Million
One Voice
One Voice
Onka's Big Monka
Dancing in the Moonlight
Oops!...I Did It Again
Lucky
Oops!...I Did It Again

(I Can't Get No) Satisfaction
Stronger
Out There and Back
Another Way
Tell Me Why (The Riddle)
Parachutes
Yellow
The Parlance of Our Time
Sundown
People like Us
Kiss This
Phil Vassar
Carlene
Just Another Day in Paradise
A Place in the Sun (Lit)
Miserable
A Place in the Sun (Tim McGraw)
My Best Friend
My Next Thirty Years
Some Things Never Change
Play
Natural Blues
Play It Loud
My Love Goes On and On
Playmate of the Year
Playmate of the Year
Pokemon: The First Movie
Don't Say You Love Me
The Polyester Embassy
Don't Call Me Baby
Power of 3
West Side Story
Pull Over
Pull Over
Purest of Pain
A Puro Dolor (Purest of Pain)
Rainbow
Crybaby
Thank God I Found You
Rascal Flatts
Prayin' for Daylight
Ready to Rumble
Bloodstains
Last Resort
Real Live Woman
Real Live Woman
Red Dirt Girl
Bang the Drum Slowly
Relationship of Command
Quarantined
Remedy
Red Alert
Renegades
Renegades of Funk
Return of Saturn
Ex-Girlfriend
Simple Kind of Life
Revelation
Give Me Just One Night (Una Noche)
Ricky Martin
Private Emotion
Riding with the King
Riding with the King
Righteous Love
Righteous Love
Risk
Breadline
The Road to El Dorado
Someday Out of the Blue
Road Trip
Early Mornin' Stoned Pimp
Mr. E's Beautiful Blues
Pumping on Your Stereo
Romeo Must Die
I Don't Wanna
Try Again
Ronan
If I Don't Tell You Now
Rule 3:36
Between Me and You
Ryde or Die, Vol. 1
Ryde or Die, Chick
What You Want
Ryde or Die, Vol. 2
Got It All
S. D. E.
What Means the World to You
Sailing to Philadelphia
Sailing to Philadelphia
Saints and Sinners
Pure Shores
Save the Last Dance
All or Nothing
Breathe and Stop
The Science of Things
Letting the Cables Sleep

Scream 3
Is This the End
What If
Screamin' for My Supper
L.A. Song
Selmasongs: Music from the Motion
Picture Dancer in the Dark
I've Seen It All
Sex and the City
Righteous Love
Sex and the City Theme
Shades of Purple
Don't Say You Love Me
Mirror Mirror
Shaft (2000)
Bad Man
Rock Wit U
Summer Rain
Theme from Shaft
Tough Guy
She Rides Wild Horses
Buy Me a Rose
Shyne
Bad Boyz
The Sickness
Down with the Sickness
Stupify
Significant Other
Break Stuff
N 2gether Now
Silver & Gold
Buffalo Springfield Again
Razor Love
Silver & Gold
Sing When You're Winning
Love Calling Earth
Rock DJ
Supreme
Single White Female
It Was
Skull & Bones
Highlife
(Rap) Superstar
(Rock) Superstar
Smile
I'm Gonna Make You Love Me
Smoke Rings in the Dark
Smoke Rings in the Dark
Snoop Dogg Presents Tha Eastsidaz
G'd Up
Snow Day
Another Dumb Blonde
Come On, Come On
My Heart's Saying Now
Picture of You
So Good Together
I'll Be
Something like Human
Hemorrhage (In My Hands)
Son by Four
A Puro Dolor (Purest of Pain)
Songs from an American Movie, Vol.
One: Learning How to Smile
A.M. Radio
Wonderful
Songs from Dawson's Creek, Volume 2
Daydream Believer
I Think God Can Explain
I Think I'm in Love with You
If I Am
I'm Gonna Make You Love Me
Songs From Dawson's Creek, Volume 2
Show Me Heaven
Songs from Dawson's Creek, Volume 2
Superman
Teenage Dirtbag
Sooner or Later
Back Here
Sound Loaded
She Bangs
Southern Rain
You Won't Be Lonely Now
Standing on the Shoulder of Giants
Go Let It Out
Stankonia
Ms. Jackson
The State
Leader of Men
Steal This Movie
My Back Pages
Time Has Come Today
Steam
No Mercy
Stiff Upper Lip
Satellite Blues
Stiff Upper Lip

Still I Rise
Baby Don't Cry (Keep Ya Head Up II)
Stories from the City, Stories from the Sea
This Is Love
Strait Up
Funeral Flights
Take It Back
Streetsoul
Plenty
Strong Heart
That's the Kind of Mood I'm In
Supergrass
Pumping on Your Stereo
Supernatural
Maria Maria
Supreme Clientele
Cherchez Laghost
Sweet Kisses
I Think I'm in Love with You
Where You Are
Swimming in Champagne
Flowers on the Wall
Ta Da
Ta Da
Take That
Take That
Tamar
If You Don't Wanna Love Me
Tattoos & Scars
Daddy Won't Sell the Farm
Tha G-Code
U Understand
Thankful
Shackles (Praise You)
There Is Nothing Left to Lose
Breakout
Thirteen Tales from Urban Bohemia
Bohemian like You
This Time Around
This Time Around
3LW
'Til I Say So
Thug Walkin'
Whistle While You Twurk
Tight Rope
You'll Always Be Loved by Me
Titan A.E.
Over My Head
Toy Story 2
When She Loved Me
TP-2.com
I Wish
Tracie
Still in My Heart
Tracks
Couldn't Last a Moment
Transcendental Blues
Transcendental Blues
Turnpike Diaries
Good Life
24/7
No Love (I'm Not Used To)
24/7
Two Against Nature
Cousin Dupree
Janie Runaway
Two Against Nature
2001
Forgot about Dre
The Next Episode
Still D.R.E.
2ge+her: Again
The Hardest Part of Breaking Up (Is Getting Back Your Stuff)
Unconditional
Unconditional
Under the Influence
It Must Be Love
Unleash the Dragon
Got to Get It
Incomplete
Thong Song
Unrestricted
That's What I'm Looking For
What'chu Like
Untamed
Another Nine Minutes
V. I. P.
V.I.P
Visit Me
That Other Woman
Vitamin C
Graduation (Friends Forever)

Vol. 3: The Life & Times of Shawn Carter
Big Pimpin'
Do It Again (Put Ya Hands Up)
Voodoo
Devil's Pie
Left & Right
Untitled (How Does It Feel)
The W
Careful (Click, Click)
Intro (Shaolin Finger Jab)/Chamber Music
The Wait
Gravel Pit
War & Peace, Vol. 2 (The Peace Disc)
You Can Do It
Warning
Minority
Water to Drink
Gladys and Lucy
We Are the Streets
Ryde or Die, Chick
Welcome II Nextasy
Wifey
Westlife
Swear It Again
Whatever It Takes
Go!
Red Alert
V.I.P
Wheatus
Teenage Dirtbag
Where I Wanna Be
Where I Wanna Be
Where the Heart Is
That's the Beat of a Heart
White Ladder
Babylon
White Pony
Change (In the House of Flies)
Elite
Who Is Jill Scott? Words and Sounds, Vol. 1
Gettin' in the Way
Who Let the Dogs Out
Who Let the Dogs Out
You All Dat
Who Needs Guitars Anyway?
Better Off Alone
Who Needs Pictures
Me Neither
We Danced
Who Wants to Be a Millionaire: The Album
I Want to Be a Millionaire
Whoa, Nelly!
I'm like a Bird
The Whole Shebang
I Will...But
This Woman Needs
Willennium
Freakin' It
Wonder Boys
Things Have Changed
The Wood
I Wanna Know
The Writing's on the Wall
Jumpin, Jumpin
Say My Name
XTRMNTR
Exterminator
Yeeeah Baby
It's So Hard
Yes!
A Country Boy Can Survive
Yes!
You Won't Ever Be Lonely
She's More
Young World: The Future
Callin' Me
You're the One
You're the One

Movie

Almost Famous
Fever Dog
The Best Man
The Best Man I Can Be
Black and White
It's Not a Game
Bounce
Need to Be Next to You
Coyote Ugly
Can't Fight the Moonlight

Dancer in the Dark
  I've Seen It All
Dude, Where's My Car
  Playmate of the Year
The Emperor's New Groove
  My Funny Friend and Me
  One Day She'll Love Me
  Perfect World
The Family Man
  This Could Be Heaven
  World Looking In
  You Stole My Bell
Frequency
  When You Come Back to Me Again
The Gift
  I'm Still Your Daddy
Girlfight
  Out for the Count
Gone in 60 Seconds
  Painted on My Heart
High Fidelity
  Let's Get It On
The Hurricane
  Hurricane
Loser
  Teenage Dirtbag
Magnolia
  Save Me
Man on the Moon
  The Great Beyond
Meet the Parents
  A Fool in Love
Million Dollar Hotel
  The Ground Beneath Her Feet
Mission: Impossible 2
  I Disappear
The Next Best Thing
  American Pie
The Road to El Dorado
  Someday Out of the Blue
Road Trip
  Pumping on Your Stereo
Shaft (2000)
  Theme from Shaft
Titan A.E.
  Over My Head
Toy Story 2
  When She Loved Me
Where the Heart Is
  That's the Beat of a Heart
Wonder Boys
  Things Have Changed

Musical

Elton John and Tim Rice's Aida
  Every Story Is a Love Story

Performer

Aaliyah
  I Don't Wanna
  Try Again
AC/DC
  Satellite Blues
  Stiff Upper Lip
Adams, Bryan
  Don't Give Up
Adams, Ryan
  My Winding Wheel
Adams, Yolanda
  Open My Heart
Adkins, Trace
  More
Aerosmith
  Angel's Eye
Aguilera, Christina
  Come On Over Baby (All I Want Is You)
  I Turn to You
  What a Girl Wants
Alice Deejay
  Better Off Alone
All Saints
  Pure Shores
Allan, Gary
  Smoke Rings in the Dark
American Cream Team
  It's Not a Game
Amil
  Do It Again (Put Ya Hands Up)
  Hey Papi
Anastacia
  I'm Outta Love
Andrews, Jessica
  Show Me Heaven

Anthony, Marc
You Sang to Me
Ashcroft, Richard
C'mon People (We're Making It Now)
A Song for the Lovers
At the Drive-In
Quarantined
ATC
Around the World (La La La La La)
A*Teens
Dancing Queen
A3
Too Sick to Pray
Avant
Separated
B-Real
Deadly Assassins
Backstreet Boys
Shape of My Heart
Show Me the Meaning of Being Lonely
Badu, Erykah
Bag Lady
Baha Men
Who Let the Dogs Out
You All Dat
Barenaked Ladies
Pinch Me
Barman, MC Paul
MTV Get Off the Air, Part 2
Basement Jaxx
Red Alert
BBMak
Back Here
Beenie Man
Girls Dem Sugar
Before Dark
Monica
Bega, Lou
Tricky, Tricky
Bell, Burton C.
Burning Inside
Beyond Gravity
Beat from Underground
Big Gipp
Connect
Big Punisher
Dramacide
Feelin' So Good
It's So Hard
Still Not a Player
Big Tymers
Get Your Roll On
I Need a Hot Girl
Bis
The Powerpuff Girls (End Theme)
Bjork
I've Seen It All
Black, Clint
Been There
Black, Jack
Let's Get It On
Black Rob
Whoa!
Blaque
As If
Blige, Mary J.
Deep Inside
Give Me You
911
Blink-182
Adam's Song
Bloodhound Gang
The Bad Touch
Bon Jovi
It's My Life
Say It Isn't So
Bosson
One in a Million
Boyz II Men
Beautiful Women
Boyzone
Picture of You
Braxton, Toni
He Wasn't Man Enough
Just Be a Man about It
Brian Setzer Orchestra
Bodhisattva
Brock, Chad
A Country Boy Can Survive
Yes!
Brooks and Dunn
You'll Always Be Loved by Me
Brooks, Garth
When You Come Back to Me Again

Browne, Jackson
My Back Pages
Bush
Letting the Cables Sleep
Byrd, Tracy
Put Your Hand in Mine
Cage, Athena
All or Nothing
Cagle, Chris
My Love Goes On and On
Calandrelli, Jorge
A Love Before Time
Cam'ron
What Means the World to You
Carey, Mariah
Crybaby
Thank God I Found You
Carrey, Jim
Grinch 2000
Carter, Aaron
Aaron's Party (Come Get It)
Carter, Torrey
Take That
Carthy, Eliza
Train Song
Case
The Best Man I Can Be
Cash, Johnny
I Won't Back Down
I'm Leavin' Now
Chambers, Kasey
The Captain
Cry Like a Baby
Changing Faces
That Other Woman
Chemical X
The Powerpuff Girls (Main Theme)
Chesney, Kenny
I Lost It
What I Need to Do
Chicane
Don't Give Up
Clapton, Eric
Riding with the King
Clark Family Experience
Meanwhile Back at the Ranch
Clark, Terri
A Little Gasoline
No Fear
Coldplay
Yellow
Collective Soul
Why Pt. 2
Colvin, Shawn
One Day She'll Love Me
Common
The Light
A Song for Assata
Corrs
Breathless
Costello, Elvis
You Stole My Bell
Cox, Deborah
Same Script, Different Cast
Crazy Town
Butterfly
Creed
Is This the End
What If
With Arms Wide Open
Crow, Sheryl
Time Has Come Today
Cult
Painted on My Heart
Cure
Bloodflowers
Where the Birds Always Sing
Cypress Hill
Highlife
(Rap) Superstar
(Rock) Superstar
Cyrus, Billy Ray
You Won't Be Lonely Now
Da Brat
That's What I'm Looking For
What'chu Like
Dandy Warhols
Bohemian like You
D'Angelo
Devil's Pie
Left & Right
Untitled (How Does It Feel)
Dangerous
Took the Bait

Davidson, Clay
Unconditional
Davis, Jonathan
Take It Back
Year 2000
Dean, Billy
Buy Me a Rose
Deftones
Change (In the House of Flies)
Elite
Destiny's Child
Independent Women Part I
Jumpin, Jumpin
Say My Name
Devo
Go Monkey Go
Dido
Stan
Thank You
Diffie, Joe
It's Always Somethin'
Disturbed
Down with the Sickness
Stupify
Dixie Chicks
Cold Day in July
Cowboy Take Me Away
Goodbye Earl
Without You
DJ Hurricane
Connect
DMX
Do You
Party Up (Up in Here)
What You Want
What's My Name
Dr. Dre
Forgot about Dre
Just Be a Man about It
The Next Episode
Still D.R.E.
Dope
You Spin Me 'Round (Like a Record)
Drama
Left Right Left
Ducent, Ricardo
It Wasn't Me
Dun, Tan
A Love Before Time
Dupri, Jermaine
I Still Got to Have It
Durst, Fred
Outside
Dylan, Bob
Hurricane
Things Have Changed
Earle, Steve
Time Has Come Today
Transcendental Blues
Edmonds, Kevon
No Love (I'm Not Used To)
24/7
Eels
Grace Kelly Blues
Mr. E's Beautiful Blues
Elliott, Missy 'Misdemeanor'
Take That
Elwood
Sundown
Eminem
Forgot about Dre
The Real Slim Shady
Stan
The Way I Am
En Vogue
Riddle
Enya
Wild Child
Estefan, Gloria
No Me Dejes De Querer (Don't Stop Loving Me)
Evan and Jaron
Crazy for This Girl
Evans, Sara
Born to Fly
That's the Beat of a Heart
Eve
Got It All
Love Is Blind
Out for the Count
Ryde or Die, Chick
Eve 6
Promise

Everclear
  A.M. Radio
  Wonderful
Everlast
  Deadly Assassins
Fabian, Lara
  I Will Love Again
Fafara, B. Dez
  Funeral Flights
Fat Joe
  Feelin' So Good
Fatboy Slim
  Demons
  Love Life
  Sunset (Bird of Prey)
  Ya Mama
Fatone, Joey, Jr.
  As If
Five for Fighting
  Superman
504 Boyz
  Wobble Wobble
Foo Fighters
  Breakout
  Have a Cigar
Fuel
  Hemorrhage (In My Hands)
Funkmaster Flex
  Do You
Furtado, Nelly
  I'm like a Bird
Getaway People
  Good Life
Ghostface Killah
  Cherchez Laghost
Gill, Vince
  Feels like Love
Gilman, Billy
  One Voice
Ginuwine
  The Best Man I Can Be
  None of Ur Friends Business
  You Owe Me
Godhead
  Break You Down
  The Reckoning
Godsmack
  Bad Religion
  Voodoo
Gomez
  Bring Your Lovin' Back Here
Goo Goo Dolls
  Broadway
Grand Theft Audio
  Stoopid Ass
Gray, David
  Babylon
Gray, Macy
  Demons
  I Try
  Love Life
Green Day
  Minority
Griggs, Andy
  She's More
Grohl, Dave
  Goodbye Lament
Groove Armada
  Sex and the City Theme
Guru's Jazzmatazz
  Plenty
Guster
  Fa Fa (Never Be the Same Again)
Guy
  Dancin'
Haggard, Merle
  I'm Leavin' Now
  I'm Still Your Daddy
  Proud to Be Your Old Man
  Wishin' All These Old Things Were New
Hall, Aaron
  Love Sets You Free
Hanson
  This Time Around
Harper, Ben
  Steal My Kisses
Harris, Emmylou
  Bang the Drum Slowly
Hart, Beth
  L.A. Song
Harvey, PJ
  This Is Love

Hathaway, Lalah
All This Time
Hayes, Isaac
Theme from Shaft
Heatherly, Eric
Flowers on the Wall
Henley, Don
Everything Is Different Now
Taking You Home
Herndon, Ty
No Mercy
Hill, Faith
Breathe
Let's Make Love
The Way You Love Me
Hoku
Another Dumb Blonde
Hollister, Dave
Can't Stay
Holy, Steve
Blue Moon
Hot Boy$
I Need a Hot Girl
Houston, Whitney
Could I Have This Kiss Forever
Same Script, Different Cast
Ice Cube
You Can Do It
Ideal
Whatever
Iglesias, Enrique
Be with You
Could I Have This Kiss Forever
IMx
Stay the Night
Incubus
Drive
Pardon Me
Stellar
Still Not a Player
Insane Clown Posse
Dirt Ball
Iommi, Tony
For Heaven's Sake 2000
Goodbye Lament
J-Shin
One Night Stand
Ja Rule
Between Me and You
Jack and Jemma
I Want to Be a Millionaire
Jackson, Alan
It Must Be Love
Jackson, Janet
Doesn't Really Matter
Jadakiss
The Best of Me
Got It All
Jagged Edge
Let's Get Married
Jay-Z
Big Pimpin'
Do It Again (Put Ya Hands Up)
Hey Papi
This Can't Be Life
Jayhawks
I'm Gonna Make You Love Me
Jean, Wyclef
It Doesn't Matter
Kenny Rogers-Pharoahe Monch Dub Plate
911
JJ72
Snow
Joe
I Wanna Know
Thank God I Found You
Treat Her like a Lady
John, Elton
Every Story Is a Love Story
Someday Out of the Blue
Jones, Donell
It's So Hard
Where I Wanna Be
Jones, Donnell
I'll Go
Jones, George
A Country Boy Can Survive
Jones, Tom
Perfect World
Jungle Brothers
V.I.P
Juvenile
U Understand

Kandi
Don't Think I'm Not
Keating, Ronan
If I Don't Tell You Now
Keith, Toby
Country Comes to Town
How Do You Like Me Now?!
Kelis
Mafia
Kelly, R.
Bad Man
I Wish
Keys, Alicia
Rock Wit U
Kid Rock
American Bad Ass
Early Mornin' Stoned Pimp
Only God Knows Why
King, B.B.
Riding with the King
Knight, Jordan
My Heart's Saying Now
Knopfler, Mark
Sailing to Philadelphia
Kool G. Rap
Dramacide
Korn
Make Me Bad
Krauss, Alison
Buy Me a Rose
The Little Girl
Kravitz, Lenny
Again
Kumbia Kings
U Don't Love Me
Kurupt
Where I Wanna Be
Lachey, Nick
Where You Are
Lambchop
Up with People
Lang, K. D.
Summerfling
Lanois, Daniel
The Ground Beneath Her Feet
Lawrence, Tracy
Lessons Learned
Lonely
Levert, Gerald
Baby U Are
Mr. Too Damn Good
Levy, Barrington
Bad Boyz
Lewis, Huey
Cruisin'
LFO (Lyte Funky Ones)
I Don't Wanna Kiss You Goodnight
LFO
West Side Story
Lil' Bow Wow
Bounce with Me
Lil' Kim
How Many Licks?
No Matter What They Say
Lil' Mo
Ta Da
Lil' Zane
Callin' Me
Limp Bizkit
Break Stuff
N 2gether Now
Take a Look Around
Lit
Miserable
Over My Head
Lonestar
Smile
Tell Her
What About Now
Lopez, Jennifer
Feelin' So Good
Love Fellowship Crusade Choir
Best Friend
Loveless, Patty
That's the Kind of Mood I'm In
Lox
Ryde or Die, Chick
Lucy Pearl
Dance Tonight
Don't Mess with My Man
Ludacris
What's Your Fantasy
Lynne, Shelby
Black Light Blue
Life Is Bad
Your Lies

Mac
He Did That
Mack 10
You Can Do It
Madison Avenue
Don't Call Me Baby
Madonna
American Pie
Music
Make It Hot
Got to Get It
Mami, Cheb
Desert Rose
Mann, Aimee
Save Me
Marilyn Manson
Break You Down
Martin, Ricky
Private Emotion
She Bangs
Mary Mary
Shackles (Praise You)
Master P
He Did That
Matchbox Twenty
Bent
If You're Gone
May, Brian
Have a Cigar
Maziarz, Mary Beth
Daydream Believer
McBride, Martina
Love's the Only House
There You Are
McEntire, Reba
I'll Be
McGraw, Tim
Let's Make Love
My Best Friend
My Next Thirty Years
Some Things Never Change
McLachlan, Sarah
When She Loved Me
Megadeth
Breadline
Meja
Private Emotion
Melanie C
Go!
Memphis Bleek
Hey Papi
Messina, Jo Dee
Because You Love Me
That's the Way
Metallica
I Disappear
Method Man
Left & Right
N 2gether Now
Y.O.U.
Milian, Christina
Between Me and You
Miller, Marcus
All This Time
Moby
Natural Blues
Monica
I Still Got to Have It
Montgomery Gentry
Daddy Won't Sell the Farm
Montgomery, John Michael
The Little Girl
Moore, Chante
Straight Up
Moore, Mandy
I Wanna Be with You
Morcheeba
Be Yourself
World Looking In
Morgan, Debelah
Dance with Me
Ms. Toi
You Can Do It
M2M
Don't Say You Love Me
Mirror Mirror
Mumba, Samantha
Gotta Tell You
Mya
The Best of Me
Case of the Ex (Watcha Gonna Do)
Free
Girls Dem Sugar
Mystikal
Shake Ya Ass

'N Sync
Bye Bye Bye
It's Gonna Be Me
Nas
I Still Got to Have It
You Owe Me
Nash, Leigh
Need to Be Next to You
Nate Dogg
Where I Wanna Be
Nelly
Country Grammar (Hot Shit)
Newman, Randy
A Fool in Love
Next
Wifey
Nickelback
Leader of Men
Nine Days
Absolutely (Story of a Girl)
If I Am
Nine Inch Nails
Into the Void
98 Degrees
Give Me Just One Night (Una Noche)
Thank God I Found You
No Authority
Can I Get Your Number (A Girl like You)
No Doubt
Ex-Girlfriend
Simple Kind of Life
North Star
4 Sho Sho
Nu Flavor
3 Little Words
Oasis
Go Let It Out
Offspring
Bloodstains
112
Callin' Me
Osborne, Joan
My Back Pages
Righteous Love
Osbourne, Ozzy
For Heaven's Sake 2000
N.I.B.
Outkast
Ms. Jackson
Tough Guy
Outlawz
Baby Don't Cry (Keep Ya Head Up II)
Paisley, Brad
Me Neither
We Danced
Paltrow, Gwyneth
Cruisin'
Pantera
Immortally Insane
Papa Roach
Last Resort
Pearl Jam
Nothing as It Seems
A Perfect Circle
Judith
Magdalena
Petty, Tom
I Won't Back Down
Pharoahe Monch
Connect
Pink
Most Girls
There You Go
P.O.D.
Lie Down
Powerman 5000
Ultra Mega
Price, Kelly
As We Lay
Love Sets You Free
You Should've Told Me
Primal Scream
Exterminator
Primus
N.I.B.
Product G&B
Maria Maria
Profyle
Liar
Puff Daddy
Best Friend
Q-Tip
Breathe and Stop
Quintanilla, A. B.
U Don't Love Me

Radiohead
Everything in Its Right Place
Morning Bell
The National Anthem
Optimistic
Raekwon
It's Not a Game
Rage Against the Machine
Renegades of Funk
Sleep Now in the Fire
Rascal Flatts
Prayin' for Daylight
Raye, Collin
Couldn't Last a Moment
Red Hot Chili Peppers
Butterfly
Californication
Otherside
Redman
Left & Right
Y.O.U.
Reed, Lou
Paranoia Key of E
Turning Time Around
R.E.M.
The Great Beyond
Rhymes, Busta
Grinch 2000
Rice, Tim
Every Story Is a Love Story
Rimes, LeAnn
Can't Fight the Moonlight
I Need You
R.L.
The Best Man I Can Be
Rock
It Doesn't Matter
Rogers, Kenny
Buy Me a Rose
Kenny Rogers-Pharoahe Monch Dub Plate
Ruff Endz
No More
RZA
4 Sho Sho
Samurai Showdown
Sade
By Your Side
St. Etienne
Tell Me Why (The Riddle)
Sammie
I Like It
Santana
Maria Maria
Savage Garden
Crash and Burn
I Knew I Loved You
Scarface
This Can't Be Life
Took the Bait
Schneider, Bob
Blue Skies for Everyone
Scott, Jill
Gettin' in the Way
Seal
This Could Be Heaven
Sedeck, Melky
It Doesn't Matter
Shaggy
It Wasn't Me
SHeDAISY
Deck the Halls
I Will...But
This Woman Needs
Sheist, Shade
Where I Wanna Be
Shyne
Bad Boyz
Sigel, Beanie
Do It Again (Put Ya Hands Up)
Silkk the Shocker
He Did That
Simon, Paul
You're the One
Simpson, Jessica
I Think I'm in Love with You
Where You Are
Sisqo
Got to Get It
How Many Licks?
Incomplete
Thong Song
What You Want
Sister Hazel
Change Your Mind

Smash Mouth
Come On, Come On
Smashing Pumpkins
Heavy Metal Machine
Stand Inside Your Love
Try Try Try
Smith, Elliott
Son of Sam
Smith, Patti
Glitter in Their Eyes
Gung Ho
Smith, Will
Freakin' It
Snoop Dogg
Crybaby
G'd Up
The Next Episode
Still D.R.E.
Son by Four
A Puro Dolor (Purest of Pain)
Sonique
It Feels So Good
Sons of the Desert
I Hope You Dance
soulDecision
Faded
Spears, Britney
From the Bottom of My Broken Heart
Lucky
Oops!...I Did It Again
(I Can't Get No) Satisfaction
Stronger
Spencer, Tracie
Still in My Heart
Splender
I Think God Can Explain
SR-71
Right Now
Staind
Home
Outside
Static X
Burning Inside
Steely Dan
Cousin Dupree
Janie Runaway
Two Against Nature
Stevie J.
Out for the Count
Stillwater
Fever Dog
Sting
Desert Rose
My Funny Friend and Me
One Day She'll Love Me
Stone, Angie
Green Grass Vapors
Stone Temple Pilots
Sour Girl
Strait, George
The Best Day
Go On
Strait Up
Funeral Flights
Take It Back
Stroke 9
Little Black Backpack
Supergrass
Pumping on Your Stereo
Supersuckers
Poor Girl
System of a Down
Shame
Tamar
If You Don't Wanna Love Me
Tamia
Can't Go for That
Taylor, James
Sailing to Philadelphia
Tha Eastsidaz
G'd Up
They Might Be Giants
Boss of Me
Third Eye Blind
Deep Inside of You
Never Let You Go
Thomas, Carl
I Wish
Summer Rain
3 Doors Down
Kryptonite
Loser
3LW
'Til I Say So

Thrust
  Faded
Timbaland
  Ryde or Die, Chick
Tippin, Aaron
  Kiss This
TLC
  Dear Lie
Toploader
  Dancing in the Moonlight
Travis
  Turn
  Why Does It Always Rain on Me?
Trick Daddy
  Pull Over
  Shut Up
Trina
  Pull Over
Tritt, Travis
  Best of Intentions
Twiztid
  Dirt Ball
2ge+her
  The Hardest Part of Breaking Up (Is Getting Back Your Stuff)
2Pac
  Baby Don't Cry (Keep Ya Head Up II)
Tyminski, Dan
  The Little Girl
Tyrese
  The Best Man I Can Be
  What'chu Like
UGK
  Big Pimpin'
Uncle Kracker
  Yeah Yeah Yeah
Union Underground
  Turn Me on 'Mr. Deadman'
U.P.O.
  Godless
Urban, Keith
  Your Everything
Usher
  Pop Ya Collar
U2
  Beautiful Day
  The Ground Beneath Her Feet
van Dyk, Paul
  Another Way
  Tell Me Why (The Riddle)
Vassar, Phil
  Carlene
  Just Another Day in Paradise
Vedder, Eddie
  Poor Girl
Vertical Horizon
  Everything You Want
  You're a God
Vitamin C
  Graduation (Friends Forever)
Walker, Clay
  The Chain of Love
  Live, Laugh, Love
Walker, Hezekiah
  Best Friend
Wallflowers
  Sleepwalker
Wariner, Steve
  Been There
Warren Brothers
  That's the Beat of a Heart
Westlife
  Swear It Again
Wheatus
  Teenage Dirtbag
Williams, Hank, Jr.
  A Country Boy Can Survive
Williams, Robbie
  Love Calling Earth
  Rock DJ
  Supreme
Williams, Victoria
  Gladys and Lucy
Winans, Mario
  Best Friend
Womack, Lee Ann
  I Hope You Dance
Worley, Darryl
  When You Need My Love
Wright, Chely
  It Was
Wu-Tang Clan
  Careful (Click, Click)
  For Heaven's Sake 2000
  Gravel Pit

Intro (Shaolin Finger Jab)/Chamber
Music
Shame
X-ecutioners
Dramacide
Xzibit
Connect
Year 2000
Yankee Grey
Another Nine Minutes
Yearwood, Trisha
Real Live Woman
Ying Yang Twins
Whistle While You Twurk
Yo La Tengo
Last Days of Disco
Yorke, Thom
I've Seen It All
Young, Neil
Buffalo Springfield Again
Razor Love
Silver & Gold
Zebrahead
Playmate of the Year
Zombie, Rob
Scum of the Earth

Television Show

At Any Cost
Beat from Underground
Jesus
I Need You
Malcolm in the Middle
Boss of Me
The Powerpuff Girls
The Powerpuff Girls (Main Theme)
The Powerpuff Girls (End Theme)
Sex and the City
Righteous Love
Sex and the City Theme
The Sopranos
The Captain
Touched by an Angel
Buy Me a Rose

Awards Index

A list of songs nominated for Academy Awards by the Academy of Motion Picture Arts and Sciences and Grammy Awards from the National Academy of Recording Arts and Sciences. Asterisks indicate the winners; multiple listings indicate multiple nominations.

2000

Academy Award
- A Fool in Love
- I've Seen It All
- A Love Before Time
- My Funny Friend and Me
- Things Have Changed*

Grammy Award
- Again
- Bag Lady
- Beautiful Day*
- Bent
- Breathe
- Bye Bye Bye
- Californication
- Feels like Love
- The Great Beyond
- He Wasn't Man Enough
- I Hope You Dance
- I Hope You Dance*
- I Try
- Independent Women Part I
- Kryptonite
- Music
- One Voice
- Save Me
- Say My Name
- Say My Name*
- Things Have Changed
- Thong Song
- Untitled (How Does It Feel)
- The Way You Love Me
- When She Loved Me*
- With Arms Wide Open*

List of Publishers

A directory of publishers of the songs included in *Popular Music, 2000*. Publishers that are members of the American Society of Composers, Authors, and Publishers or whose catalogs are available under ASCAP license are indicated by the designation (ASCAP). Publishers that have granted performing rights to Broadcast Music, Inc., are designated by the notation (BMI). Publishers whose catalogs are represented by The Society of Composers, Authors and Music Publishers of Canada, are indicated by the designation (SOCAN). Publishers whose catalogs are represented by SESAC, Inc., are indicated by the designation (SESAC).

The addresses were gleaned from a variety of sources, including ASCAP, BMI, SOCAN, SESAC, and *Billboard* magazine. As in any volatile industry, many of the addresses may become outdated quickly. In the interim between the book's completion and its subsequent publication, some publishers may have been consolidated into others or changed hands. This is a fact of life long endured by the music business and its constituents. The data collected here, and throughout the book, are as accurate as such circumstances allow.

A

Abilene Music Inc. (ASCAP)
c/o Songwriters Guild
1500 Harbor Blvd.
Weehawken, New Jersey 07087

ABKCO Music Inc. (BMI)
1700 Broadway
New York, New York 10019

Absinthe Music (BMI)
see Warner-Chappell Music

Acrynon Publishing (BMI)
2214 West Erwin
Tyler, Texas 75702-6717

Acuff Rose Music (BMI)
65 Music Square West
Nashville, Tennessee 37203

Bryan Adams Publishing (BMI)
see Almo Music Corp.

Aftermath Music
Address Unavailable

Christina Aguilera Music (ASCAP)
c/o Douglas Mark
1424 2nd St., 3rd Fl.
Santa Monica, California 90401

List of Publishers

Ah Choo Music (ASCAP)
see Universal-MCA Music Publishing

Ahe Belle Music (ASCAP)
see Famous Music Corp.

Ain't Nothin' Goin on But F****n Music (ASCAP)
see Sony ATV Music

Ain't Nothing but Funkin' (ASCAP)
see Warner-Chappell Music

Air Chrysalis Scandinavia
see Chrysalis Music Group

Air Control Music (ASCAP)
see EMI Music Publishing

Air Station Seven (SESAC)
see EMI Music Publishing

Airstream Dreams Music (ASCAP)
see Famous Music Corp.

Al West Publishing (BMI)
c/o Sony ATV Songs
P.O. Box 1273
Nashville, Tennessee 37202

J. Albert & Son Music (ASCAP)
c/o Carlin America, Inc.
126 East 38th St.
New York, New York 10016

Almo/Irving
1358 N. LaBrea
Los Angeles, California 90028

Almo Music Corp. (ASCAP)
2440 Sepulveda Blvd.
Suite 1119
Los Angeles, California 90064

Alto Chroma (SESAC)
see EMI Music Publishing

Alva Music (BMI)
P.O. Box T
PMC Frazier Park, California 93222

Andre'sia Music
Address Unavailable

Angel Music Ltd. (ASCAP)
PO Box 1276
Great Neck, New York 11024

Antraphil Music (BMI)
c/o Antra Music Group
1515 Locust Street
Philadelphia, Pennsylvania 19102

Anwa Music (ASCAP)
see Almo Music Corp.

Appletree Songs (BMI)
see Warner-Chappell Music

Ariose Music (ASCAP)
PO Box 5085
Brentwood, Tennessee 37024

Armo Music Corp. (BMI)
c/o Lois Publishing Co.
1540 Brewster Ave.
Cincinnati, Ohio 45207

Arrival Music (BMI)
see Warner-Chappell Music

Art of War Publishing
Address Unavailable

As You Wish Music (BMI)
c/o Jeffrey H. Cohen
240 Waverly Pl., No. 2
New York, New York 10014

Asifits Music (BMI)
Paul Norris Nelson Jr.
3021 Smith Lane
Franklin, Tennessee 37064

Ayatollah Music Publishing (ASCAP)
c/o Collin Dewar
18 Edgewood Ave., 1st Floor
Yonkers, New York 10704

Aynaw Music (BMI)
see Famous Music Corp.

B

Ba-Dake Music (BMI)
c/o Super Songs Unlimited
200 W. 51st St., Ste. 1009
New York, New York 10019-6208

Baby Mae Music (BMI)
c/o Hamstein
PO Box 163870
Austin, Texas 78716

Babyboys Little Pub Co (SESAC)
c/o Mr. Bryan-Michael Paul Cox
8931 Sage Place Dr.
Houston, Texas 77071-3271

Back from the Edge (ASCAP)
c/o Chris Weber
967 Hammond St., #5
West Hollywood, California 90069

Badams Music Ltd.
Address Unavailable

Baldy Baldy Music (ASCAP)
c/o Leslie Hall Matakosky
1608 Ash Valley Dr.
Nashville, Tennessee 37215

Bambaataa Music (BMI)
c/o Taylor
3410 Dereimer Avenue, No. 4 M
Bronx, New York 10475-1536

Banana Tunes Music (BMI)
see BMG Music

Bar R Music (SESAC)
c/o Mr. Rivers Rutherford
1241 Clifftee Dr.
Brentwood, Tennessee 37027-4125

Barland Music (BMI)
see Bug Music

Teron Beal Songs (ASCAP)
see BMG Songs Inc.

Beatle Boots Music (ASCAP)
c/o VWC Management
13343 Belleview-Redmond Rd.
Bellevue, Washington 98005

Bedknobs and Broomsticks Music (BMI)
c/o Tim James Price
19923 Lorne Street
Canoga Park, California 91306

Beechwood Music (BMI)
see EMI Music Publishing

Beef Puppet (ASCAP)
c/o Grakal & Bond
1541 Ocean Ave., Suite 200
Santa Monica, California 90401

Bendan Music (ASCAP)
c/o Bruce Malament
11668 Erwin St., #B
North Hollywood, California 91606

Bernard's Other Music (BMI)
see Warner-Chappell Music

Bertam Music Co. (ASCAP)
see EMI Music Publishing

Bertam Music Publishing
Address Unavailable

Beyonce Publishing (ASCAP)
see Sony ATV Tunes LLC

Bicycle Music (ASCAP)
8075 W. 3rd St., Suite 400
Los Angeles, California 90048

Bidnis Inc Music (BMI)
c/o Stuart Ditsky CPA
733 Third Ave., 19th Floor
New York, New York 10017

Big Bizkit Music (ASCAP)
see Zomba Enterprises

Big Black Jacket Music (BMI)
see Warner-Chappell Music

Big on Blue Music (BMI)
see Warner-Chappell Music

Big P Music (BMI)
c/o Richard Joseph
116 N. Robertson Blvd.
No. 705
Los Angeles, California 90048

Big Red Tractor Music (ASCAP)
1503 17th Ave. South
Nashville, Tennessee 37213

Big Scary Tree Publishing
Address Unavailable

Big Sky Music (ASCAP)
PO Box 860, Cooper Sta.
New York, New York 10276-0860

Benny Bird Co., Inc. (BMI)
P.O. Box 307
Camden, Maine 04843-0307

BKY Music (ASCAP)
see BMG Songs Inc.

Black Bull Music (ASCAP)
Attn: Stevland Morris
4616 Magnolia Blvd.
Burbank, California 91505

Black at Cha Publishing (ASCAP)
c/o Darin Jeffrey Black
1640 Sunset Ave., #1
West Covina, California 91790

Black Fountain Music (ASCAP)
see EMI Music Publishing

Black Hand Music (ASCAP)
see Universal-MCA Music Publishing

Black Ice Publishing (BMI)
c/o Lisa Thomas Music Services
22287 Mulholland Hwy., #417
Calabasa, California 91302

Black Lava (ASCAP)
see Universal-MCA Music Publishing

Black Panther Publishing (BMI)
see Famous Music Corp.

Blackened Music (BMI)
c/o Prager & Fenton
12424 Wilshire Blvd., Ste. 1000
Los Angeles, California 90025

Blanc E Music (BMI)
c/o Burt Goldstein
156 W. 56th St., Ste. 1803
New York, New York 10019

Mary J. Blige Music (ASCAP)
see Universal-MCA Music Publishing

Blind Sparrow Music (BMI)
7015 Boone Trail Circle
Brentwood, Tennessee 37027

Blizzard Music (BMI)
14 Wheeldon Lane
Palm Coast, Florida 32164

Blondie Rockwell Music (ASCAP)
see Universal-MCA Music Publishing

Blue Khakis Music (SESAC)
see Put It Down Music

Blue Mountain Music Ltd.
Address Unavailable

Blue Plate Music Publishing (BMI)
see Bug Music

Blue's Baby Music (ASCAP)
see Universal-MCA Music Publishing

BMG Music (ASCAP)
1540 Broadway
New York, New York 10036

BMG Music Publishing Ltd.
Address Unavailable

BMG Songs Inc. (ASCAP)
8750 Wilshire Blvd.
Beverly Hills, California 90211

Bocephus Music (BMI)
c/o Deon Burgess
P.O. Box 40929
Nashville, Tennessee 37204-0929

Bon Jovi Publishing (ASCAP)
see Universal-MCA Music Publishing

Boobie and DJ Songs (BMI)
see Warner-Chappell Music

Boomer X Publishing (ASCAP)
60 E. 42nd St., Suite 1064
New York, New York 10165

Rory Bourke Music (BMI)
212 Robin Hill Rd.
Nashville, Tennessee 37205

Nick Bracegirdle Publishing
Address Unavailable

Ji Branda Music Works (ASCAP)
see Wonderland Music

Braxtoni Music (BMI)
Address Unavailable

Breakthrough Creations (ASCAP)
see EMI Music Publishing

Bridgeport Music (BMI)
c/o Jane Peterer Music Co.
P.O. Box 1011
New York, New York 10268

Brill Building Songs (ASCAP)
see BMG Songs Inc.

Brother Jumbo Music (ASCAP)
see Warner-Chappell Music

Browder and Darnell Publishing (BMI)
c/o Raineyville Music
315 S. Beverly Dr., Ste. 206
Beverly Hills, California 90212-4310

Bruin Music Co. (BMI)
see Famous Music Corp.

Bubalas Publishing (SOCAN)
see BMG Music

Bubba Gee Music (BMI)
see Warner-Chappell Music

Bud Dog Music (ASCAP)
9320 Wilshire Blvd., #200
Beverly Hills, California 90212

Bug Music (BMI)
Bug Music Group
6777 Hollywood Blvd., 9th Fl.
Hollywood, California 90028

Bughouse (ASCAP)
see Bug Music

Built on Rock Music (ASCAP)
see Ensign Music

Buna Boy Music (BMI)
see Glitterfish

Burbank Plaza Music (ASCAP)
see EMI Music Publishing

Burning Music Ltd.
Address Unavailable

Gary Burr Music (BMI)
see Tree Publishing Co., Inc.

Bust a Nut in Your Eye Music (BMI)
8833 Sunset Blvd., Penthouse West
Los Angeles, California 90069

Butt Nugget and the Squirrels Music (BMI)
8833 Sunset Blvd., Penthouse West
Los Angeles, California 90069

Butter Jinx Music (BMI)
c/o Margo Matthews
P.O. Box 92004
Los Angeles, California 90009-2004

Buzz Cut Music (BMI)
c/o Richard C. Giles
1007 Deep Woods Trail
Brentwood, Tennessee 37027

C

C Town Music (BMI)
c/o Crosstown Records Inc.
2080 Bruns Lane
Cincinnati, Ohio 45244

Cal-Gene Music (BMI)
see EMI Music Publishing

Cal IV Entertainment Inc. (ASCAP)
c/o Daniel Hill
808 19th Ave. S.
Nashville, Tennessee 37203

Cal Rock Music (ASCAP)
see EMI Music Publishing

Caliber Music (ASCAP)
P.O. Box 58070
Nashville, Tennessee 37205

Cappagh Hill Music (BMI)
see Careers-BMG Music

Caraljo Music Inc. (BMI)
23 Park Timbers Drive
New Orleans, Louisiana 70131

Careers-BMG Music
8750 Wilshire Blvd.
Beverly Hills, California 90211

Joseph Cartegena Music (ASCAP)
see Jelly's Jams L.L.C. Music

Casadida Publishing
Address Unavailable

Johnny Carter Cash Music (ASCAP)
700 Johnny Cash Pkwy.
Hendersonville, Tennessee 37075

Buzz Cason Publications (ASCAP)
2804 Azalea Pl.
Nashville, Tennessee 37204

Celebrity Status Entertainment (BMI)
c/o Chaka Kimithi Blackmon
16661 Princeton
Detroit, Michigan 48221

Champion Music (BMI)
1755 Broadway 8th Fl.
New York, New York 10019

Champion Music UK
Address Unavailable

Chappell & Co., Inc. (ASCAP)
see Warner-Chappell Music

Chappell Music Publishers Ltd.
Address Unavailable

Chase Chad Music (ASCAP)
see EMI Music Publishing

Checkman Music (ASCAP)
see Warner-Chappell Music

Cherry Lane Music (ASCAP)
6 E. 32nd St., 11th Fl.
New York, New York 10016

Cherry River Music (BMI)
6 East 32nd St., 11th Floor
New York, New York 10016

Child Bride Music (SESAC)
c/o Harlan P. Howard
1902 Wedgewood Ave.
Nashville, Tennessee 37212-3733

Children of the Forest Music (BMI)
c/o Manatt et al.
11355 W. Olympic Blvd.
Los Angeles, California 90064

Choice Is Tragic Music (BMI)
see Famous Music Corp.

Chrysalis Music Group (ASCAP)
Attn: Jeff Brabec
8500 Melrose, 2nd Fl.
Los Angeles, California 90069

Chrysalis Songs (BMI)
see Chrysalis Music Group

Chuch Wagon Gourmet Music (ASCAP)
see Famous Music Corp.

Sonia Clarke Publishing
Address Unavailable

Coburn Music (BMI)
33 Music Square West
Suite 110
Nashville, Tennessee 37203

Colgems-EMI Music (ASCAP)
see EMI Music Publishing

Tom Collins Music Corp. (BMI)
Box 121407
Nashville, Tennessee 37212

Collipark (BMI)
c/o Michael A Crooms
135 Rockfort Ct.
College Park, Georgia 30349

Colpix Music (BMI)
P.O. Box 8500 (2320)
Philadelphia, Pennsylvania 19178

Janice Combs Music (ASCAP)
see EMI Music Publishing

Justin Combs Publishing (ASCAP)
see EMI Music Publishing

Common Green Music (BMI)
see Irving Music Inc.

Complete Music (England)
Address Unavailable

Connotation Music (BMI)
see Warner-Chappell Music

Conversation Tree Entertainment (ASCAP)
see Zomba Enterprises

Don Cook Music (BMI)
P.O. Box 1273
Nashville, Tennessee 37202

Cool Abdul Music (ASCAP)
see Zomba Enterprises

Jemma K. Cooper Music (ASCAP)
355 S. End Ave., #28G
New York, New York 10280

Coopick Music (ASCAP)
c/o Craig T. Cooper
P.O. Box 191009
Los Angeles, California 90019

Copyright Management Services (BMI)
1625 Broadway, 4th Floor
Nashville, Tennessee 37203

Corner of Clark and Kent (ASCAP)
see EMI Music Publishing

Cota Music (BMI)
see Warner-Chappell Music

Cotillion Music Inc. (BMI)
see Warner-Chappell Music

Covina High Music (BMI)
P.O. Box 4474
Palm Desert, California 92261-4474

Coyote House Music (ASCAP)
see Famous Music Corp.

Cradle the Balls Music (ASCAP)
3737 Evans St.
Los Angeles, California 90027

Crazytown Music (ASCAP)
c/o David Weise
16000 Ventura Blvd., #212
Encino, California 91436

Cream Teamsters (BMI)
c/o Kendall A. Minter
432 Park Ave. South
New York, New York 10016

Creeping Death Music (ASCAP)
c/o King, Purtich, Holmes et al.
1900 Avenue of the Stars
Suite 2500
Los Angeles, California 90067

Crisler Edizioni Musicali SR
Address Unavailable

Crited Music (BMI)
see Warner-Chappell Music

Crooked Chimney Music (BMI)
P.O. Box 147050
Gainesville, Florida 32614

Cross Keys Publishing (ASCAP)
attn: Donna Hilley
PO Box 1273
Nashville, Tennessee 37202

Crutchfield Music (BMI)
P.O. Box 50314
Nashville, Tennessee 37205

Cryn'er Way to the Bank Music (SESAC)
see Child Bride Music

Curb Magnasong Music Publishing (BMI)
Address Unavailable

Curb Songs
47 Music Square East
Nashville, Tennessee 37203

Cut Out Music (ASCAP)
PO Box 158206
Nashville, Tennessee 37215

Cutlass Music (BMI)
310 E. 102nd St., Apt. 6A
New York, New York 10029

Cuts R Us Songs (BMI)
c/o Anita Hogin
1105 16th Ave. South
Ste. C
Nashville, Tennessee 37212

Cyptron Music (BMI)
see EMI Music Publishing

D

Da Crippler Publishing (BMI)
Address Unavailable

Da Youngest and Da Crunkest (ASCAP)
see EMI Music Publishing

Daddy Rabbitt Music (ASCAP)
704 Huckleberry Trail
Nashville, Tennessee 37221

Dandy Warhol Music (BMI)
c/o Purtich Holmes et al
1900 Ave. of the Stars, Ste. 2500
Los Angeles, California 90067

Lashawn Daniels Productions (BMI)
see EMI Music Publishing

Dat Nigga Funky (ASCAP)
see Universal-MCA Music Publishing

Dead Game Publishing (ASCAP)
see Warner-Chappell Music

Demis Hot Songs (ASCAP)
see EMI Music Publishing

Demolition Man Music (BMI)
see Put It Down Music

Demon of Screamin Music (ASCAP)
see EMI Music Publishing

Demonoid Deluxe Music
Address Unavailable

Desmone Music (BMI)
c/o Jeff Smarr, Sony ATV Songs LLC
P.O. Box 1273
Nashville, Tennessee 37203

Desmophobia (ASCAP)
see Polygram Music Publishing Inc.

Diamond Rob Music (ASCAP)
see EMI Music Publishing

Diamond Storm Music (BMI)
c/o Mike Curb Music
47 Music Square East
Nashville, Tennessee 37203

Diana Music Corp. (BMI)
c/o NKS Management
10100 Santa Monica Blvd.
Suite 1300
Los Angeles, California 90067

Diggs Family Music (BMI)
99 University Pl., 9th Fl.
New York, New York 10003

Dinky B. Music (ASCAP)
see EMI Music Publishing

Walt Disney Music (ASCAP)
c/o Disney Music Publishing
500 S. Buena Vista St., MC 6174
Burbank, California 91521

Divided Music (BMI)
see Zomba Enterprises

Divine Mill Music (ASCAP)
see Warner-Chappell Music

Divine Pimp Music (ASCAP)
see BMG Music

DJ Irv (BMI)
see EMI Music Publishing

Donril Music (ASCAP)
see Zomba Enterprises

Doors Music Co. (ASCAP)
c/o Ruminating Music
23564 Calabasas Rd., #107
Calabasas, California 91302

Dove Daniels Music (BMI)
c/o The Royalty Network Inc.
246 Fifth Avenue
Suite 300
New York, New York 10001

Dow Tone Music (ASCAP)
see BMG Songs Inc.

Dowhatigotta Music
Address Unavailable

Dream Image IDG Publishing (BMI)
156 W. 56th St., 4th Fl.
New York, New York 10019

Dreamworks Songs (ASCAP)
see Cherry Lane Music

Druse Music Inc. (ASCAP)
c/o Codikow, Carroll, Guido, et al.
9113 Sunset Blvd.
Los Angeles, California 90068

Dub Notes (ASCAP)
see Warner-Chappell Music

Dungeon Rat Music (ASCAP)
see EMI Music Publishing

Dunson Twin Music (ASCAP)
c/o Sean Dunson
620 Symphony Pl.
Davenport, Florida 33837

Dystopia (SESAC)
see EMI Music Publishing

E

E D Duz It Music (BMI)
c/o Eric Dawkins
4560 Coldwater Cyn
Apt. 106
Studio City, California 91604

E One Music (BMI)
see EMI Music Publishing

E Two Music (ASCAP)
see EMI Music Publishing

E W C Publishing Co (BMI)
Address Unavailable

Early Morning Productions (ASCAP)
350 Davenport Rd.
Toronto, Ontario
Canada

Ecaf Music (BMI)
c/o Sony Songs, Inc.
P.O. Box 8500 (2320)
Philadelphia, Pennsylvania 19178

Eclectic Music Co. (BMI)
c/o Barry Kornfeld
190 Waverly Pl.
New York, New York 10014

Ecstasoul Music (ASCAP)
see Chrysalis Music Group

Eddie F. Music (ASCAP)
100 Piermont Rd.
Closter, New Jersey 07624

Edition Alex C Music (BMI)
Address Unavailable

Edition Kosmo
Address Unavailable

Edition Syndicate Songs
Address Unavailable

Eight Mile Style Music (BMI)
c/o Jeffrey Irwin Bass
1525 East Nine Mile Rd.
Ferndale, Michigan 48220

Eight/Twelve Music (BMI)
see Warner-Chappell Music

Ekop Publishing LLC (BMI)
550 Madison Avenue
New York, New York 10022

Ella and Gene's Son's Music (ASCAP)
c/o Toni L. Tolbert
PO Box 390703
Edina, Minnesota 55439

Jack D. Elliot Music (ASCAP)
355 S. End Ave., Apt. 16G
New York, New York 10280

Ellipsis Music (ASCAP)
c/o Julie Lipsius
9 Prospect Park West
Room 14B
Brooklyn, New York 11215

Elvis Mambo Music (ASCAP)
see Music of Windswept

Emerald Forest (ASCAP)
c/o Monileigh Music
374 Poli St., Ste. 203
Ventura, California 93001

EMI April Canada
Address Unavailable

EMI-April Music (ASCAP)
see EMI Music Publishing

EMI Blackwood Music Canada Ltd. (BMI)
Address Unavailable

EMI-Blackwood Music Inc. (BMI)
see EMI Music Publishing

EMI-Full Keel Music (ASCAP)
see EMI Music Publishing

EMI-Grove Park Music (BMI)
see EMI Music Publishing

EMI Music Publishing
810 Seventh Ave.
New York, New York 10019

EMI Music Publishing Ltd.
Address Unavailable

EMI Robbins Catalog Inc. (ASCAP)
see EMI Music Publishing

EMI Songs Ltd.
see EMI Music Publishing

EMI U Catalogue (ASCAP)
see EMI Music Publishing

EMI United Catalogue (BMI)
see EMI Music Publishing

EMI-Virgin Music (ASCAP)
see EMI Music Publishing

EMI Virgin Music Ltd. (BMI)
Address Unavailable

EMI-Virgin Songs (BMI)
see EMI Music Publishing

EMOA Music Publishing (ASCAP)
c/o Sony /ATV Discos Music Publishi
605 Lincoln Rd.
Miami Beach, Florida 33139

Encore Entertainment LLC (BMI)
121 17th Ave. South
Nashville, Tennessee 37203

Enot Publishing LLC (ASCAP)
see Sony ATV Tunes LLC

Ensign Music (BMI)
see Famous Music Corp.

EPHCY Music (ASCAP)
see Universal-MCA Music Publishing

Escatawpa Songs (BMI)
c/o Frascogna Courntey PLLC
P.O. Box 23126
Jackson, Mississippi 39225-3126

Essex Music International (ASCAP)
c/o The Richmond Organization
11 West 19th St.
New York, New York 10011

EV Music Publishing (BMI)
c/o Provident Financial Management
10345 W. Olympic Blvd., 2nd Fl.
Los Angeles, California 90064

Evadon Ltd.
Address Unavailable

Evergleam Music (BMI)
see Rondor Music

Everything I Love Music (BMI)
see Universal-MCA Music Publishing

Excellent Classical Songs (BMI)
see Roshashauna

Ez Elpee Music (BMI)
c/o Lamont J. Porter
825 Boyton Ave., Apt. 5B
Bronx, New York 10473

F

Fade 2 Black Music (ASCAP)
see Polygram Music Publishing Inc.

FAF Publishing (BMI)
c/o Jose Flores, Sonido Inc.
112 West 31st St.
4th Floor
New York, New York 10001-3402

Fake and Jaded Music (BMI)
see Southfield Road Music

Famous Music Corp. (ASCAP)
10635 Santa Monica Blvd.
Ste. 300
Los Angeles, California 90025

Fancy Footwork Music (ASCAP)
52 Meadow Ln.
Roslyn, New York 11577

Far Out Music (ASCAP)
7417 Sunset Blvd.
Hollywood, California 90046

Faust's Haus Music (BMI)
c/o King, Purtich, Holmes, et. al.
1900 Avenue of the Stars
Suite 2500
Los Angeles, California 90067

Fede Yon Music (BMI)
PO Box 8500
Philadelphia, Pennsylvania 19178-0002

Fiction Songs Ltd. (ASCAP)
see BMG Songs Inc.

Fifty-Seven Varieties Music (BMI)
c/o Tim Heintz
P.O. Box 6061-597
Sherman Oaks, California 91413

Fingaz Goal Music (ASCAP)
see EMI Music Publishing

Finger Lickin Good Music (ASCAP)
see Emerald Forest

Firm Body Music (BMI)
c/o Tenyor Music
246 Fifth Avenue
Suite 300
New York, New York 10001

First and Gold Publishing (BMI)
99 Miami Gardens Dr.
Suite 128
Miami, Florida 33169

Five Card Music (BMI)
see Music of Windswept

Five for Fighting Music (BMI)
see EMI Music Publishing

563 Music Publishing (ASCAP)
see Zomba Enterprises

Floyd's Dream Music (BMI)
4409 Park Ave.
Nashville, Tennessee 37209

Flybridge Tunes (BMI)
see EMI Music Publishing

Flying Earform Music (BMI)
8935 Lindblade St.
Culver City, California 90023

Flyte Tyme Tunes (ASCAP)
see EMI Music Publishing

Follazoo Crew Music (ASCAP)
see Encore Entertainment LLC

Foot in the Door (BMI)
230 Lexington Ave.
West Hempstead, New York 11552-1520

For My Son Publishing
Address Unavailable

Foray Music (SESAC)
see EMI Music Publishing

Foreign Imported Productions (BMI)
555 Jefferson Ave.
Miami, Florida 33139

420 Music (ASCAP)
c/o Michael Simpson
1801 Country Ln.
Pasadena, California 91107

4MW (ASCAP)
see Burbank Plaza Music

Fox Film Music Corp. (BMI)
c/o Twentieth Century Fox Film Corp
PO Box 900, Bldg. 18
Beverly Hills, California 90213

Fox Tunes (SESAC)
see Fox Film Music Corp.

Foxy Dead Girl Music (ASCAP)
see EMI Music Publishing

Fozman Music LLC
Address Unavailable

Len Freedman Music
719 Lilac Drive
Santa Barbara, California 93108

Freejunket Music (ASCAP)
c/o Salter St. Music
719 Lilac Drive
Santa Barbara, California 93108

Dwight Frye Music (BMI)
72 Madison Ave., 8th Floor
New York, New York 10016

Full of Soul Music (BMI)
see EMI Music Publishing

Fun with Goats Music (ASCAP)
see EMI Music Publishing

Funk So Righteous Music (BMI)
2355 NW 89th St.
Miami, Florida 33147

Funky Noble Productions (ASCAP)
see Famous Music Corp.

G

Gaje Music (BMI)
Address Unavailable

Gang Music Ltd.
Address Unavailable

Gangsta Boogie Music (ASCAP)
see Warner-Chappell Music

GC Publishing
Address Unavailable

Gee Jaz Music (BMI)
c/o Eugene A. Peoples
P.O Box 100175
Brooklyn, New York 11210-0175

Gee Street Sounds (ASCAP)
see BMG Songs Inc.

Geomantic Music (BMI)
Address Unavailable

Get the Bo (ASCAP)
see EMI Music Publishing

Ghetto and Blues (ASCAP)
see EMI Music Publishing

Ghetto Fabulous Entertainment (ASCAP)
c/o Ivan Matias
105-84 Flatlands
10th St.
Brooklyn, New York 11236

Gibbon Music Publishing
Address Unavailable

Gifted Pearl (ASCAP)
see EMI Music Publishing

Gimme Back My Publishing (ASCAP)
see Bug Music

Glitterfish (BMI)
P.O. Box 50314
Nashville, Tennessee 37205

Gnat Booty Music (ASCAP)
see Chrysalis Music Group

Go to Del Music (ASCAP)
see Volunteer Jam Music

Goathead Music (ASCAP)
see Zomba Enterprises

Godchildren Music (BMI)
see EMI Music Publishing

Golddaddy Music (ASCAP)
see EMI Music Publishing

Golden Wheat Music (BMI)
see Warner-Chappell Music

Gone Gator Music (ASCAP)
c/o Wixen Music Publishing
23564 Calabasas Rd., #10
Calabasas, California 91302

Grand Master Chimp and Da Cronies Music (BMI)
8833 Sunset Blvd., Penthouse West
Los Angeles, California 90069

Grantsville Publishing (ASCAP)
see Zomba Enterprises

Green Daze Music (ASCAP)
1100 Third St.
San Rafael, California 94901

Greenfund (ASCAP)
see Warner-Chappell Music

Grindtime Publishing (BMI)
c/o Myron L. Avant
8015 South Yates
Chicago, Illinois 60617

Group Productions
Address Unavailable

Grunge Girl Music (ASCAP)
see EMI Music Publishing

Gumbo Woman Music (BMI)
711 W. Avery St.
Pensacola, Florida 32501

Gyz Muzik (ASCAP)
see EMI Music Publishing

H

Merle Haggard Music (BMI)
Address Unavailable

Hale Yeah Music (BMI)
see EMI Music Publishing

Hamstein Cumberland Music (BMI)
see Hamstein Music Co.

Hamstein Music Co. (BMI)
Box 163870
Austin, Texas 78716

Happenstance Music
Address Unavailable

Happy Mel Boopy's Cocktail Lounge (BMI)
see Zomba Enterprises

Happy Valley Music (BMI)
1 Camp St.
Cambridge, Massachusetts 02140

Ron Harbin Music (ASCAP)
c/o Ron Harbin Sr.
118 16th Ave. S., Ste. 215
Nashville, Tennessee 37203

Hard Working Black Folks (ASCAP)
see Warner-Chappell Music

Hay Wagon Music (ASCAP)
see Big Red Tractor Music

Hazel Songs (ASCAP)
see Warner-Chappell Music

Heavy Harmony Music (ASCAP)
6433 Topanga Canyon Blvd.
Suite 445
Canoga Park, California 91303

Hempstead Live (ASCAP)
see EMI Music Publishing

Henchi Music (SESAC)
see EMI Music Publishing

Hennesy for Everyone (BMI)
15250 Ventura Blvd., Ste. 900
Sherman Oaks, California 91403

Herbalicious Music (ASCAP)
see EMI Music Publishing

Hey Rudy Music Publishing (BMI)
see Universal-MCA Music Publishing

Hidden Kuu Music (SESAC)
Address Unavailable

Hidden Pun Music (BMI)
see EMI Music Publishing

Hierophany Music (ASCAP)
c/o Oliver Ray
45 MacDougal St.
New York, New York 10012

Hit Boy Music (BMI)
Address Unavailable

Hit & Run Music (ASCAP)
1841 Broadway, Ste. 411
New York, New York 10023

Hitco Music (BMI)
see Warner-Chappell Music

Hitco South (ASCAP)
see Windswept Pacific Entertainment

Hits from Da Bong Music (ASCAP)
c/o Curtis Management
417 Denny Way, 2nd Fl.
Seattle, Washington 98109

Hope Chest Music (BMI)
see Universal-MCA Music Publishing

Hot Cha Music (BMI)
c/o Gelfard, Rennert & Feldman
1301 Avenue of the Americas
10th Floor
New York, New York 10019

Hot as Fire (ASCAP)
c/o James Travis III
811 N. Linwood Ave.
Baltimore, Maryland 21205

House of Fame (ASCAP)
PO Box 2527
Muscle Shoals, Alabama 35662

Melanie Howard Music (ASCAP)
1902 Wedgewood Ave.
Nashville, Tennessee 37212

Howie Tee Music (BMI)
see Irving Music Inc.

Howlin' Hits Music (ASCAP)
PO Box 163870
Austin, Texas 78716

Human Boy Music (ASCAP)
see Warner-Chappell Music

Hunglikeyora (ASCAP)
see EMI Music Publishing

Huss-Zwingli Publishing (ASCAP)
see Sony ATV Tunes LLC

I

Enrique Iglesia Music (ASCAP)
see EMI Music Publishing

Ignorant (ASCAP)
see Almo/Irving

Ill Kid Music (ASCAP)
c/o Lodinguer, Erk & Chanzis
15 East 26th St, Suite 1803
New York, New York 10010

Ill Will (ASCAP)
see Zomba Enterprises

I'm Nobody Music (ASCAP)
see Warner-Chappell Music

Imposto (SESAC)
see EMI Music Publishing

In My Dreams (ASCAP)
5750 Wilshire Blvd., #590
Los Angeles, California 90036

Innocent Criminal (ASCAP)
see EMI Music Publishing

Interior Music (BMI)
c/o Margo Matthews
5750 Wilshire Blvd., Suite 565W
Los Angeles, California 90036

Irving Music Inc. (BMI)
2440 Sepulveda Blvd., Suite 119
Los Angeles, California 90064

Irving Music Inc.-East Memphis (BMI)
see Irving Music Inc.

Island Music (BMI)
6525 Sunset Blvd.
Los Angeles, California 90028

It's Tea Time (ASCAP)
see EMI Music Publishing

J

J Rhone Music (BMI)
3346 Altura Ave.
La Cresenta, California 91214

Jackelope Publishing (BMI)
c/o Jacques Levy
P.O. Box 252
Hamilton, New York 13346-1311

Jackie Frost Music
Address Unavailable

Jae'wans Music (BMI)
see EMI Music Publishing

Jagermaestro (ASCAP)
see EMI Music Publishing

Jahque Joints (SESAC)
see Universal-MCA Music Publishing

Jam N' Bread Music (ASCAP)
see Heavy Harmony Music

Jam Yo Music (BMI)
c/o Yolanda Adams
10402 Reading Rd.
Richmond, Texas 77469

Jat Cat Music Publishing (ASCAP)
see Universal-MCA Music Publishing

Jay E's Basement (ASCAP)
see Universal-MCA Music Publishing

Jazz Merchant Music (ASCAP)
see Zomba Enterprises

Jelly's Jams L.L.C. Music (ASCAP)
235 Park Avenue South
10th Floor
New York, New York 10003

Rodney Jerkins Music (BMI)
see EMI Music Publishing

Fred Jerkins Publishing (BMI)
see Famous Music Corp.

Jermaine Music
Address Unavailable

Jezebel Blues Music (BMI)
Address Unavailable

Jinsoo Lim Music (ASCAP)
see Wixen Music

Jo Skin Music (ASCAP)
see Zomba Enterprises

Jobete Music Co. (ASCAP)
see EMI Music Publishing

Johnny Handsome Music (BMI)
250 W. 57th St., Ste. 1517-18
New York, New York 10019

Jones Music America (ASCAP)
c/o Dorothy Mae Rice Jones
416 W. 9th St., No. 1312
Cincinnati, Ohio 45203

Hudson Jordan Music (ASCAP)
6047 Tampa Ave., Suite 302
Tarzana, California 91356

Montel Jordan Music (ASCAP)
see Famous Music Corp.

Steven A. Jordan Music (ASCAP)
see Warner-Chappell Music

Joshua's Dream Music (BMI)
see Warner-Chappell Music

Juicy Time (ASCAP)
see EMI Music Publishing

JuJu Rhythms (ASCAP)
see EMI Music Publishing

Jungle Brothers Music
Address Unavailable

Jungle Fever Music
Address Unavailable

K

K Money Music (ASCAP)
c/o Marquis T. Collins
3823 Elmley Ave.
Baltimore, Maryland 21213

Kamakaze Zero Music (BMI)
8833 Sunset Blvd., Penthouse West
Los Angeles, California 90069

Kandacy Music (ASCAP)
see EMI Music Publishing

Karima Music (BMI)
127 West 141st St., No. 36
New York, New York 10030

KDH Publishing (SESAC)
Address Unavailable

Kelendria Music (ASCAP)
see Sony ATV Tunes LLC

R. Kelly Music (BMI)
see Zomba Enterprises

Kevin Hicks Music (BMI)
5290 Carrick Rd.
Cocoa, Florida 32927

Kierulf (BMI)
see Zomba Enterprises

Kilosheem Publishing (ASCAP)
c/o Rasheem Pugh
639 W. Christopher St., Apt. 2B
Orange, New Jersey 07050

King Nummy Publishing (BMI)
c/o Provident Financial Management
2020 Union St.
San Francisco, California 94123

Stephen A. Kipner Music (ASCAP)
Attn: Stephen A. Kipner
19646 Valley View Dr.
Topanga, California 90290

Kodeko Music (ASCAP)
c/o Tena Clark
35 W. Dayton St.
Pasadena, California 91105

Kohaw Music (ASCAP)
see Bicycle Music

Kreditkard Music (ASCAP)
c/o Cal IV Entertainment Inc.
808 19th Ave. S.
Nashville, Tennessee 37203

L

Lakshmi Puja Music (ASCAP)
see The Songwriters Guild

Larsiny (ASCAP)
c/o Barry Reese
7835 Provident St.
Philadelphia, Pennsylvania 19150

Lastrada Music (ASCAP)
1344 Broadway, Suite 208
Hewlett, New York 11557

Latavia Music Publishing (ASCAP)
see Sony ATV Tunes LLC

Leaving Hope Music (ASCAP)
20325 Center Ridge Rd.
Penthouse
Cleveland, Ohio 44116

Lehsem Songs (BMI)
see EMI Music Publishing

Less Than Zero (BMI)
see Southfield Road Music

Let Me Show You Music (ASCAP)
235 Park Ave. South, 10th Floor
New York, New York 10003

Lethal Dose Music (BMI)
Address Unavailable

Letoya Music Publishing (ASCAP)
see Sony ATV Tunes LLC

LFS III Music (ASCAP)
c/o Spectrum VII Music
9044 Melrose Ave., Ste. 200
Los Angeles, California 90069

Lil Lu Lu Publishing (BMI)
see EMI Music Publishing

Lil Mob Publishing (ASCAP)
see EMI Music Publishing

Lil Rob Entertainment (BMI)
c/o Robin Andre Mays
141-25 182nd St.
Springfields, New York 11413

Lion Hearted Music (ASCAP)
35 Music Sq. East
Nashville, Tennessee 37215

Lissome Songs (ASCAP)
c/o John Cvoizer
5152 Xevxes Ave. S.
Minneapolis, Minnesota 55410

Little Big Town Music (BMI)
see MCA Music Publishing

Little Cricket Music (ASCAP)
see EMI Music Publishing

Little Diva Music (BMI)
see Heavy Harmony Music

Little Shop of Morgansongs (BMI)
1800 Grand Ave.
Nashville, Tennessee 37212-2118

Living Under a Rock Music (ASCAP)
see Universal-MCA Music Publishing

Livingsting Music (ASCAP)
see Malaco Music Co.

Llerol Music (ASCAP)
see Universal-MCA Music Publishing

Lonesome Dove Music (BMI)
c/o Carl Eugene Jackson
1720 Hickory Trace Dr.
Gallatin, Tennessee 37066-5801

Loot on Loose Leaf Music (ASCAP)
c/o Brian Anthony Bailey
1206 S. Bronson, #1
Los Angeles, California 90019

Lopsided (SESAC)
see EMI Music Publishing

Love Monkey Music (BMI)
c/o Robert J. DiPiero
803 18th Ave. South
Nashville, Tennessee 37203

Low Crawl Music (ASCAP)
see Universal-MCA Music Publishing

LT Music Publishing (BMI)
see Warner-Chappell Music

Ludacris Music (ASCAP)
see EMI Music Publishing

M

Ma Ma Bev's Music (BMI)
Address Unavailable

Mad Dog Winston Music (BMI)
see Warner-Chappell Music

Magnasong (ASCAP)
see Tom Collins Music Corp.

Magnetic Music Publishing Co. (ASCAP)
5 Jones St., Apt. 4
New York, New York 10014

Magnolia Hill Music (BMI)
Box 50
Nashville, Tennessee 37202

Major Bob Music (ASCAP)
1111 17th Ave. S
Nashville, Tennessee 37212

Make Shift Music (BMI)
c/o Anita Hogin
1105 16th Avenue South
Suite C
Nashville, Tennessee 37212

Malaco Music Co. (BMI)
PO Box 9287
Jackson, Mississippi 39286-9287

Malloy's Toys Music (BMI)
c/o Starstruck Angel Music, Inc.
40 Music Square West
Nashville, Tennessee 37203

A. Maman Music
Address Unavailable

Aimee Mann
c/o Provident Financial Mgmt.
268 Newberry St., 4th Floor
Boston, Massachusetts 02116

Manuiti LA Music (ASCAP)
c/o Haber Corp.
16830 Ventura Blvd., Suite 501
Encino, California 91436

Marc 'n Tha Dark Music (BMI)
c/o Marc D'Andrea
836 East Vine Ave.
West Covina, California 91790

Marketwright Music (BMI)
see Universal-MCA Music Publishing

Marsky Music
Address Unavailable

Adam Martin Music (BMI)
see EMI Music Publishing

Mascan Music (ASCAP)
see Warner-Chappell Music

Mass Confusion Productions (ASCAP)
see Warner-Chappell Music

Mat Music
Address Unavailable

Matanzas Music (ASCAP)
c/o Stan Lynch
1093 A1A Beach Blvd., PMB 347
St. Augustine, Florida 32080

MCA Music Canada
Address Unavailable

MCA Music Publishing (ASCAP)
see Universal-MCA Music Publishing

McHuge Music (BMI)
c/o Thomas E. McHugh
163 Clarendon Circle
Franklin, Tennessee 37069

Mcud Music (ASCAP)
see Zomba Enterprises

Meeengya Music (ASCAP)
see Universal-MCA Music Publishing

Megasong Publishing
see BMG Music

Mel Boopie Music (BMI)
c/o King et al.
1900 Avenue of the Stars
25th Floor
Los Angeles, California 90067

Merokee Music (ASCAP)
Address Unavailable

Mewtwo Music (ASCAP)
see Cherry Lane Music

Jessica Michael Music (ASCAP)
see Warner-Chappell Music

Mick Dog (ASCAP)
see Universal-MCA Music Publishing

Mick Hits Music (ASCAP)
c/o Michael Wayne Hiter
PO Box 110375
Nashville, Tennessee 37222

Mighty Moe Music (ASCAP)
c/o Jerome Earnest
PO Box 26158
Austin, Texas 78755

Mighty Nice Music (BMI)
see Universal-MCA Music Publishing

Mijac Music (BMI)
see Warner-Chappell Music

Mike City Music (BMI)
c/o Michael C. Flowers
51 Gardenbrook Lane
Willingboro, New Jersey 08046

Mike Curb Music (BMI)
c/o Brad Kennard
47 Music Square East
Nashville, Tennessee 37203

Milene Music (ASCAP)
c/o Opryland Music Group
P.O. Box 128469
Nashville, Tennessee 37212

Minneapolis Guys Music (ASCAP)
see EMI Music Publishing

Miss Bessie Music (ASCAP)
c/o Provident Financial Mgmt.
10345 Olympic Blvd.
Los Angeles, California 90064

MJ Twelve Music (BMI)
see EMI Music Publishing

Mo Better Grooves Music (ASCAP)
see Famous Music Corp.

Mo Lovin' Music
Address Unavailable

Moebetoblame Music (BMI)
c/o Myman et al.
11777 San Vicente, Suite 880
Los Angeles, California 90049

Mondeenise Productions
Address Unavailable

Money Mack Music (BMI)
Address Unavailable

Charlie Monk Music (ASCAP)
3001 Hobbs Rd.
Nashville, Tennessee 37215

Montalupis Music (BMI)
see Irving Music Inc.

Montauk Mantis Production (BMI)
see EMI Music Publishing

Rufus T. Moore (SESAC)
Address Unavailable

Moose Music Ltd. (SOCAN)
see Early Morning Productions

Mother Culture Publishing (ASCAP)
see Warner-Chappell Music

Ms. Mary's Music (BMI)
see Warner-Chappell Music

Ms Trina Music Publishing (BMI)
c/o Katrina Taylor
99 Miami Gardens Dr.
Ste. 128
Miami, Florida 33169

Mugsy Boy Publishing (BMI)
c/o Joshua Michael Schwartz
14 Tuscany Drive
Jackson, New Jersey 08527

Mumblety Peg (BMI)
see BMG Music

Murlyn Songs (ASCAP)
see Chrysalis Music Group

Music Hill Music (BMI)
see Careers-BMG Music

Music of Windswept (ASCAP)
see Warner-Chappell Music

Mustaine Music (BMI)
see EMI Music Publishing

Muy Bueno Music (BMI)
1000 18th St., S.
Nashville, Tennessee 37212

My Blue Car Music (ASCAP)
see Warner-Chappell Music

My Life's Work Music (BMI)
see Windswept Pacific Entertainment

My Own Chit Publishing (BMI)
see EMI Music Publishing

My Rib Is Broke (ASCAP)
see Warner-Chappell Music

N

N-The Water Publishing (ASCAP)
P.O. Box 924190
Houston, Texas 77292

Naked Under My Clothes Music (ASCAP)
see Chrysalis Music Group

Nate Dogg Music (BMI)
see Sony ATV Music

Nature's Finest Music (BMI)
Address Unavailable

Nelstar Publishing (SOCAN)
Address Unavailable

New Columbia Pictures Music (ASCAP)
see Sony ATV Tunes LLC

New Enterprises Music (BMI)
see Fox Film Music Corp.

New Haven Music (BMI)
see PolyGram Records Inc.

New Monarchy Music (SESAC)
see Fox Film Music Corp.

New Regency Music (ASCAP)
see TCF

Randy Newman Music (ASCAP)
c/o Gelfand, Rennert & Feldman
1880 Century Park, E., Ste. 1600
Los Angeles, California 90067

Gary Nicholson Music (ASCAP)
see Sony ATV Tunes LLC

Nick 'n Ash Music (BMI)
c/o Paul N. Worley
P.O. Box 22359
Nashville, Tennessee 37202

Glen Nikki Music (ASCAP)
see Starstruck Writers Group

Nik's Place Publishing (ASCAP)
c/o Philip Douglas
PO Box 20404
1134 Roselawn Way
Bowling Green, Kentucky 42102

Nine Street Songs
Address Unavailable

19 Music
Address Unavailable

98 Degrees and Rising (ASCAP)
see EMI Music Publishing

Ninth Street Tunnel Music (BMI)
c/o Sony/ATV Songs
P.O. Box 1273
Nashville, Tennessee 37202

NNC Publishing (ASCAP)
see Warner-Chappell Music

No Fences Music (ASCAP)
c/o O'Neil, Hagamon & Co.
1025 16th Ave. South, #202
Nashville, Tennessee 37212

No Gravity Music (ASCAP)
see EMI Music Publishing

No Hassle (ASCAP)
c/o Mayer Nussbaum Katz & Baker
75 Rockefeller Plaza
New York, New York 10019

Charlie Noble Music (ASCAP)
1770 Century Blvd. NE, B
Atlanta, Georgia 30345

Noontime South (SESAC)
see Warner-Chappell Music

Noontime Tunes (ASCAP)
see Chrysalis Music Group

Notes to Music (ASCAP)
see Warner-Chappell Music

Nothing But the Wolf Music (BMI)
7587 River Rd.
Nashville, Tennessee 37209

Notorious Kim Music (BMI)
Queen Bee Entertainment, Inc.
23 Old Quarry Rd.
Englewood, New Jersey 07631

Nuevo Dia Publishing (BMI)
see Songs of Windswept Pacific

Nuyorican Publishing (BMI)
c/o Rigney Friedman Business Mgmt.
1200 Wilshire Blvd., No. 850
Los Angeles, California 90025

Nyrraw Music (ASCAP)
see EMI Music Publishing

O

O' Brook Music (BMI)
c/o Gelfand, Rennart & Feldman
1880 Century Park East
Suite 1600
Los Angeles, California 90067

O Tex Music (BMI)
1000 18th Ave. SO
Nashville, Tennessee 37212

October Eighth Music (SESAC)
see Warner-Chappell Music

Oh My God Music (ASCAP)
see Universal-MCA Music Publishing

On Board Music (BMI)
1007 Montana Ave., Suite 341
Santa Monica, California 90403

One Ol' Ghetto Hoe Music (ASCAP)
see Warner-Chappell Music

1802 Music Publishing (ASCAP)
1802 Palisade Ave.
Teaneck, New Jersey 07666

1972 Music (SESAC)
see EMI Music Publishing

Ooky Spinalton Music (ASCAP)
see EMI Music Publishing

James Osterberg Music (BMI)
see Bug Music

P

Painkiller Publishing (BMI)
c/o Scott D. Sanders
740 Sidney Marcus Blvd.
Apt. 5202
Atlanta, Georgia 30324

Pathetic Hindsight Music (BMI)
see Bug Music

Shawn Patrick Publishing (BMI)
see Famous Music Corp.

Pearl White Music (BMI)
see EMI Music Publishing

Peermusic III LTD (BMI)
5358 Melrose Blvd.
Suite 400
Los Angeles, California 90038

Peermusic Ltd. (BMI)
c/o APRS Peer International
5358 Melrose Blvd., Suite 400
Los Angeles, California 90038

Peertunes LTD (SESAC)
see EMI Music Publishing

Pener Pig Publishing (BMI)
see Universal-MCA Music Publishing

Penn State Urban Legends Music (BMI)
Address Unavailable

Penny Annie Music (BMI)
1400 South Street
Nashville, Tennessee 37212

Pentagon Lipservices Two PSW Music (BMI)
see Pentagon Music Co.

Pentagon Music Co. (BMI)
c/o Lipservices
9 Prospect Park West, #14B
Brooklyn, New York 11215

Perk's Music, Inc. (BMI)
see Universal-MCA Music Publishing

Perren Vibes Music, Inc. (ASCAP)
Attn: Christine Perren
4028 Colfax Ave.
Studio City, California 91604

Pez (BMI)
9 Dolly Corn Ln.
Old Brookeville, New York 11545

A Phantom Vox Music (BMI)
c/o Anthony, Peyrot, Tanner et al.
10866 Wilshire Blvd., 10th Floor
Los Angeles, California 90024

Philmore Publishing (ASCAP)
c/o Philmore Fleming
PO Box 42583
Portland, Oregon 97242

Phreakas Ada Phunk (ASCAP)
8125 Acacia Cir.
Cypress, California 90630

Harve Pierre Publishing (BMI)
143-55 228th St.
Laurelton, New York 11413

Pimp My Pen International
Address Unavailable

Pimp Yug (ASCAP)
see Warner-Chappell Music

Pink Panther Music (ASCAP)
see EMI Music Publishing

Pixar Talking Pictures (ASCAP)
c/o Robert Taylor
1011 W. Cutting Blvd.
Richmond, California 94804

Plagiarism Publishing (BMI)
8833 Sunset Blvd., Penthouse West
Los Angeles, California 90069

Platinum Firm Music (ASCAP)
see Zomba Enterprises

Platinum Plow (ASCAP)
see Warner-Chappell Music

Po Ho Productions (ASCAP)
see Universal-MCA Music Publishing

Pokey Dog Music (BMI)
Address Unavailable

Polygram International Music (ASCAP)
see Universal-MCA Music Publishing

Polygram International Music B.V.
Address Unavailable

Polygram Music Publishing Inc. (ASCAP)
see Universal-MCA Music Publishing

PolyGram Records Inc. (ASCAP)
see Universal-MCA Music Publishing

Poodlebone Music
Address Unavailable

Post Oak Publishing (BMI)
c/o Friedman and LaRosa
747 3rd Ave.
New York, New York 10017

Pretty Blue Songs (BMI)
7424 George Gaines Rd.
Nashville, Tennessee 37221

PRI Music (ASCAP)
see Polygram Music Publishing Inc.

Price is Right Music (ASCAP)
see MCA Music Publishing

Prinse Pawl Musick (BMI)
see Tommy Boy Music

Proceed Music (BMI)
652 Valley Rd.
Upper Montclair, New Jersey 07043

Promuse (BMI)
see Protoons Inc.

Protoons Inc. (ASCAP)
c/o Profile Records Inc.
740 Broadway, 7th Floor
New York, New York 10003

Psychopathic Music Publishing (BMI)
Address Unavailable

Pugwash Music (BMI)
c/o Tom Long, Creative Director
Balmur Entertainment, Inc.
1105 17th Ave. South
Nashville, Tennessee 37212

Pulling Teeth Music (BMI)
c/o Kathryn D. Lang
P.O. Box 790
Victoria, British Columbia V8W 2R7
Canada

Put It Down Music (SESAC)
11684 Ventura Blvd., Ste. 286
Studio City, California 91604

Q

Queen Isabella's Subjects (ASCAP)
see Bug Music

R

Radio Legs Music (BMI)
c/o Mark Helias
PO Box 20364, Tompkins Sq. Sta.
New York, New York 10009

Rainyville Music (BMI)
see Island Music

Ramecca Publishing (BMI)
see BMG Music

Ram's Horn Music Co., Inc. (ASCAP)
see Big Sky Music

Ranger Bob Music (ASCAP)
see Polygram Music Publishing Inc.

Rats God Music (BMI)
see Bug Music

Reach Music International (ASCAP)
217 E. 86th St., Ste. 117
New York, New York 10028

Real an Ruff Muzik (ASCAP)
see Warner-Chappell Music

Realsongs (ASCAP)
Attn: Diane Warren
6363 Sunset Blvd., Ste. 810
Hollywood, California 90028

Recombinant Music (BMI)
Address Unavailable

Red Brazos (BMI)
Box 163870
Austin, Texas 78716

Lou Reed Music (BMI)
c/o Sister Ray Enterprises
584 Broadway, Suite 609
New York, New York 10012

Retribution Music (BMI)
P.O. Box 8500 (2320)
Philadelphia, Pennsylvania 19178

Rex Benson Music (BMI)
see Copyright Management Services

Taylor Rhodes Music (ASCAP)
210 Lauderdale Rd.
Nashville, Tennessee 37205

Riddum Music (BMI)
c/o Jeff Smarr
PO Box 1273
Nashville, Tennessee 37202

Right Bank Music (ASCAP)
c/o Haber Corp.
16830 Ventura Blvd., Suite 501
Encino, California 91436

Rising Gorge Music (BMI)
see EMI Music Publishing

Roastitoasti Music (ASCAP)
see Wixen Music

Bobby Robinson Sweet Soul Music (BMI)
c/o Spirit One Music
137 5th Ave.
New York, New York 10010

Rock Willows Music (BMI)
Address Unavailable

Rokstone Music
Address Unavailable

Rondor Music (ASCAP)
see Almo Music Corp.

Roshashauna (BMI)
533 Madison St., Apt. 3C
Hoboken, New Jersey 07030-1707

J & J Ross Co. (ASCAP)
see The Songwriters Guild

Ruff Ryders Entertainment (ASCAP)
312 West 53rd St., Suite 208
New York, New York 10019

Rusty Knuckles Music (BMI)
see Warner-Chappell Music

Rutland Road (ASCAP)
c/o Haber Corp.
16830 Ventura Blvd., Suite 501
Encino, California 91436

Connor Ryan Music (BMI)
see Universal-MCA Music Publishing

Rye Songs (BMI)
P.O. Box 8500 (2320)
Philadelphia, Pennsylvania 19178

S

Sailandra Publishing (ASCAP)
see Universal-MCA Music Publishing

St. Nathanson Music (ASCAP)
1500 Ocean Pkwy., Apt. 4G
Brooklyn, New York 11230

St. Swithin's Songs (BMI)
c/o Serling, Rooks & Ferrara
254 West 54th St.
14th Floor
New York, New York 10019

Saja Music Co. (BMI)
see Lastrada Music

Sarangel Music (ASCAP)
c/o Sussman and Associates
1222 16th Ave. S., 3rd Fl.
Nashville, Tennessee 37212

Scantz Music (SESAC)
c/o Mr. Darnley Scantlebury
BDB Management
Studio City, California 91604-0000

Scorpiorock Tunes (ASCAP)
see Warner-Chappell Music

Harvey Scott Music
Address Unavailable

Scott & Soda (ASCAP)
see Encore Entertainment LLC

Scrapin' Toast Music (ASCAP)
see Bug Music

Screen Gems-EMI Music Inc. (BMI)
see EMI Music Publishing

Scribing C-Ment Songs (ASCAP)
c/o W C, PS
13343 Bellevue-Redmond Rd.
Suite 201
Bellevue, Washington 98005

Sea Gayle Music (ASCAP)
see EMI Music Publishing

Second Decade Music (BMI)
c/o Kool World Ltd.
43 Enfield Ave.
Montclair, New Jersey 07042

Second Generation Rooney Tunes (BMI)
c/o Spivak et al.
1010 Northern Blvd., Suite 304
Great Neck, New York 11021-5306

Sell the Cow Music (BMI)
see Warner-Chappell Music

Senseless Music (BMI)
see Universal-MCA Music Publishing

September Six Music
Address Unavailable

Erick Sermon Enterprises (ASCAP)
see Zomba Enterprises

Seven Angels Music (BMI)
see Sony ATV Tree Publishing

703 Music (ASCAP)
see EMI Music Publishing

Sexy Grandpa Music (ASCAP)
see Rondor Music

Shae Shae Music (ASCAP)
c/o Shae V. Jones
9211 N. Tryon St., #4-170
Charlotte, North Carolina 28262

Shakin Baker Music, Inc. (BMI)
c/o Howard Comart, C.P.A.
1775 Broadway, Rm. 532
New York, New York 10019

Shakur al Din Music (ASCAP)
see Windswept Pacific Entertainment

Shame on You (ASCAP)
c/o Shawn Albro
1156 Beachwood Dr.
Hollywood, California 90038

Dan Shea Music (BMI)
Address Unavailable

Shek' Em Down Music (BMI)
see Windswept Pacific Entertainment

Shellayla Songs (BMI)
Address Unavailable

Shep and Shep Publishing (ASCAP)
see Famous Music Corp.

Shoecrazy Publishing (SESAC)
c/o Integreated Copyright Group
P.O. Box 24149
Nashville, Tennessee 37202-4149

Shokorama Music (ASCAP)
see Bug Music

Showbilly Music (BMI)
P.O. Box 1273
Nashville, Tennessee 37202

Silktone Songs (ASCAP)
3250 Oregon Trail
Olympia Fields, Illinois 60461

Silliwak (ASCAP)
see EMI Music Publishing

Silly Bo Music (BMI)
2605 Nightingale
Memphis, Tennessee 38127

Silver Fiddle Music (ASCAP)
c/o Segel & Goldman Inc.
9200 Sunset Blvd., Ste. 1000
Los Angeles, California 90069

Silverkiss Music (BMI)
see Careers-BMG Music

Paul Simon Music (BMI)
1619 Broadway, Suite 500
New York, New York 10019-7412

Sin Drome Music (BMI)
c/o Henry Marx
18344 Oxnard St., Suite 101
Tarzana, California 91356

Single's Only Music (BMI)
c/0 Cliftee Dr.
Brentwood, Tennessee 37027

Sixty Four Square Music
Address Unavailable

Siyeeda's Publishing (ASCAP)
c/o Jimmy Cozier Jr.
84 Sterling Street
Brooklyn, New York 11225

SKG Music Publishing LLC (ASCAP)
see Cherry Lane Music

Slam U Well Music (ASCAP)
c/o Track Masters Entertainment
555 Madison Ave., 3rd Floor
New York, New York 10022

Slea Head Music (ASCAP)
see Bug Music

SLL Music (ASCAP)
see Copyright Management Services

Smash Mouth Music
Address Unavailable

Smitty's Son (BMI)
c/o Sony Songs Inc.
P.O. Box 8500 (2320)
Philadelphia, Pennsylvania 19178-0002

SMY Music (ASCAP)
see Sony ATV Tunes LLC

Sneaky Snake Music (BMI)
c/o The Law Offices of Gary S. Wish
9200 Sunset Blvd., Ste. 505
Los Angeles, California 90069

Snook Life (SESAC)
c/o Mr. Jovonn Alexander
191 West Sneden Place
Spring Valley, New York 10977-3971

So So Def Music (ASCAP)
see EMI Music Publishing

Soda Creek Songs (ASCAP)
see Universal-MCA Music Publishing

SODRAC
Address Unavailable

Solomon's Works Music
Address Unavailable

Sondance Kid Music (ASCAP)
see Universal-MCA Music Publishing

Song Matters Music (ASCAP)
see Ensign Music

Songs of Dreamworks (BMI)
see Cherry River Music

Songs of Hamstein Cumberland (ASCAP)
PO Box 160870
Austin, Texas 78716

Songs of Lastrada (BMI)
see Lastrada Music

Songs of Nashville Dreamworks (BMI)
see Cherry River Music

Songs of Otis Barker (ASCAP)
see Howlin' Hits Music

Songs of Polygram (BMI)
see Universal-MCA Music Publishing

Songs of Teracel (BMI)
c/o Sony ATV Songs
P.O. Box 1273
Nashville, Tennessee 37202

Songs of Universal (BMI)
see Universal-MCA Music Publishing

Songs of Windswept Pacific (BMI)
see Windswept Pacific Entertainment

The Songwriters Guild (ASCAP)
1500 Harbor Blvd.
Weehawken, New Jersey 07087

Sontanner Music (BMI)
see Careers-BMG Music

Sony ATV Music (ASCAP)
550 Madison Ave.
New York, New York 10022

Sony ATV Songs LLC (BMI)
8 Music Square West
Nashville, Tennessee 37203

Sony ATV Tree Publishing (BMI)
1111 16th Ave. S.
Nashville, Tennessee 37212

Sony ATV Tunes LLC (ASCAP)
8 Music Square West
Nashville, Tennessee 37203

Sony Songs Inc. (BMI)
see Warner-Chappell Music

Soul Assassin Music (ASCAP)
c/o Gelfard, Rennert & Feldman
1880 Century Park East
Suite 1600
Los Angeles, California 90067

Soul on Soul Music (ASCAP)
see EMI Music Publishing

Souljah Music (ASCAP)
see Famous Music Corp.

Soulsuck Music (ASCAP)
see Cherry Lane Music

Soulvang Music (BMI)
see EMI Music Publishing

Sounds of Da Red Drum (ASCAP)
c/o Jerome Foster
2250 Newbold Ave.
Bronx, New York 10462

Sounds Heard Everywhere Music (BMI)
c/o Derrick Ladd
11271 Ventura Blvd.
Suite 176
Studio City, California 91604

Sounds from the Soul (ASCAP)
c/o DeWayne J. Rogers, Jr.
5903 Fallbrook Ave.
Woodland, California 91367

Soundtron Tunes (BMI)
Butter Jinx Music Inc
P.O. Box 92004
Los Angeles, California 90009

Southfield Road Music (BMI)
c/o Manatt et al.
11355 W. Olympic Blvd.
Los Angeles, California 90064

Special Ed Music (BMI)
Address Unavailable

Special Rider Music (SESAC)
PO Box 860, Cooper Sta.
New York, New York 10276

Spent Bullets Music
see BMG Music

Spinnaker Music (BMI)
521 Logan Ave., Box 12-A
Laredo, Texas 78040-6633

Spurburn Music (BMI)
c/o Paul Barker
208 McConnell Drive
Austin, Texas 78746-4433

SPZ Music (BMI)
c/o Richard Eisner and Co.
575 Madison Ave.
New York, New York 10022-2511

Squamosal Music (BMI)
see Warner-Chappell Music

Squish Moth Music (ASCAP)
see Warner-Chappell Music

Starstruck Angel Music (BMI)
see Starstruck Writers Group

Starstruck Writers Group (ASCAP)
40 Music Square West
Nashville, Tennessee 37203

STD Music Publishing (ASCAP)
c/o Steve Standard
418 Atlantic Ave.
Brooklyn, New York 11217

Stellabella Music (BMI)
see Len Freedman Music

Stephanye Music (BMI)
see Warner-Chappell Music

Still Digging Music (ASCAP)
see BMG Songs Inc.

Stone Diamond Music (BMI)
see EMI Music Publishing

Stone Forest Music (BMI)
c/o Michael A. Palmer
904 Christina Dr.
Mt. Juliet, Tennessee 37122

Scott Storch Music (ASCAP)
see TVT Music

Straitjacket Songs
see Almo Music Corp.

Stratinum Songs (BMI)
see Famous Music Corp.

Strawberry Blonde Music (BMI)
see Bug Music

Street Warfare Publishing (BMI)
c/o Art of War Music
40 W. 57th St.
New York, New York 10019

Strong Songs (BMI)
750 Park Ave.
New York, New York 10021

Tom Sturges Music (ASCAP)
see EMI-April Music

Sugar Hill Music Publishing, Ltd.
96 West St.
Englewood, New Jersey 07631

Sugarfuzz Music (BMI)
P.O. Box 467399
Atlanta, Georgia 31146-7399

Suge Publishing
Address Unavailable

Superman Music (ASCAP)
see Warner-Chappell Music

Sushi Too Music (BMI)
see EMI Music Publishing

Swizz Beats Publishing (ASCAP)
c/o Madison Smallwood Financial Gro
400 Interstate North Pkwy.
Suite 1220
Atlanta, Georgia 30339

T

T Girl Music LLC (BMI)
Address Unknown

T. Scott Style Music (SESAC)
see Put It Down Music

Tabulous Music (ASCAP)
see Famous Music Corp.

Tallest Tree Music (ASCAP)
see Warner-Chappell Music

Tanner Music (ASCAP)
c/o John Tanner
5307 S. 92nd St., Ste. 104
Hales Corners, Wisconsin 53130

Taxicaster Music (BMI)
see Warner-Chappell Music

TCF (ASCAP)
see WB Music Publishing

TCF Music Publishing (ASCAP)
see Twentieth Century-Fox Music Corp.

Te Bass Music (BMI)
see EMI Music Publishing

Techwood Music (ASCAP)
c/o Turner Music Publishing
1 CNN Center, Box 105366
Atlanta, Georgia 30348

Teflon Hitz (ASCAP)
c/o Sheldon Harris
11 Jackson Ave.
Scarsdale, New York 10583

Temporary Music (BMI)
see Warner-Chappell Music

Ten Fifty Music (BMI)
c/o Brad Baker
1 CNN Center, Box 105366
Atlanta, Georgia 30348-5366

Tenom Music (ASCAP)
c/o Conesha Owens
442 D Folsom Dr.
Anitoch, California 94509

Terri Ooo Tunes (ASCAP)
see Universal-MCA Music Publishing

That's Plum Song (ASCAP)
see EMI Music Publishing

Thea Later Music (BMI)
c/o Thea Tippin
P.O. Box 40129
Nashville, Tennessee 37204-0129

Them Damn Twins Music (ASCAP)
see EMI Music Publishing

Third Lug Music (BMI)
Address Unavailable

Thirty Two Mile Music (BMI)
see Warner-Chappell Music

Three EB Publishing (BMI)
5715 Claremont Ave., Suite C
Oakland, California 94618

353 Music (SESAC)
c/o Chad James Elliot
P.O. Box 650442
Fresh Meadows, New York 11365-0442

3EB Publishing
Address Unavailable

3rd I Musicworks (ASCAP)
c/o Jess S. Morgan & Co. Inc.
5750 Wilshire Blvd., Ste. 590
Los Angeles, California 90036

Throwin' Tantrums Music (ASCAP)
see EMI Music Publishing

Thumb Print Music (BMI)
Address Unknown

Tiarra's Daddy Music (BMI)
see Universal-MCA Music Publishing

Cori Tiffani Music (BMI)
c/o Spivak & Meiselas
1010 Northern Blvd., Suite 304
Great Neck, New York 11021

Tight 2 Def Music (ASCAP)
580 Stoneglen Chase
Atlanta, Georgia 30331

Till Death Do Us Part (ASCAP)
c/o Sean M. Lassiter
9714 Roosvelt Blvd., #2
Philadelphia, Pennsylvania 19115

Time for Flytes Music (BMI)
1876 Independence Square
Dunwoody, Georgia 30338

Tintoretto Music (BMI)
110 West 57th St.
New York, New York 10019

Tiny Buckets O'Music (ASCAP)
see Chrysalis Music Group

Tokeco Tunes (BMI)
c/o Sussman & Associates
1222 16th Ave. South
3rd Floor
Nashville, Tennessee 37212

Tommy Boy Music (BMI)
902 Broadway, 13th Floor
New York, New York 10010

Tony! Toni! Tone! Music (ASCAP)
see PRI Music

Toolshed Music (ASCAP)
see EMI Music Publishing

Touched by Jazz Music (ASCAP)
see EMI Music Publishing

Trans Con Publishing (ASCAP)
see Zomba Enterprises

Trans Continental Music (ASCAP)
see Zomba Enterprises

Transfixed Music (ASCAP)
c/o Provident Financial
10345 W. Olympic Blvd., #200
Los Angeles, California 90054

Tray Tray's Music (ASCAP)
c/o Tracey Davis
15665 Willow Dr.
Fontana, California 92337

Tree Publishing Co., Inc. (BMI)
see Sony ATV Tree Publishing

Tremonti Stapp Music (BMI)
c/o Wind Up Records
72 Madison Ave.
New York, New York 10016

Trescadecaphobia Music (BMI)
c/o Troy Jamerson
110 33 157th St.
Jamaica, New York 11433

Treyball Music (ASCAP)
c/o Gelfand, Rennert & Feldman
1880 Century Park East
Suite 1600
Los Angeles, California 90067

Trick N Rick (BMI)
c/o Maurice Young
99 Miami Gardens Dr.
Apt. 128
Miami, Florida 33169

Trinity of Relative Evil Music (BMI)
7225 Santa Monica Blvd.
Los Angeles, California 90046

Tripptunes (BMI)
c/o Dan Tripp
2500 Bonita Place
Monroe, Louisiana 71201

TRO-Andover Music, Inc. (ASCAP)
10 Columbus Circle, Ste. 1460
New York, New York 10019

Tsanoddnos Music (BMI)
see Ensign Music

Tuff Huff Music (BMI)
see Zomba Enterprises

Tunes on the Verge of Insanity (ASCAP)
see Famous Music Corp.

TVT Music (ASCAP)
23 E. 4th St.
NYC, New York 10003

Twentieth Century-Fox Music Corp. (ASCAP)
P.O. Box 900
Music Dept., Bldg. #18
Beverly Hills, California 90213

Twenty Seven Songs (BMI)
c/o RZO
110 W. 57th St.
New York, New York 10019

27th and May Music (ASCAP)
see EMI Music Publishing

Twenty Three West Music (BMI)
71 W. 23rd St., No. 1611
New York, New York 10010-4102

Two Guys Who Are Publishers (ASCAP)
c/o Bradley Music Management
1100 18th Ave. S., Ste. D
Nashville, Tennessee 37212

Two Tuff-Enuff Publishing (BMI)
5765 Lowell St.
Oakland, California 94621

Ty Land Music (BMI)
1660 Rachel Way
Old Hickory, Tennessee 37138

Tycon Music (BMI)
Address Unavailable

Tzitzis What We Do Music (BMI)
see EMI Music Publishing

U

U Betta Like My Muzic (ASCAP)
see Zomba Enterprises

Ugmoe Music (ASCAP)
see Universal-MCA Music Publishing

Uh-Oh Entertainment (ASCAP)
see Famous Music Corp.

Undeas Music (BMI)
266 Washington Ave., Suite D16
Brooklyn, New York 11205

Unicade Music (ASCAP)
c/o Shukat Arrow Hafer and Weiser
111 W. 57th St., Ste. 1120
New York, New York 10019

Unichappell Music Inc. (BMI)
see Warner-Chappell Music

United Artists Music Co., Inc.
6753 Hollywood Blvd.
Los Angeles, California 90028

Universal Duchess Music (BMI)
see Universal-MCA Music Publishing

Universal-MCA Music Publishing (ASCAP)
2440Sepulveda Blvd., Ste. 100
Los Angeles, California 90064

Universal Music Publishing Int. Ltd.
Address Unavailable

Universal-Polygram Intl Tunes (SESAC)
c/o Ms. David Renzer
99440 Collection Center Dr.
Chicago, Illinois 60693-0994

Universal Songs of Polygram Intl. (BMI)
see Universal-MCA Music Publishing

Urban Warfare (ASCAP)
c/o University Music Entertainment
156 West 56th St., Suite 1803
New York, New York 10019

V

Vallallen (ASCAP)
c/o Beldock, Levin & Hoffman
99 Park Ave., Suite 1600
New York, New York 10016

Vanderpool Publishing (BMI)
see Famous Music Corp.

Vaporeon Music (BMI)
see Cherry River Music

Phil Vassar Music (ASCAP)
see EMI Music Publishing

VDPR Music (BMI)
see Warner-Chappell Music

Vibe Like That Music (ASCAP)
see Cherry Lane Music

Vinny Mae Music (BMI)
50 West Main
Ventura, California 93001

Violent Publishing
Address Unavailable

Virginia Beach Music (ASCAP)
see Warner-Chappell Music

Viva La Curcaracha Music (ASCAP)
see Dreamworks Songs

Voco Music
Address Unavailable

Volunteer Jam Music (ASCAP)
c/o Charles E. Daniels
1217 16th Ave. S.
Nashville, Tennessee 37212

W

Wacissa River Music (BMI)
1102 17th Ave. S., Ste. 400
Nashville, Tennessee 37212

Wallflower Music (BMI)
see Copyright Management Services

Wally World Music (ASCAP)
see Sony ATV Tunes LLC

Waltz Time Music (ASCAP)
see EMI Music Publishing

Steve Wariner Music (BMI)
P.O. Box 157
Nashville, Tennessee 37135

Warner-Chappell Music (ASCAP)
10585 Santa Monica Blvd.
Los Angeles, California 90025

Warner/Chappell Music Canada Ltd.
Address Unavailable

Warner-Tamerlane Music (BMI)
see Warner-Chappell Music

Waterdance Music (BMI)
c/o Jonnie Barnett
1007 McMahan Ave.
Nashville, Tennessee 37216

Watermelon Girl Music (BMI)
c/o Dawn S. Robertson
Copyright Department
10635 Santa Monica
Los Angeles, California 90025

Roger Waters Music Overseas Ltd.
Address Unavailable

Waters of Nazareth Publishing (BMI)
see EMI Music Publishing

WB Music Publishing (ASCAP)
see Warner-Chappell Music

WCR Publishing (BMI)
Address Unavailable

Webo Girl (ASCAP)
c/o Grubman, Indursky, Schindler, e
152 West 57th St.
New York, New York 10019

Wee Small Hours Music (ASCAP)
see Warner-Chappell Music

White Rhino Music (BMI)
c/o Stephen Finfer
23 East 4th St.
3rd Floor
New York, New York 10003-7023

Who Knows Music (BMI)
see EMI Music Publishing

Why Walk Music (ASCAP)
c/o Flood, Bumstead, McCready et al
P.O. Box 331549
Nashville, Tennessee 37203

Willarie Publishing Co. (ASCAP)
see EMI Music Publishing

Windfall Music Enterprises (BMI)
P.O. Box 505
Millwood, New York 10546

Windswept Pacific Entertainment (ASCAP)
9320 Wiltshire Blvd., Suite 200
Beverly Hills, California 90212

Wishart Songs (BMI)
c/o Stuart Brawley
834 Grant St.
Ste. 4
Santa Monica, California 90405

Wisteria Music (BMI)
c/o Nigro et al
10100 Santa Monica Blvd.
Suite 1300
Los Angeles, California 90067

Without Anna Music (ASCAP)
1700 Hayes St. Bldg.
Nashville, Tennessee 37203

M. Witmark & Sons (ASCAP)
see Warner-Chappell Music

Wixen Music (BMI)
24025 Park Sorrento, Suite 130
Calabasas, California 91302

Womanly Hips Music (BMI)
c/o Joan Osborne
P.O. Box 99440
Chicago, Illinois 60693-9440

Wonderland Music (BMI)
see Walt Disney Music

Woolly Puddin' Music (BMI)
see Bug Music

World of the Dolphin Music (ASCAP)
see Universal-MCA Music Publishing

Write on Music (BMI)
C.O. Sussman and Associates
1222 16th Ave. South
3rd Floor
Nashville, Tennessee 37212

Wu-Tang Publishing (BMI)
see BMG Music

Y

Yellow Desert Music (BMI)
1609 17th Ave. South
Nashville, Tennessee 37212

Yellow Elephant Music
see Sony ATV Tunes LLC

Yellow Man Music (BMI)
Address Unavailable

Yessiree Bob Music (ASCAP)
see BMG Songs Inc.

Young Fiano Music (SESAC)
see Put It Down Music

Young Lord Music (SESAC)
PO Box 23766
Baltimore, Maryland 21203-5766

Z

Zeon Music (ASCAP)
see Len Freedman Music

Zomba Enterprises (ASCAP)
138 West 25th St., 8th Floor
New York, New York 10001

ISBN 0-88099-229-8